HELLCAT
OF
THE HAGUE

HELLCAT
OF
THE HAGUE

THE NEL SLIS STORY

PIONEERING JOURNALIST

CAROLINE STUDDERT

Contents

Introduction

A quest and a tribute

She struck me first with her deep, smoky voice on the telephone. I was looking for a job, and the famous old pioneering Dutch journalist immediately gave me every conceivable contact in the Netherlands. And she told me to use her name. Thanks to Nel, in spring 1981 I got my first regular job as a journalist.

I didn't actually meet her until later, when she agreed to do a magazine interview with me. It took place in The Hague in her apartment by the sea. She was a surprisingly difficult interviewee. She rattled happily through her dramatic life on her own terms, but was reticent to the point of obstinacy about anything more personally revealing.

Nel must have been 68 then, thin, tough and weather-beaten with a dark complexion. She had a long craggy face like a gloomy monkey, until it lit up with a dazzling smile. She was very smartly dressed, an elegant woman. I was embarrassed when the editor headlined her interview 'Hellcat of The Hague.' But she loved it. After the interview, I said I would look forward to her autobiography. She said yes, she must write one.

Some dozen years on, I asked her, what about your book? We were lingering amid empty white-clothed tables, about to be swept out with the crumbs after some press function in The Hague. She said immediately, we will write it together – in short story form. Unfortunately, I was starting a new financial news bureau in Amsterdam at the time, so I didn't get a chance to start visiting her regularly for several more years.

But by then she had lost her memory.

I didn't realize this immediately, as it hadn't completely gone and she could still churn out her oft-told life story on auto-pilot. But I couldn't get her to pause, expand on any scene or depart from her own script. However, I kept on coming to her apartment most weeks and recording her repetitions. I was working on the book plan, starting with her island beginnings, and I tried to cheer her on with hopelessly over-optimistic ideas about the book's progress.

Then came the final blow. I phoned as usual to tell her helper, Sonia, that I planned to visit, but Sonia said I couldn't come because Nel was going into a care home that day. I did visit her there a few times, but by then her memory had really gone. One of her minders, journalist Friso End, reckoned it lasted about six seconds. Not even the length of a sentence.

So what was I to do next? I had no idea how to write this book on my own, but still wanted to tell Nel's story. That is, if I really knew what it was. A long struggle followed, collecting anything I could find about her, and interviewing anyone who knew her. This was difficult too, as they kept dying on me – Nel was no spring chicken. Things were further complicated by my move to Prague in 2001. To cap it all, only a former colleague was thoughtful enough to let me know when Nel died at the end of that year. Uninvited and facing a work deadline, I didn't make it to the funeral. Nel would have respected my deadline. Afterwards, I went on slowly collecting pieces in the jigsaw puzzle of Nel's life and writing draft after draft, plonking everything in as best as I could. Later I put it away for a few years, before being irresistibly if nervously drawn back again.

I have asked myself, what is the point of it all now after such a long time? The point is Nel herself, her life and struggles as a groundbreaking woman journalist. It's her highly coloured personality, the impression she made on people and they on her. Her charm, rages, tiresomeness and reticence, all are part of Nel. The point is one woman's struggle and one woman's views on journalism, on women and feminism, on her country, on the EU at a formative time, and on the wider world. It wasn't an easy ride for her. There are sacrifices involved in breaking new ground. But she has left us a valuable legacy. She's left us a generous slice of 20th century history, seen through the eyes of someone who was *there*

Caroline Studdert

Acknowledgements

So many people have helped me on the long road I have trodden in search of Nel that it is impossible to pay tribute properly to everybody. One thing is certain though. Without Brad Gaiennie's patient and expert piloting through the lengthy line-by-line editing process here in Prague, Hellcat of The Hague would never have made it into print. Deepest thanks to Brad.

Without the encouragement of Yolanda Frenkel-Frank from the start, I doubt that I would have gone on with the book. Yolanda, a producer in The Hague, was fascinated as a child by Nel, a close friend of her parents, and knew her all her life. I am also much indebted to her suggestions from reading various versions of the book. Tyna Wyneaerds, OECD librarian in Paris when I met her, was Nel's heir and the daughter of her best friend on the island where she grew up. She added a vital thread that runs through the book as she knew all the families from the island and was in touch with Nel throughout her life. I am also greatly indebted to Tyna's brother Piet Wackie-Eysden, a lawyer in The Hague, and Nel's most important 'minder' in the last years of her life, for access to his published 'Life Sketch' of Nel containing a large quantity of very valuable material. Friso Endt, fellow-journalist and another key 'minder,' also provided quantities of information and helped me with access to Nel's archives. Nel's nephew Hans van Nieuwenhuyzen talked to me about Nel and the Slis family and took a great interest in the book, as did his wife Janny. In Middelharnis on Goeree-Overflakkee, the town hall's archivist Jan Both enthusiastically provided a picture of the history of Nel's island.

Special thanks are due to former Dutch Premier Ruud Lubbers for sitting on the steps in the Nieuwe Kerk with me and talking about Nel when the Dalai Lama was visiting Amsterdam a few years back. Famous US journalist and commentator Daniel Shorr, one-time partner of Nel, and old friend and Financial Times journalist Reginald Dale both gave key telephone interviews from Washington. Former AFX News colleagues Sarah Borchersen-Keto put me in touch with Schorr and John Buckley updated me on events in Holland after I moved to Prague. Interviews and anecdotes were generously provided by Foreign Press Association former chairmen Helmut Hetzel and Friso Endt, former president Vera Vaughan Bowden and Nel's vice-chairpeople David Post and Laura Raun among many others. Further interviews and sources are listed in the Appendix, but I'm afraid I keep remembering more vital people almost daily, so a special thank you to those the black hole I call my memory has yet to disgorge. Members of Prague Writers Group gave many useful suggestions and helped me when I was stuck. My daughter Isabella Montgomery and Prague friend Christi Brooks rescued me with last-minute edits and technical problem-solving for a computer illiterate like myself. Special thanks also to Sybille Yates and Marcus Bradshaw for creating the cover and for much vital support. All the deficiencies and errors which undoubtedly remain in the book despite all this help are entirely my own work and responsibility.

Beginnings:

DISCOVERING EUROPE

(1913-1939)

1.
The Islander

Growing up on Goeree-Overflakkee

Christened Neeltje Adriana Slis, Nel was born on 2 September 1913 on the island of Goeree-Overflakkee. Lying off the foot of the Netherlands in the province of Zuid-Holland, Goeree-Overflakkee is separated from the mainland by the wide Haringvliet channel. Nowadays, its chief town of Middelharnis is little more than half an hour's drive from Rotterdam. Dyke-bridges have long anchored the island to the mainland. But for Nel as a child, visiting Rotterdam was a major expedition into another world. She reminisced about this once in a radio interview she gave late in life.

> "You could go once a day over the Haringvliet, with the boat to Hellevoetsluis and then with a little tram to Rotterdam. That was my first impression of the big world... I do still remember well the meal that we had there and the coffee or tea... We went to have chicken soup in a restaurant that was called 'Wolf'. That was tres chique at that time. And then at four o'clock – that was already late because we had to go back with the tram – we had tea with appelbollen (apple dumplings). And then you went back – it took a while. First with that little tram from Rotterdam in the Rozenstraat to Hellevoetsluis. And then you went on this boat, sometimes in awful

weather, that took three-quarters of an hour, or sometimes an hour…Then you went on a little tram again, to Middelharnis."

i. A Gentleman Farmer who never touched the Soil

Nel was born in the tiny village of Ooltgensplaat, near Middelharnis. Her mother, Lena Koert, died on 8 December, 1917 when she was just four. The following year, her father, Johannes Aren Slis, then 42, moved back to Middelharnis where he had grown up. Johannes came from a prosperous family of 'gentleman farmers' and he bought himself a fine house on the corner of Stationsweg (Station Road). Nel's nephew Hans Nieuwenhuyzen described it to me as a large and beautiful house, but it has long since been demolished to make way for undistinguished modern housing. Naturally, our 'gentleman farmer' had put in a farm manager to run his farm.

Middelharnis town council archivist Jan Both searched through the council's old records for me and discovered that Johannes Slis had a very substantial amount of land, and would have been considered quite wealthy. As Nel was fond of telling me, this was rated the best land in the Netherlands. Exactly how much land he had was difficult to work out from the archives, as farming families intermarried and there would be parcels of land in different areas. Inherited land was divided up between the males, making it a great advantage to have few or preferably no brothers. As far as I know, Johannes had no brothers.

Jan Both was remarkably easy to locate when I asked for an archivist in Middelharnis' tidy modern town hall. He was a dark-haired young man, small and neat, and quite unlike my image of an ancient, dusty grey and reclusive archivist. He would happily have spent all day talking about the island's history. As he rummaged in the archives, Both kept up a running commentary.

> One married a farmer's daughter, and she had land too, so one married land actually, that was what they said then. Johannes' first wife also came from a farming family, Kadoek, I don't think that farm was so enormously big. The second wife also came from a good house, also with land. The third wife, the widow Mosselman, that was actually not a farming family, but in trading. But her previous husband Overdorp, who was the mayor, was also from a farming family. So it was always in these farming circles that marriages took place. And they were always fighting about land

Most likely, Johannes' land ran to over a hundred hectares. The largest farmer at the time had 257 hectares, an impressive spread in Europe even by today's standards. The prominent status of the whole Slis clan is obvious from the large collection of imposing Slis tombstones in Middelharnis churchyard. Nel once told me the family can be traced back to 1545.

Johannes Slis turns out to have been more interested in buying and selling horses than in farming, and not at all interested in looking after his motherless daughter. As Nel put it,

> "A gentleman farmer who never touched the soil. He more or less didn't need to, he was well-padded (rich), so to say, coming originally from a shipping family, and he lived in a nice, big house. He was totally oblivious to the difficulties of life, I suppose because he always had money, was born with money. He had a comfortable life and never did much. He gave more to his horses than to the soil – he was always away buying and selling these big horses."

Johannes would travel all the way up the country to Groningen, where the breeding of black carriage horses is still kept alive today by groups of enthusiasts. I have seen these horses in action, in a vignette that felt quite romantic to me. I was sitting in Papeneiland café at a crossroad between two canals in Amsterdam's historic Jordaan district one frosty autumn evening. All of a sudden, we were transported back a century or so in time as twenty or more teams of big, heavily handsome black horses clattered and slipped over a bridge across the canal, snorting breathily behind beautifully preserved carriages. Drivers were well-muffled atop, and passengers waved from the windows.

Horses were not at all romantic for Nel. She simply saw them as her distant, egotistical father's hobby which took him away from home.

> "He was always on the go, he always found an excuse to go somewhere, especially to horse fairs. He travelled constantly back and forth to Groningen and Oldenburg, because there were these big, thick, heavy horses. My father… I sometimes think, a kind of Bluebeard. His first wife died when my oldest sister was two; he remarried a woman who also died when I was two. Perhaps that is why I don't especially like horses. He was not what you'd call a father, not that interested, except that he was interested to be told about when I came first at school - then he was proud of me in a way. Then I got some attention from him."

Once she described him:

> A dark man, with green eyes, not bad looking. He could
> be very charming, if you were not dependent on him."

Nel's parents Lena Koert and Johannes Aren Slis

Johannes Slis (L) Johannes Slis with "the widow" (R)

ii. Island Life

While Johannes Slis was away from home indulging in his passion for buying and selling carriage horses, his farm manager was in charge of a very different type of horse. These were not bred as carriage horses, but were powerful beasts for ploughing and tilling the island's fertile arable land.

Farmers in those days had special 'knechts' or servants who had to get up early to take care of the horses and get everything ready for the arrival of the hordes of farm labourers. The knechts were socially closer to the household than the farm labourers, and were also expected to help out with other tasks. In high season, they stood by at the harbour to manage shipments of produce. Isolated as the island may have been, it was surely more populated than today and not necessarily quieter. Instead of cars, I imagine the constant rumble of carts and clopping of horses' hoofs, and busy scenes of loading and unloading at the harbour.

Island society was headed by a small elite clan of wealthy farmers, a sprinkling of people in the shipping industry and a few 'notables' like the notary, the pharmacist, the doctor, the bank manager and the mayor – all very likely also from farming families. The wealthy farmers were on the big polders in the southeast part called Goeree, with some of the best arable land in the Netherlands. On the poorer land in the northwest Overflakkee part, holdings were small-scale, with farmers often employing only one or two workers.

It occurs to me that while Nel may have been lonely and often unhappy, she was also a child of the wealthy island elite. Perhaps this, along with her innate island toughness and democratic bent, helps explain why she was never overawed by anyone in later life, including people in very powerful positions.

At the bottom of the island's social heap was an army of impoverished farm labourers, who had a terrible struggle getting through the winter, when there was little or no work . In the autumn, there would be hand threshing for a couple of weeks, and then virtually no work until it was time to plough again the next spring. A labourer's family would keep a pig, slaughter it and live off it all winter. The family would have a small patch of ground where they could grow some vegetables and thus struggle through to spring. All of which makes me think there must have been a lot more people around on the island than today, though presumably busy labouring in the fields and in their vegetable patches - or falling exhaustedly to sleep in their shacks.

In the middle of the social strata was a small group of artisans such as carpenters and shopkeepers. There was also a sizeable Jewish community, generally in retail trades such as clothes shops, but also quite often butchers and meat traders. They must have prospered, as there is a large group of Jewish gravestones in the old churchyard on the left-hand side of the entrance, facing the Slis contingent on the right. Oddly enough, many people thought Nel was Jewish, though she wasn't. It did turn out however that the great love of her life was a Jewish man. I often wonder if she was a little fascinated as a child by such a distinctive group of people.

The farm workers were virtually wiped out after the second world war by the introduction of tractors and harvesters. This happened very quickly as a result of the postwar Marshall Aid reconstruction programme. Efforts were made to bring some industry to the island to create employment, but with no bridge yet built and little interest among the business community, these ventures did not last. Many workers began commuting to Rotterdam to work in the port, for which special boats were provided by the Rotterdam port authority.

The final diffusion of the island culture began after the first dam/bridge was built in 1964, providing an umbilical cord to connect it with Rotterdam. People could now easily commute to Rotterdam, and many actually moved there. A reverse migration also occurred, as many Rotterdammers moved out to live on the island, and the two-way flow gradually created a socially flatter and less 'rural' society. Still, even at the beginning of the 21st century, quizzing a local barkeeper in Middelharnis revealed that he came from a farming family. Not far below the surface, the island's farming roots are still there. Middelharnis itself, though covering a bigger area due to more spacious modern housing, has only about doubled in population in over a century, from around 3,500 when Nel was a child.

The Slis farmland, like the rest of the fertile land in Goeree, was used for various crops, chiefly wheat and corn. Some sheep farming was seen from around 1900, but on the smaller farms outside the dykes. In an era predating artificial fertilizers, cattle were mainly valued for manure. Most of the manure was imported by boat from Rotterdam, where it was collected from the streets, and landed on the 'manure wharfs' in Middelharnis. The few cattle on the island were looked after by herdsmen, who would have ten or twelve head and drive them up onto the dykes to graze, keeping a sharp eye on them to make sure they did not stray off the dykes into the crops.

For Nel as a child, the island was a farming-centred world. Harsh for the majority, it was presumably reasonably pleasant for the elite. Small children generally take their social environment for granted, and I don't know what Nel thought of the numerous poor farm labourers as I didn't find out about them myself until she was incommunicado. Interestingly, Nel did say her mother was serious-minded and had "social inclinations." It seems she used to talk about the poor and this was 'not done' at the time. There was a group of women around that time who formed a club called Dorcas, getting together to make clothes for the poor and run soup kitchens. This sounds like the kind of activity in which Nel's mother might have got involved, on account of her social interests.

Along with the frequent absences of her father, Nel found herself cut off from her mother's family because of the internecine family feuds. She said she never actually met them until she inherited some land from her mother when she was 21. Nel also told me she didn't remember her mother. "I'd just seen her in pictures and heard about her," she said. This seems to me an odd statement from Nel, who had a proverbially brilliant memory before she lost it. My earliest memory is of an incident when I was two, and plenty of people have even earlier memories, so one would expect her to have at least some of her mother by the time she was four. For some unknown reason, she also sometimes said her mother died when she was two or three, not four.

Another curiosity was Nel's completely non-religious upbringing. Archivist Both did not find this as amazing I did, because of a class difference in religious matters at the time. The big farmers took a liberal and quasi-agnostic stance, though this did not stop some of them from sitting on the church board, as community leaders. The farm workers by contrast gravitated to the more extreme, strict orthodox 'Gereformeerd' pole. No doubt they would grumble vociferously about the libertine and godless elite. This elite was technically Reformed or 'Hervormd' and would be baptised, but was otherwise free-thinking.

Still, Nel's case seems extreme. She claimed a completely a-religious childhood.

> "I only understood the difference between God, Jesus and the whole club later, let's say when I was 12 or 13. Because no attention was paid to it…. When I was eight, I asked my father what's the difference between God and Jesus. He said, that you learn when you go to catechism."

It seems a safe assumption that Nel never made it to catechism.

Nel's heir Tyna Wynaendts also remembered that the well-heeled families of Middelharnis would never go to church or have anything to do with religion. But like me, she found it remarkable that Nel didn't even know the difference between God and Jesus. As she said,

> "I mean, that's difficult to do, even for a non-believing family. I must say, my family still sent me to Sunday school because they thought I had to know a minimum even if they themselves only went to church at Christmas, because it was part of the general culture. But nobody ever told her anything – she was so lonely, she only talked to the maid."

Nel described herself as a serious, ambitious child, always very busy doing her homework, and very curious about life. She liked animals apart from horses, and owned a dog and a couple of cats. She led an active outdoor life as well, with plenty of skating in winter and swimming and tennis in summer. "I have always needed the outdoors, throughout my life," she often told me. She learned to swim and ride a bicycle early and drove a car at the age of 10. "We were one of the first to have a car on the island," she said, adding more surprisingly, "and a radio."

She was inclined to say that before her father remarried when she was 10, she was on her own but not unhappy, and enjoyed the island. But Tyna said she was very lonely even before the remarriage, because of her father's lack of interest. Tyna put this down to his character plus the fact that the importance of 'parenting' was relatively unknown or at least not much discussed at the time. To quote Tyna,

> "I think her father was aloof and very egotistical; he looked after his horses and his pleasure, and he spent a lot of money apparently too. And he didn't really care what other people thought. Also, nowadays parents know a little about the impact they have on their children by their own behaviour, but in that generation, I don't think it occurred to people that it might not be good for their daughter if they were not more present, not more loving. Modern parents, well, they can't open a newspaper without reading about how it should be, but in those days, they didn't even think about it, they just had their own lives, and if they weren't very interested in children, that was it."

iii. A Surrogate Family

Nel particularly hated the period after her father remarried. 'That widow' brought Nel a younger step-sister, Trinette, to add to her older half-sister, Jaan, from her father's first wife. As Nel liked to remind people, her 'Bluebeard' father's first wife had also died when her daughter Jaan was young. Jaan's son Hans Nieuwenhuzyen remembered that Nel could not get along with the widow and there were always rows. Hans himself was clearly fond of Nel and got on well with her. He and his wife, who was also from the island, told me they kept in touch with her intermittently almost until the end of her life. I found out later that the widow's daughter Trinette did not die until 2000, apparently in Amsterdam, but Nel said nothing at all to me about her. Perhaps they did not get along either. At any rate, Nel did complain vociferously about Trinette's mother:

> "A woman I had absolutely nothing in common with. Alone with this strange woman...it was an unhappy time. I was stuck, the only one at home, as my father's eldest daughter was already married at that time."

In her loneliness, Nel clung to her Aagie, variously described as her father's 'housekeeper', charwoman or maid.

> "Aagje was the simplest woman you could think of, with a good heart. Really I was brought up by the housekeeper; she was a sort of mother…Everyone was married, and I was left over with Aagje."

However, Nel did have one great friend, Tyna's mother Jenneke. She was two years older than Nel and "understood the family situation," as Nel put it. Jenneke was the daughter of the notary, and in his big house and office on the Achterweg, Nel found the family cosiness and warmth she missed at home. Tyna's brother Piet was to become a lifelong support to Nel as well. Telling me sadly in our first interview that her friend Jenneke had eventually died, Nel said:

> "Her son is a lawyer with one of the biggest firms in the Netherlands and if I was totally lost with anything, I always went to him, throughout my life."

This was the first time I heard about Piet Wackie Eysden. It was Piet who provided one telling detail about Jenneke's mother. He said Nel kept a portrait of her beside her bed throughout her life. Nel was extremely grateful to Jenneke's mother, who she described as:

> "A very exceptional woman. She had us do handicrafts one evening a week, and then she read to us, preferably from books by Selma Lagerlof." (Appendix)

Janneke effectively provided Nel with a surrogate home, with the warmth of family life. Tyna said her grandmother was like that:

> "She had Hungarian children staying with her when a whole trainful of Hungarian children was sent to Holland - I think they lived with her for more than a year. She was very much like that: 'Oh, if you don't have your mother, welcome, stay with us'. And a lot of Nel's generosity to all of us was based on that, I think. She probably was a remarkable woman. A little bit like Nel in a way; my grandmother told people what was what, and if she liked or disliked somebody, you would know it in a few minutes - very outspoken. And she loved Nel."

It turns out that many children were sent to Holland after the Communists crushed the 1956 uprising in Hungary.

Tyna also told a story about Nel and Jenneke as little girls skating, an activity which is in the blood of everyone in Holland.

> "In Holland, that's what you do. Even when I was a child, the first day the ice was strong enough to go skating, the schools would close down for at least one

afternoon, and the whole country was on skates. So my mother and Nel were on skates, and Nel had to go to the toilet very frequently, especially when it was cold. So it happened when they were skating, and they wanted to hide, so they went under a bridge because getting on the land is difficult when you're skating. But of course the ice under a bridge is not so thick, so they both went through it and they were completely wet and miserable going home, with everybody laughing at them.

Nel believed the lack of her own family in her childhood made her more inclined to strike up friendships

> "I think you tend to make more friends when you have less family. I'm very lucky, I'm not so much extrovert but an easy mixer. Even if I feel immense dislike, it's with great gusto. Even on the island, there were one or two girls of my own age and I remained very close friends with one of them (Jenneke) throughout my life. Our lives went in different directions, but later, circumstances brought us together again. Her husband died and she remarried later – I followed all of that."

Tyna explained that her mother was originally engaged to a Mr. Mais on the island.

> "Then my father came along and she married him, and years later, when my father died, she married the first, Mr. Mais. So they all knew each other and grew up together."

> Looking at a photograph of her mother with Nel, Tyna mused

> :"Here you see my mother, who really considered Nel one of the family, knowing she was so lonely and unhappy at home. So my mother and Nel were the closest friends...for more than 70 years."

Nel had several other extraordinarily long-standing friendships spanning fifty or sixty years. Many were made as she lived and worked around Europe as a young woman. And for years after she retired, Nel did her "Tour de France/Italy/Denmark/Spain/Portugal" and stayed with her friends in turn - but not for more than three days, she told me in 1981:

> "Since I was freelance, I could not go away for three or four months; it was usually two to three weeks, country by country, sometimes combining Italy and Switzerland

together, or France; Spain and Portugal and so on. I believe the saying that 'guests are like fish and stink after three days'. I also have friends in Holland, but I haven't LIVED so much in Holland. In The Hague, they're mostly very good acquaintances - my friends are scattered all over Europe."

iv. A Very Peculiar Country: The Great Flood of 1953

Before leaving the island, I should describe where it is in this strangely-shaped country called the Netherlands. On the map, Goeree-Overflakke is one of a group of islands off the southwest coast of the Netherlands below Rotterdam, attached to each other and the mainland by dams and bridges. The islands look like slices of land bitten off by the sea.

Goeree-Overflakke is connected via four bridge/dams to the other islands and thence eastward to Rotterdam. Below the islands, the southwest base of the Netherlands is completed by the long Zuid Beveland and Walcheren peninsular, along which the A99 snakes from Bergen op Zoom to Vlissingen.

The island slices form the southwest corner of a triangle whose base runs from Vlissingen on the coast to Venlo inland to the east. From Venlo, motorways run all the way up to the northern apex of the triangle at Den Helder. Following the line of the coast at the apex is the procession of Frisian islands: Texel (pronounced Tessel), Vlieland, Terschelling, Ameland, Schiermonnikoog, Rottumerplaat and Rottumeroog and their smaller companions. The islands trail in a westerly curve round the north coast of Friesland and Groningen, the North Sea on their outside and the Waddenzee between them and the mainland.

The Waddenzee is cut off from the freshwater IJsselmeer lake by the Afsluitdijk (closing-off dyke), a great Dutch engineering feat built between 1927 and 1933 and visible from outer space. Before that, the IJsselmeer was the salty Zuiderzee. Together, the Waddenzee and IJsselmeer cut a swathe between Noord-Holland province and the northwesterly bulk of the country. The northwestern provinces are Friesland, Groningen, Friesland, Drenthe, Gelderland, Overijssel and the almost entirely man-made polderland province of Flevoland. That is, apart from the God-made former island of Urk.

Down at the east end of the base of our Netherlandish triangle, the strange limb of the appropriately named Limburg province stretches south along the Maas river and ends up at the Roman city of Maastricht.

This charming Dutch city is almost completely surrounded by Germany and Belgium.

This completes the picture of Nel's whole peculiar country, so intimately connected with the sea and the great rivers. Essentially, the Netherlands is the delta of the great Rhine river, which meets the ocean to create the perfect location for Europe's largest port of Rotterdam. It is a 'peculiar' country in the sense of being 'unique'. And Goeree-Overflakee played a peculiar role in Nel's formative early years.

Goeree-Overflakkee is actually in Zuid-Holland, but close to Zeeland province. For a long time, I thought it was in Zeeland, as Nel sometimes used to say she was a Zeelander. Both provinces are intimately connected with the ocean and its great shipping highways. Goeree-Overflakee and neighbouring Zeeland were among the areas that suffered the most from the great flood of 1953. Writing at the end of the 1950s, the novelist Hammond Innes recalled how he first saw the Netherlands, sailing into the Hook of Holland:

> "A vast expanse of sea and sky with only the spire of a church or the sails of a windmill to show that we were coming into land. We sailed up to Rotterdam, past oil refineries and cranes and miles of warehouses; it was hard to realise that this, the greatest port in the world, was all built on piles in a quaking land of bog. And then down through the rivers and canals to Flushing – locks and bridges and barges everywhere, and from the deck no land visible except the dykes on either side, their green tops in silhouette against the cloud-spattered sky. But when I climbed the mast, I could see all the rich land of Holland laid out below the level of the water on which we sailed – way, way below it, as much as twenty feet."

Innes wrote movingly of the 1953 flood disaster.

> "Saturday evening, January 31, 1953 – I remember listening to the radio with that sense of disaster that both fascinates and appalls. Gale warnings, tide warnings… all the coasts of the North Sea were threatened." He quotes Jean Ingelow's *The High Tide on the Coast of Lincolnshire* (1571):
>
> *Men say it was a stolen tyde*
>
> *The Lord that sent it, He knows all*
>
> "A stolen tide! It swept in over England's east coast… and Holland stood in the direct path of the storm. Wind

force close on a hundred knots, and almost one quarter of that country below sea level – five million people, half the population, with no protection against the elements but the dykes they themselves had erected over the century.... In that first onslaught, the sea did not breach the protecting dykes; it swept in over the top of them. In places a twelve-foot wall of water rampaged through farm and village. And in that and succeeding nights, 1,800 people lost their lives; 10,000 farms and houses were destroyed, a further 40,000 damaged."

Recalling the apocryphal story of the boy sticking his finger into the sea dyke to save Haarlem, Hammond Innes said:

"A ludicrous story for anybody who has actually seen a dyke, but it captured the world's imagination as a symbol.. But on the night of January 31,1953, a group of men did in fact what the little boy did in fiction ...all that night they lay shoulder to shoulder against their crumbling dyke at Kalijnsplaat, supporting it and holding back the waters by the sheer weight of their bodies. They were not heroes. Or if they were heroes, then half Holland was heroic that night, for they were just one of many groups who did what they could in a desperate situation and fought the flood tide the way their fathers had fought it before them."

When this happened, Nel had already been a working journalist for some eight years.

While it must have been harrowing for her to cover, it was a big story, and she knew the character of the people on her island.

"I was born on Goeree-Overflakee, I knew the country and the mentality. I reported that people on Tholen island were sitting in black skirts on the roof waiting to be saved, and when a German boat came along that wanted to help them, they shouted: 'Oh, no, no Germans!' They stayed sitting on the roof."

Archivist Jan Both said many Germans came to help.

"Yes, they came from far and near, from America, Sweden, Belgium...Because the Netherlands only had one helicopter. Fishermen came from other places, even from north Netherlands. There was also a Bavarian pilot who was immediately involved when he heard about it on the radio, and he was able to pick up a lot of people from the rooftops.

Goeree-Overflakkee was one of the worst affected areas, especially under Oude Tonge. Around Dirksland and Melissant it stayed dry, but the rest was flooded and a large number of people drowned – over 300 in Oude Tonge alone. In Middelharnis, it was a bit less; that had to do with the dykes still holding in the polders; the outer dykes had already been flooded, but some of the inner ones held.

But the flood happened in the middle of the night, and took most people by surprise, for they were sleeping. It was in the middle of winter, it snowed and the water was ice-cold. So if you just fell in, you quickly drowned. And such an enormous flood, you couldn't escape – you just had to grab something, and you had to be rescued quickly, because if you're not dressed, you are freezing…There are gruelling stories of people on a roof… at a certain moment, one after the other let go from the cold... A whole family on the roof. And you could see nothing of course, it was extremely dark, because all the lights were out."

v. Leaving Goeree-Overflakkee: Secondary school in Haarlem

Before Nel left the island, she attended the local R.S.G. Goeree-Overflakkee primary school in Middelharnis. This school must have made a big impression on its pupils. In 1994, a local paper described the school's 75-year jubilee reunion as attracting an estimated fifteen hundred former pupils to the town, including a 78 year old man from Mexico city. A photo shows groups of pupils from 1930-1934 and 1925-1929. The oldest group, from 1917-1924, followed the procession in a minibus. Nephew Hans Nieuwenhuyzen's wife also attended the school, and his aunt on the other side of the family was at the reunion, and remembered that Nel was there too. Nel also said she met her first boyfriend on the island, though she was only 13 when she left:

Middelharnis school reunion 27 June 1992

> "Very kindly, very nice, he wrote to me when I went away to school in Haarlem. He was a young Dutchman, the son of the mayor of the island. It was all bicycling, going on the back of his bicycle. We just went to the beach, swimming, tennis, because there was nothing else to do on the island. There were horses, but that horse business, it wasn't so fashionable then for women. I learned about that more in England later. But it never appealed to me. I was afraid of horses, perhaps they reminded me of my father."

When she 13, Nel was sent away to a school in Overveen, near Haarlem.

> "At that time, the 'nobility' of the island so to say, sent their sons and daughters away as soon as they could walk, talk and be sensible to the 'outside world', to The Hague or Amsterdam, to go to school."

As Nel put it, her father had big ideas, and chose the Kennemer Lyceum because no school nearer by was good enough for him. He made this choice after being turned down for reasons unknown by the Zeister Christelijk Lyceum. Possibly they considered the family a little too non-religious. In his sketch of Nel's life, Piet Wackie-Eysten wondered whether she was 'sent away' because she was hard to handle, as Piet's mother had sometimes implied. Or alternatively, whether she was not doing well at the local school, which seems very unlikely. His final suggestion was that the village high school was considered too limited for her talents. This rings true to me and fits in with those big ideas of Johannes. In any event, it turned out to be a good choice. As Nel said,

> "I very much enjoyed it; I was very happy there. Sometimes I went back to the island for holidays, but also to the home of one of the girls in the house where I was living."

Still, it was a big move.

> "I had come from this little island which is somewhere down there at the bottom of the Netherlands to this chic school, Kennemer Lyceum, and it was populated at that time by boys and girls whose parents were in Indonesia, and so they had no family around - they were just left there. At least half the pupils were like that. But they stayed in some special institution near the Kennemer Lyceum, the Kiho. I was not put up in one of these homes, but at a widow's, who was very nice. But she got sick and I went from one place to another while I was at the school, because of sicknesses and god knows what else. I was never sick, though. I had a good time - I loved that school."

Nel also had high praise for the school's rector, De Vletter.

> "He always stood by me. A big man, with a big personal interest. I have very good memories of the school. There I gradually grew up. I had no head for science, but languages spurred me on. For them, I really had a talent."

Reminiscing about the school, she went on:

> "In my last year at school, my father was still living on the island with the third wife, and I had to leave the place where I was staying again, not because of problems or anything but because the people were sick. I preferred to take a room, as if I was a lone student, with people who just gave me breakfast, but that was all. And then I was called in to see the head of the Kennemer Lyceum, Mr De Vletter. He knew that I still had a father, and he said, does your father know that you are just living in a room? It was most unusual for someone to be still at

high school and rooming already, as if you were an older student - not staying in a family. I said, yes, he does, he has my address, and I didn't want to say that he couldn't give a damn anyway."

In a similar story involving Mr. De Vletter, the offence was having a boyfriend. This version starts with a glimpse of the impression she made at the school, and also repeats Nel's constant refrain about her father turning her off marriage.

'Friends later told her how she looked when she came to school. "I talked back and I knew what I wanted." And she had a boy-friend. An offence for which she was called up to see the rector. "Did my father know? Of course my father knew. Naturally, I said. That was the first friend," she says, "and not the last, who I told that I would never marry. I find affairs great fun, but I didn't want to marry. That is, I think, because of my father, he has coloured my picture of men."'

Sometimes, one felt, the lady doeth protest too much. There did after all turn out to be one man she wanted to marry, but we will get to that later.

Writing a contribution for a class reunion 50 years later on 23 April 1982, Nel complained that when she returned to the Netherlands in 1974 after a stint in Brussels, she found newspapers, radio and especially television provincial and complacent. Dutch journalists had a total lack of languages, especially as they were "deprived of the entire Latin horizon," she grumbled. Nel went on:

"Then I think nostalgically of our Kennemer Lyceum where we had to write, talk and read in at least three foreign languages every week."

At the end of her piece, she says warmly:

"On my many roads in the world, I have met many old-Kennemers and always with much pleasure"

Incidentally, the peripatetic Nel's contribution was typed on the stationery of Les Freres Charbonnel restaurant in Brantome, in France's Dordogne.

A very blurry photo shows Class 5 LE (literature, economics) back at the school desks after 50 years. The eleven pupils have been ingeniously listed under their first initials to compose the word Wachtplan NH. "P", who appears from the list to be one Piet Schmal, writes a piece on those "in front of and in" the class of 1927-1932. Nel's teachers included the world-famous creator of quaint fairytale Dutch paintings, Anton Pieck, on whose work a whole theme-park in the south of the Netherlands, De Efteling, was modelled. Schmal's piece begins with a dig at 'modern' teaching methods:

> "In thankful remembrance of our socially-motivated educators – professional specialists with great cultural interests… not yet hampered by modern concepts like project education, youth culture, broadening care, multiple choice, study guidance roles, professional sections and other didactical approaches."

Schmal goes on to list the teachers and their subjects, which included history, natural history,

German, economics, political science, bookkeeping and geography with a teacher whose specialities were India and Papuans, English appropriately taught by "The Iron Lady", beating the UK's Maggie Thatcher to the soubriquet, French, singing, music and "physical and mental sport." He further records that eighteen sat their finals iApril 1932. Of these, twelve "apostles" were still alive and meeting annually 50 years later. These formed Wachtplan NH, according to Schmal a cross-section of the Dutch population. A contemporary survey he cites apparently showed a remarkable 72% would like to have their schooldays over again.

In his next paragraph, he reminds his readers that school-leavers faced hard times in 1932:

> "As far as your future is determined in your youth by Family, Association/Church or School, for all of us it was the school most of all that formed us…Every school-day it was impressed on us that we were learning not for the School but for Life and WE too fell – just as today – after the summer 1932 into the vacuum of an Economic Crisis… no place for school-leavers… Delft engineers working as conductors on the trams… but WE had had the *"Umwertung aller Werte"* and economic lessons about Keynes at school.

> Of our Class – the family Cross-section after all – one was able to carry on to further study and that was because the Psycho-technical Laboratory of Kuiper and van Lennop of Utrecht had visited our class for a two-week long psychological test, out of which he emerged with an exceptionally high I.Q.! The rest were happily normal and began with a job and certainly…at the bottom of the ladder…therefore with both feet on the ground, as the youngest employee or as voluntary worker

or apprentice nurse. We were motivated and wrestled our way up, not to be held back!"

Finally, Schmal, or P., comes into the home straight:

> "Proposition: Youth always has the future and that has NOTHING to do with brains/knowledge or background but everything to do with the level and engagement of the education and the mentality thus formed."

Clearly, times were not easy for people leaving school in 1932, but Nel would certainly prove to be motivated and wrestle her way up. She also felt in retrospect that her unusual and ultimately unhappy home life probably made her more enterprising and independent.

> "I didn't really want to go back to the island, after the unhappy experience with my father's third wife. But I had enjoyed the life until then even though I lacked a mother figure - I suppose that made me more enterprising and aggressive. I think I'm a very independent person."

With great satisfaction, she told me a story to prove this point.

> "It must be obvious: I remember one time I drove from Brussels to Antwerp in a frightful fog. I couldn't see anything, and I stopped at a petrol station and there was a man filling his tank and he said, 'Are you ready to drive to Antwerp?' I said, is it possible and he said yes, if you follow me. So I followed him very slowly and when we got there, he invited me for coffee. While we were having it, he said: "I'm sure that's the first time in your life that you've followed someone." I never saw the man again, but the incident always stayed with me."

Nel was never again to live on Goree-Overflakkee, but she always remained proud of her island origins. Trying to understand Nel had me 'searching for something on an island'. This is a phrase Liv Ullmann uses in her book 'Changing'. On the Swedish island of Faro, Ullmann found a people living close to the earth, close to the sea, characterized by simplicity. There is surely an echo of this feeling coming down the years from the small, remote island of Goeree-Overflakkee. Admittedly, Ullman described her islanders as living in harmony with themselves, which does not sound much like Nel's islanders with all their squabbling over land and money. But elsewhere she says:

"No outsiders could point at them and make them feel inferior. People who had trust in their place on earth. They were far from uncomplicated, nor without demands, hatreds and aggressions. But they had pride, a dignity which they allowed no one to crush."

This seems to me a perfect match for the islander character that I found in Nel. When she left the island to go to school in Haarlem, Nel stood in front of her mirror, rolled up her sleeves and said to herself that it would not matter what people said about her later, as long as it was not, "that poor Slis." She, too, took pride and dignity with her from her island. Ullmann goes on to say that old people and children are also islanders in our society:

"People who don't care to keep the mask and the facade in order. Who dare to show who they are."

As her friend the renowned writer and columnist Flora Lewis said of Nel.

"What you saw was what you got."

Origins foreshadow what is yet to come; later events take us back again to our origins. This is how the jigsaw puzzle of Nel's life is built up, though with many missing pieces.

2
A moveable feast: Paris and onward

Searching for a role

It is a fact that time seems to stretch out and almost stand still in childhood. But once we are grownup, it starts to accelerate. After Nel left school, I felt the pace heating up as she set out eagerly into the world beyond the Netherlands, with all her senses on high alert.

In old age, people often go on remembering their earliest years when they can't remember what they had for breakfast. In Nel's case, it seemed to be the period after leaving the island that lingered longest in her memory, at least when she spoke to me. At first, I wondered whether this might have been because her childhood and adolescence had ended so unhappily with the hated widow. And secondary school, though she enjoyed it, was a means to an end. The end was getting away from the island, and out into the wider world. Although this was clearly a very exciting period for Nel, I eventually decided that the apparent memory quirk was simply because she was speaking to an outsider. Tyna, who was part of her surrogate family on the island, found that after she lost her memory, she could still be prompted to remember her early years by showing her photos from those days.

Everything Nel told me from those 1930s years *felt* fresh and new, and painted in bright, bold brushstrokes. This was before the shadow of war fell, and also before the postwar struggle to build her long career in journalism. At the same time, Nel's account of this chapter of her life is patchy and sometimes contradictory. Nor is it long on detailed descriptions of people and places. However many times she returned to the period with pleasure and great animation, she would still swing through it at a headlong gallop. It was impossible to get her to pause and elaborate, or to fill out the picture at some interesting point. The brushstrokes remained entirely impressionistic, dramatic and significant from a distance, but dissolving into disconnected fragments on closer inspection.

The story begins in Paris. Iman Slis, a pharmacist in Utrecht who had married the sister of Nel's mother, persuaded Nel's father to let her go there after she finished secondary school. This uncle Iman kept an eye out on Nel from afar and evidently had some influence with her father. It seems likely he was also related to him, though from a different branch of the Slis family. Nel's stay in Paris was to be the start of a lifelong love affair with the French language and culture. Some hints of an exotic Parisian lifestyle were picked up by Piet Wackie Eisden. Piet was curious about a laconic telegram from Uncle Iman summoning Nel home. 'Viens - Slis', it said. It was addressed to mlle slis, rue tournefort, paris and dated 27 June 1933. The cause of the summons, and whether she responded to it, are unknown.

In autumn 1932, Nel began her studies in Paris with a language course at the Alliance Française.

> "Later, I took a *cours de la civilisation française* at the Sorbonne. That was a very wonderful time, because I came there sort of wide-eyed and everything was interesting to me. I liked the language of course, and I liked the country, I always have. But I also found it fascinating meeting people, whether they were French, Russian or Yugoslav. They were a motley crowd. Some, very few I may say, were Dutch; then there were Yugoslav students and White Russian emigres.
>
> "I shared a flat with a very nice girl called Tamara who was also at the Sorbonne. She was from a previously very rich Russian family who were also totally out of money at that time. She had five older sisters including Veshti, the one I liked best, who I used to see later on in Rome. Tamara was born in Harbin in China and her father was pure Russian, but her mother was German. From Russia, they escaped first to China, and later they were all over the place. I got to meet all the other sisters, Dasha, Veshti and the eldest I met later, she was a lawyer in

America. There was another one who had an affair with this horrible Jewish Russian, I don't know how HE made his money, but he scared me a little. But anyway, Dasha was a nice, handsome girl, who later went to live in Venice. I spent all my Christmases with Vesti until a few years ago."

In Nel's bureau, there was a wonderful photo of Vesti looking very theatrical in a café in Rome. How I wish I had seized that and many others when I had the chance. Nel had a couple of drawers full of photos, which we browsed through for a while on one of my early visits. But at that time I hadn't even realized that her memory was disappearing, let alone the speed at which this was happening. The drawers also contained a lot of very glamorous photos of her as a young woman which I was unable to find later.

In Paris, Nel said somewhat boastfully:

"I forgot all about my first boyfriend on the island. My second boyfriend was a Frenchman, this son of the famous artist Royarts. He also wanted to marry me. He was a nice guy, Felix Conbruna. But I had to meet his parents and I thought oh Christ, no. The parents were very bourgeois, and the only thing they thought of me was that I was 'une jeune Hollandaise'. But then they saw me and they thought, not too Hollandaise, perhaps, I don't know. But I think it's because I so hated my father, there was so little affection, that I couldn't face being married to a man."

The reactions of the bourgeois Parisians to the young Dutchwoman ring true. They probably expected a bovine blonde in clogs and were quite surprised by the slim, chic young woman they met. Nel went on:

"After a year, I went back to the Netherlands for family reasons. That concerned the property. I had got a letter in a totally unknown hand, from my mother's sister who I'd never met. She sent me a note to come back because she didn't want my father to get his hands on the property. I'd never seen my uncle and aunt because my father was damned by my mother's family because he spent too much. They had told my mother that she was foolish to marry my father because he was a spendthrift. He had money of his own, but the LAND was very important on the island, because there's so little of it. My aunt said my mother had land and they said that if ever I needed it, I was welcome in Utrecht. It turned out I inherited 11 hectares from my mother, quite a lot, and I didn't realize the importance of it at the time, but later, I was able to sell the land and buy my flat in The Hague."

"While I was staying with my aunt and uncle, a professor of pharmacology at Utrecht University, he said, why don't you study pharmacy? It was easy, because he also owned two pharmacies. After a few months, my uncle decided I should live on my own, and he was right. So I found a place with a widow in Utrecht who had lost her money and she already had two school teachers staying there who were very nice. But I thought Utrecht was well, very nice too but I'm not going to stay there for the rest of my life, I must get out of there."

Nel said she couldn't stay there for ever because they paid her living expenses out of rent from the land, but I wonder whether Uncle Iman found Nel a bit too hot to handle when she was actually staying with them. However, it is clear that this part of the family was at pains to make sure the land and its income went to Nel and did not fall into the hands of her father.

"I never went back to the island until I came to live in The Hague after the war… Remember, they said, that you must never sign anything that your father puts in front of you. He must not get hold of the land of your mother, because he will swallow it up."

Nel claimed that when her father died, "there was nothing left, not of the money and not of the land, everything was squandered." This may be true, but to amend his overall record slightly, there is evidence that he did pay for her to do the nursing course she took later in the 1930s. It also seems a safe assumption that he must have paid for the year in Paris, and probably for a subsequent year in England.

Nel's nephew Hans van Nieuwenhuyzen also told me she did in fact occasionally return to Goeree-Overflakkee after she set out on her travels around Europe, even though she said she didn't. When he was a child of around ten or twelve, Nieuwenhuyzen remembers the father giving Nel money:

"It struck me then, because it was a thousand guilders, at that time a very large amount of money."

Nel herself never mentioned to me any meetings with her father at all after she left school. Yet he died nearly a quarter of a century later, on 9 May 1956.

Back in Utrecht in 1933, Nel worked in Uncle Iman's pharmacy for six months,

> "but then I got fed up with all those pills and I said I wasn't interested. The pills came out of my nose, I can tell you. So my uncle said, why don't you go to England for a year – 'so good for your character', he said."

So Nel went to England.

> "When I arrived off the boat, I went to Ilfrey Park in the neighbourhood of Harrow, a beautiful, enormous house. A sort of castle, which was then a guest-house run by Ione Sherry, as British as they came. She came to meet me at Waterloo Station and I said to her, how did you know that I was Nel Slis, and she said, because you looked Continental. In England I was very happy, because there were many people whose parents were overseas. There was a man who came from India and gave some riding lessons, and I met some very nice Irish people there who sort of took to me. Later I was billeted with people who actually washed their teeth using the crockery."

The teeth-washing bit was one of Nel's more mystifying remarks that I never cleared up with her.

> "I was reading English at Rhodes College in Oxford. I had a French boyfriend who was staying in the same house. He wanted to marry me too. We didn't sleep with boys in those days - that came later. I met a very nice Swiss girl who became a famous doctor, and later I went out with her brother and the brother wanted to marry me. I said, well, I don't want to marry - but he had said, of course, if I am going to marry you, then you have to get up early in the morning, and take a cold shower. Extraordinary.... "

Indeed.

> "Then all of a sudden I decided to be a nurse. I don't know why, but that often happens with girls - I lacked close relationships when I was young - girls want to make up for it themselves, I think. Maybe it was compensation for my lack of family ties. I was never part of a family – nobody knew what to do with me, sort of, and I was always moving from one place to another.

Lack of affection is, I think, the reason I wanted to be a nurse."

Nel applied to a very well-known nursing school outside Paris, but it didn't work out. As she explained, this was

"because they were too Catholic and I was brought up not strictly but with the idea that the world consisted mostly of Protestants. The training was very famous, the director was a niece of the cardinal and I had to go to Mass at six in the morning. After 24 hours, I walked out of there with all my luggage...

"About that time, I had a letter from this White Russian friend of mine, Tamara, inviting me to join her in Munich, and I went up there for the winter, went skiing in Garmisch and studied languages in Munich. Tamara had said to me before, you must come with me on your vacations, my mother lives in Munich and she'd like to have you there. So Paris had already proved to be my great opening to stay with families that were spread all over the world. Tamara's mother was divorced - she had lost her husband in China."

History doesn't relate whether she literally lost her husband somewhere in China or just metaphorically, on account of being divorced. Nel went on:

"Munich didn't terribly impress me, but I thought it was very nice staying with Tamara's mother. She used to say, Nel, you're spending too much, because I did, too. Because, you see, I felt embarrassed, and I spent to give them something to repay their hospitality, because I didn't pay a 'pension', and I felt that being a guest in the house, I should bring them things. My German wasn't terrific, but we had all talked French, German and English at school and I had a knack for languages. The mother talked German, and she said to me, '*Nel, du wirdst nochmal mit dem naktenpopo an der Strasse kommen*' - one day, you'll land on the street on your bare behind. I never forgot that.

"While I was following German courses in Munich, I found out there was an excellent nursing course in Lausanne, La Source, which was a very Protestant business. I started at La Source in April 1935, when I was 21, and I got my nursing diploma in November 1938. It was *tres serieux*, La Source, *Premiere Ecole des gardes-*

malades independante et evangelique. I found the evangelical part a silly business. You sung songs, '*A toi Jesus toute ma jeunesse.*' I thought: you won't get me, "a toi Jesus", never! But then we were sent out to work. I worked first in Lausanne, then a year in France in Metz and after that, a year in Geneva."

"You could take long vacations and I always went to Italy, following courses in Italian first in Perugia and later in Florence. In Florence, I stayed with Florentine people, very nice, and they had a young man there and I was young too, not beautiful but I was young. He used to say, can you sing in Dutch and I said, I can't sing but I'll talk to you in Dutch. These boys used to say, oh, it's like pulling the chain in the W.C.

"Then I thought, what shall I do now. I wanted to do another year in psychiatry actually. Because I was after all aware – I have a very good nose for this – that a lot of people are sick, physically, but that there are many more that are sick in another way. I talked with a couple of doctors in Switzerland and they said, if you want to do psychiatry with this diploma from La Source, then go to Vienna. But first I planned a long vacation in Rome to perfect my Italian."

While she was doing the nursing course in Lausanne, Nel shared a room with Inez Forel, daughter of a well-known psychiatrist, Auguste Forel.

"A crazy, but amusing person. Unfortunately, she had an affair with the gardener and had to leave the school."

Apparently Auguste Forel's influence was the reason why Nel wanted to study psychiatry in Vienna, its Mecca. However, the Utrecht Slis family had already decided in 1938 that even though Vienna might be the cradle of psychiatry, it was also a viper's nest of Nazism. So Nel went to Rome to study psychiatry and wound up staying there for a year. According to Piet Wackie Eysten, not much came of the psychiatry course because she fell in love with an Italian doctor, from whom she did learn Italian but not psychiatry. Nel did not enlighten me on any such details, but she did give me a strong sense of how much she enjoyed Rome. As in Paris, this was in large part thanks to White Russian connections:

"Italy I loved, of course. I like the Italians, of course, but I was so lucky to stay with these Russians in Rome. I was staying with a White Russian family. They have played a great part in my life, these White Russians. This family was stranded in Rome in 1917 as the husband, Massoyedo, had been number two at the Russian embassy before the revolution. They managed by taking in paying guests.

"It was a wonderful year. I did voluntary work for the forerunner of the UN's FAO (Food and Agriculture Organisation). I learned Italian. I have kept that up all my life. I took lessons here in The Hague for years and I didn't pay because the Italian government pays to keep up the culture. I went every Thursday at nine o'clock in the evening, and the teacher was a good friend, charming - she only spoke in Italian and you could only reply in Italian. There were also Italian children in the class, there to keep up their culture.

(*Back in Rome*), "Messoyedo was a very nice guy. His wife had been very rich, a Baltic baroness – but no longer, of course, after the Russian revolution. As ex-diplomats, they knew many other diplomats. So when they were stranded, they bought a house with extra rooms where they could receive *pensionaires*, like myself when I came to Rome to learn Italian. I got the contact through Jonkheer van Panhuis, who was a Dutch diplomat who knew them from the earlier diplomatic period. So they sent Dutch girls and boys there.

"Apart from Messoyedo, there was Mikalina, the maid, who impressed me. She looked after the household because 'madame' liked her. I remember there was a cat, I was very fond of cats. There was a strange collection of people. There was a tremendous homosexual, very big, from Berlin, Combodel, who spoke with his hands when he recited poems, with ten big fingers on the table. His big hands were always on the table when he wanted to make a point. At that time, we didn't even quite know what homosexuals were. It was shady, sort of. There was also a Spanish woman whose husband was in Cuba, and there were British women with husbands in the services. There was one woman whose husband was serving in the navy in Malta and she simply HATED Malta, and there was also this British military man. So it was a strange mixture, a strange potpourri of people. And I thrive on that."

I had the impression that she called Combodel a 'tremendous' homosexual because he was overtly gay in a way that she had not encountered before. Her ignorance about homosexuals is not at all surprising at that time. When I went to a girls boarding school in the UK much later, in the 1950s, a schoolteacher mystified us completely by lecturing us on the evils of having what we called 'gone-ons', or crushes, on other girls. We knew nothing about lesbianism and anyway she avoided using the term. Having a 'gone-on' at that school seemed to be more of a convention to which I conformed like everybody else. I can only think of a couple of girls who might really have been gay.

Nel went on:

> "And then the Russians themselves, there were many Russian Contessas, numerous receptions and God knows what, and I quickly came across the name of a prince... I knew nothing about Russia - I came from Goeree and Haarlem. I learned much about these things. Knowing people, that was the thing, and since I never forgot names, I got to know a lot of people because I thought it was very fascinating. So different from my island and Haarlem - when you're young, and all these characters with titles…There was no talk of the Russian revolution, but it was a kind of 'court-in-exile'. They were all refugees, some with lots of money. They talked a lot in Russian, but also in French, and they name-dropped like hell - I can't remember all the Russian princes and princesses that passed through my hands…. There was a whole pecking order - at receptions, they were all there, dropping names. They didn't talk about the communists, they only talked about have you seen the countess this, baroness that. *Terrible, trés terrible.* A lot of the Russian aristocracy of course went to Paris, but lots also to Rome, because the wife of the last king, Emanuel, was something Montenegro and had been brought up at the Czar's court."

Talking about the magnificent baroque photo of Vesti in a plush Roman café that I liked so much prompted Nel to recount an incident that was clearly important to her.

> "That photo of Vesti in the cafe - you WENT there to be seen! Vesti was a theatre woman, she did everything to do with the theatre. She was brought up very rich, but *"il ne reste plus beaucoup…* I used to go and have a drink on the Via Venezia, which was the Champs Elysee of Rome,

and that was always amusing because it was near the gardens of Rome where you walked - it was very chic. Messoyedo didn't want me to be late for lunch, as that would annoy the baroness, so he said: 'I come and get you at the Via Venezia'. Then he came with the taxi and I don't know what sort of nonsense we talked, but then he put his hand on my knee and said, *"Nel, vous avez l'ame d'un Slav"* - you have a Slav soul. And I think I have too, a little bit. The soul of a Slav? Generous, yes, and also not thinking about putting money in shares or this type of thing - not like the Germans, no, no, no. Yes, yes - for years, people used to say to me, are you Russian? I think it was the way the Russians talked, I started to talk like them."

Nel also very much liked the Italians, though she never told me anything about her medical boy-friend in Rome. But Mussolini was on the rise.

"I got on fine with the Italians, I must say. But there was a big contrast between these white Russians living in Rome in an older world and the rise of Mussolini and his followers. With the Fascists in power, I listened to them - it was fascinating in a way. We saw the Mussolini rallies in Rome - we were mocking them at first. Certainly we saw Mussolini, yes, we used to go to the piazza to hear him expound. Everyone laughed then, but all the same... he was *pas très sympathique*, no, no, no. We went there to see the show. But Mussolini was starting to get louder and louder and there had been the Anschluss in Austria in 1938. Most of the instructors in Vienna were Jewish doctors, and I didn't feel like going to that country with the Anschluss, so I was quite stymied."

The Anschluss (Union) was the political union of Austria and Germany (1938-45). Hitler's plans for union had been checked in 1934 when Mussolini sent troops to the Brenner Pass to safeguard Austria's independence. But by 1937, Mussolini was in the Axis camp and Hitler could put pressure on Chancellor Schuschnigg to legalise the Austrian Nazi party. The party stirred up unrest and in 1938, Schuschnigg resigned and Nazi Arthur Seyss-Inquart then became chancellor. He invited the Germans to occupy the country and restore order. After the occupation, Hitler held a plebiscite in which an overwhelming majority approved Austria's inclusion in 'Greater Germany.'

After I discovered that Nel once had an unhappy affair with a Russian, I wondered whether this could have been Messoyedo. I don't think so, however, as she would not have described the little incident in the taxi to me with such pride, and besides, she was always very reticent about personal matters.

A sentence in an interview about Nel leaving Rome struck a chord with me. "When the Jews in the tennis club started to flee to Brazil, it was time to get out…. " evokes shades of the film 'Tea with Mussolini."

It's easy to see where Nel's abidingly elegant dress-sense came from, between the influence of Paris and Rome and all the aristocratic people she met along the way.

WAR

(1939-1945)

3.
To the Finland station. Grand Balls, Ball-bearings and the BBC

"Like a hair in the soup"

In the summer of 1939, Nel's pharmacist uncle wrote to her, telling her: "You can't stay, they're all fascists now. There's going to be a war - come back to Holland." Nel left Rome at the end of August and reached Holland on September 1st, and on the 3rd, "there was the phoney war." The phoney war was the ominous lull following Germany's invasion of Poland, for which the Nazi-Soviet pact had cleared the way. The invasion of Poland caused Britain and France to declare war on Germany and marked the start of World War II. During the phony war, lasting until the German onslaught in the West in 1940, there was little hostile action except in Poland and at sea.

i. Nursing war-wounded in Finland

Nel was staying with her uncle and aunt in Utrecht again.

> "They had one son in Indonesia, I remember. I was disoriented, one, because I hadn't been therefor a long time and two, what to do. Utrecht was not the gayest place. I volunteered for hospital work, but in Holland, they're very snooty, they think the best of nursing is Dutch. If I wanted to work in a Dutch hospital, I had to do a refresher course for a year. So I started to do shorthand and typing, and I also learned to drive. I had a

wonderful winter then, lots of skating. Then there was this war in Finland...

"There was a big, big ball in the Witte Brug (a hotel that no longer exists), a very smart, well-known place in The Hague, and I was dancing with this guy and talking to him. I said, I'm back here now after so many years and I'm ever so bored, and he said well, I know something for you. He was the top man in the Red Cross, André de la Porte was his surname, from a "*trés grande famille*", and he knew I was a trained nurse - you know, La Source was a great school.

"Then he said, we are sending an ambulance team to Finland, would you like to come? Finland had been at war with Russia, but the war was finished, and everyone was helping. Apparently it didn't matter there that I had a Swiss diploma. So I went to nurse war-wounded on the Finnish-Russian front."

The ball had in fact been held for the victims of the Finnish-Russian war.

Nel left for Finland on 21 March 1940 with the ambulance team, consisting of 19 nurses, six doctors, an interpreter and a driver. The team was cheered on its way at the Red Cross head office on Prinsessegracht in The Hague by Princess Juliana, then chairwoman of the Dutch Red Cross. Then, Nel shuddered,

"We went by air to Copenhagen and Stockholm. It scared the wits out of me, I hated flying."

This was the only time Nel ever flew. She also had a lifelong aversion to using elevators, which gave her claustrophobia.

From Stockholm, Nel insisted on taking a boat to Finland.

"I arrived via Helsingborg, stuck on the Baltic Sea, virtually alone, because most had flown, but I got there anyway and they were all in Vierumaeki (about 150 kilometres northeast of Helsinki). That was really a magnificent building, which was originally meant as a training site for the Canada 1938 Olympics, but the Olympics never came off because of the war. There we had a contract for three months."

As things turned out, it was to be over five years before Nel returned to the Netherlands.

A Dutch newspaper reported shortly after the team's arrival that the ambulance started work on 1 April in a sports school in Verumaeki, converted into a surgical clinic and hospital. The report went on:

> "On that day, the operating room saw two operations, while the first six photos were made in the X-ray room. The ambulance functioned with all its own surgical and medical equipment, which, thanks to good packing, arrived completely undamaged after difficult transportation via plane, ship, rail and truck."

The number of war-wounded received and nursed by the Dutch Red Cross team in Verumaeki soon ran into the hundreds. One of the doctors recounted his experiences in the Dutch Magazine for Medicine.

> "By weak lamplight, the patients lay cheerlessly staring in front of them, their eyes sunk deep in their exhausted faces, dyed green by the light. Visitors entering from the daylight suddenly found themselves plunged deep in immense distress. In one bed, a blind man was vegetating, no longer bothered by the half-light. Next door, a completely paralysed patient had quietly withdrawn in the dusky hell to die unnoticed, and a young farm boy with amputated arms tossed restlessly around and around."

On 10 May, 1940, the Germans invaded Holland. Nel said most of the doctors and nurses wanted to go back and applied for visas, but there were three doctors who were not married and didn't want to ask the Germans for a visa. "They got away somehow with the aid of the Finns, in an aeroplane," she said with a touch of asperity. Nel herself had no wish to return to Holland. As she put it, she had

> "no fiancé, no family and not even a canary. I wanted to go to England to do something against the Nazis. We were hearing this dreadful Blitzkrieg on London all the time on the radio…I did not want to go back, but the Finns were also not terribly funny."

By the end of June, the Vierumaeki sports school was no longer available and its entire medical inventory was taken to Helsinki. A month later, when the last patients had been taken elsewhere, it was presented to the Finnish Red Cross. At the end of August, a message was received from Berlin that visas were approved for the ambulance team members. Most of them then travelled via Sweden and Germany back to occupied Holland, arriving there on 8 September 1940.

In a more acid comment on the rest of the team, Nel fulminated in one interview that

> "Three of the seven doctors oiled themselves away like hares, without any discussion, when we heard the krauts had occupied the Netherlands. The others went back to the Netherlands, also without any discussion. Just like most nurses, Dutch women were milksops then, they were always too late getting there. And now they still do nothing", said Nel with a sudden flare of anger.

It is difficult to imagine Nel in the frumpy, Victorian uniforms of the nurses in the photo of the Finland ambulance team on its return to the Netherlands on page... She was to don nursing gear one last time again in England later in the war. No doubt she still managed to look slim and trim and dashing. I am sure she was a practical and efficient nurse with a 'no-nonsense' approach, very likely giving short shrift to petty malingerers and complainers. Her great curiosity and interest in what was going on would have stood her in good stead, and she would have been quite fearless and calm in the face of horrendous wounds or diseases. Her warmth, honesty and sympathy would then have come across. She must have been a good person to have at your bedside if you were really in trouble.

I found no record of Nel speaking about her nursing experiences in Finland. She was ever reticent about matters she regarded as private or did not wish to go into for whatever reason. Although it was not a lengthy period, it must have been a deeply affecting experience.

Nel and her fellow-nurses were awarded the Finnish bronze Bravery Medal. There was also a hand-written statement "to certify that Miss N.A. Sliss (sic) has been working as a diplomed nurse during the whole stay of the Dutch ambulance in Finland to the utmost content," signed by Dr J.A.C. Schepel, 1st surgeon of the Dutch Ambulance in Finland. A few months later, a letter was sent from The Hague to inform her that she had been awarded a silver Red Cross medal for her services in Finland. The letter was addressed to Middelharnis, and took years to reach Nel, at the time somewhere on the high seas between Finland and America.

**Dutch nurses on their return from nursing war-wounded in Finland,
September 1940**

ii. A long road to America

Meanwhile, back in Finland after the other nurses had left, Nel and two other nurses camped out in the woods by the lakes, with reindeer wandering around the paths. They made fires to cook fish and even managed to smoke some, and they fetched bread by boat.

> "One was like me, a freebooter with practically no family, the other was Jewish, so she certainly had some reason to be afraid. So the Jew and I decided to try to get out some other way."

This was a lean and difficult period, I learned obliquely, with little to eat and great uncertainty about what to do. Plus there was the fear of the ever-encroaching Nazis. But Nel had contacts.

> "The then chargé d'affaires, a very nice man, said he could take us and give us shelter with an old man who lived just outside Helsinki. So there we sat and played gin rummy, and I remember I even gave Dutch lessons to the Belgian ambassador's daughter. We were still trying to get out - the two nurses wanted to go to Indonesia, but I didn't - I wanted to go to England."

First, the three decided to go to America via Sweden, but the Dutch ambassador in Sweden advised them to go via Russia.

> "There was no direct way, so we thought we would go via Russia and Japan to the States and then I could go to England and the others to Indonesia."

Even Nel conceded this wasn't easy.

> "For Russia, we needed to get a visa; for a visa, we had to go to Sweden, so we went to Sweden, the Jew and I, and I had one boyfriend there from Perugia University, who...I didn't feel very much like asking aid from him, because he wanted to marry me. He was a philology student, working on an English dictionary - not the most interesting thing...His mother was in a mental home and his father had shot himself. For several reasons, I didn't want to marry him, though he was a very nice man."

With his family record, no wonder.

Piet Wackie Eysten discovered a telegram sent from Stockholm on 11 May, 1940, the day after the Germans invaded Holland, and addressed to Nel Slis, Dutch Ambulance, Vierumaeki. It said: "Keep strong, stick to me, love Gustav Warburg." Piet had no idea who this Gustav was, but he also found a letter from him kept by Nel among her papers and dating from nearly four years later. This was apparently written in reply to one sent by Nel from London at the end of 1943.

> "I am so glad you are all right, satisfied with your work and so on", he wrote. "I am sorry you did not get my last letter of last summer where I told you that I am married since 17/7."

Gustav had bought a house outside Stockholm, but was called up for military service.

> "Poor Finland and the Baltic States. Is there no other solution for Europe than the choice between brown and red barbarism? Please write me soon about your self", the last sentence underlined.

> "There are so many things I can't write in this letter, one has to think of the examiner."

No doubt he was referring to censorship. Whether this was the same former boyfriend as the depressive Swede from Perugia University, history does not relate, but she must have been fond of him as she kept his letter.

Back in 1940, Nel said,

> "I sat there in Helsingborg and I went to see my embassy people and I said I'd like to go to America and the man

said well, we can arrange that.......We got a visa for Japan, but not for Russia, so we had to go on, you know, standing in the queue."

Failure to get a visa for Russia was not for want of trying. Armed with an introduction to the Soviet Embassy from the Dutch ambassador to Sweden, Nel managed to speak to the Russian ambassadress, commonly described as the 'famous' Aleksandra Kollontai, *La Kollontai*. She owed her fame to being Russia's first woman ambassador. Asked later whether La Kollontai was charming, Nel said:

"She was at least human and she saw a possibility that I could get to America via Russia and Japan. From there, I could then get to England. Nonetheless, she did refuse the visa: La Kollontai accurately observed: 'Lady, your country has never recognised mine'."

That somewhat circuitous route via Russia and Japan to America and England was now barred, but another epic journey soon took its place.

"Suddenly we got news from a friend I'd made, a friend of the mayor of Helsinki, and he said come over, there's a boat going from Petsamo (then in northern Finland) to Baltimore - quicker than all this circus. So we dropped all the Japanese and Russian part - we already had visas for America."

The ship, a 3,000 tonne freighter, took 26 days. At one point, it nearly sunk after hitting a submerged iceberg. Nel and her companions slept on the floor. "(The boat) cavorted over the ocean and I was dead sick the whole journey", Nel said. The vessel was Finnish, and the Finns were neutral at the time. Also on board were two maids bound for the Finnish embassy in Washington and two Jewish people, one from Czechoslovakia and one from Denmark.

"We stopped in Tromso, in the extreme north of Norway. There the krauts boarded the boat, and the Finns said, who have we got here? But then they let the Nazis through all the same. The captain said, I don't think that they will do anything, because they are people from the German Navy. They did leave the two Jewish people and the nurses alone. They also said, I actually heard one say, 'Ach, these Red Cross sisters are not interesting'. If he had just known how interesting we were!

> After that visit, there was not a drop of alcohol left for the rest of the trip, nearly a month... The radio on board also went on the blink then"'.

Conceding that the boarding of the Germans was a risky moment, Nel said:

> "Well, of course. But if you're about 26, then you only think of one thing: 'I must get to America as soon as possible'. Nowadays I would have shit my pants three times, probably. But at that time... But yes, I was very happy when I reached land"'.

At any rate, she insisted she was not scared at the time.

> "No, I only had one idea--that I must get away from these godforsaken Nazis.

> But I did talk once with the captain, though that was a very difficult conversation. He knew a little bit of German and a little English, I knew no Finnish, so we just wormed our way around. Then I said: Will we ever get there? And he said, 'Well, if only the load does not shift' Because he had to go on to Japan. That was one of the few things (I learned) from our conversation."

In her conversation with the captain, Nel managed to discover that the boat was carrying ball-bearings from Sweden to Japan.

> "Which I promptly reported to the British Naval attaché in New York - I don't think the boat ever got to Japan............"

Altogether, it was a gruelling trip.

> "That Finnish boat, the Britta Thorden - I shall never forget it. It was stormy all the time, I was sick as a dog, and when I stepped onto the quay green in the face, still in this lovely Carl Denig (nurse's) outfit, along with the stateless Jews, the maids for the Finnish embassy in Washington and two fellow-nurses, there were these rich American ladies on the quay, saying: 'How interesting - refugees from Europe."

Nel arrived in the U.S. in November 1940. It then took her until the following May to get to England:

> *(In New York)* "I stayed with my Russian friend Tamara, who had got married to an American diplomat there. But they were just married, you know...Since I had only my

uniform, she gave me clothes for New York. I was applying for jobs...I was a graduate nurse, so I was going round all the agencies; I spoke Dutch, German, French, Italian, English. But I wasn't at my best after Finland, there was very little to eat there, so they told me at last they were really looking for a blonde receptionist, something like that", Nel snorted.

She ended up working at the Netherlands Purchasing Commission of the Dutch government-in-exile. There, she translated pilots' handbooks for the Brewster fighter aircraft they were optimistically hoping to buy to defend Dutch Indonesia, but she told me they never got the planes.

"But I got so tired of America - it was not at war, it was before Pearl Harbour, and I felt out of place and uncomfy... I was going mad from these Americans, who just did not want to participate in the war, and from these American wives, who hadn't got anything better to do than knit socks for those poor Europeans"'.

iii. England!

In New York, Nel nagged the consulate to get her to England and eventually got herself into the second Canadian naval division convoy, which left for the U.K. in May 1941.She sailed on a Union Castle Line ship. As the only person not in uniform, she aroused some suspicion on arrival in the U.K. and was allowed in only after a two-hour screening. This was conducted by

"the already famous Colonel Oreste Pinto, a British security officer of Amsterdam-Portuguese origins, who had put a rope around the neck of many Pieter Gerbrandy about the screening, but finally admitted:

"I did find him (Pinto) a nice guy." After all, she conceded, "I was the only one not in uniform. There were American girls, all in nice uniforms, and all kinds of uniformed boys, who had come from far and near. I arrived in Scotland with this boat, an Union Castle liner. There I got a night train - I had never seen a blacked-out train before. It was war, but I didn't realise that myself yet. I was accompanied, because they didn't really trust me much - that woman not in uniform, who is she? So I was under escort by a man and a woman, obviously from the Brits, to see if I was kosher and not a spy. If the

English hear that you speak two or three languages, then they think, hmm, suspicious."

By 1 August, Nel had found work, joining the Netherlands Voluntary Red Cross in New Cross Hospital in Wolverhampten, where the Princess Irene Brigade was stationed. She described this as nursing a "colony of Dutch exiles."

> "But I didn't like the Dutch colony there. Anyway, these colonies are always uninteresting. They were not sick, of course - it was just ingrown toenails and blackheads, and there'd be a great feast if someone got appendicitis."

Her nursing work was however appreciated. Miss F. Cain, the hospital's Matron, gave her a reference on her departure, which said Miss Adriana N. Slis had acquired

> "very valuable experience in the up-to-date surgical technique and treatment of acute surgical and accident patients."

The document also wished her every success in her future career, little knowing that Nel was then about to leave the nursing profession forever.

In Wolverhampton, Nel had nursed Cees Fock, then working in London with the government in exile, who became a lifelong friend. Fock was to prove a staunch ally and advisor during Nel's initial years as a journalist in The Hague, as he became Secretary-General of the General Affairs Ministry (in UK terms, this approximates to the Prime Minister's Office). Nel clearly felt somewhat sidelined in Wolverhampton after battling to get to England to do something about the Nazis, but her next move did make her part of the war effort. It also landed her in London when it was under siege from V-2 bombing.

> "I moved to London and stayed with one of the Russians I knew from Paris (Lottie), who had married an Englishman in Singapore and was happy to take me in," Nel told me. "I got a job with the BBC monitoring service in January 1943 - by taking a test. I monitored various languages, in the first place Dutch and Flemish, of course. I found the food horrifying. We were sitting in the country in Evesham, later in Reading and Cavendish."

There were monitors from all over the world - Swedes, Kenyans, Arabs, a Dutch woman with a Kenyan background, a whole slew of Czechs and Slovakians, a contingent of Danes and other northerners. As well as

Dutch and Flemish, Nel's linguistic talents meant she could fill in on monitoring French and Italian broadcasts.

Everything was monitored and translated, from military business to rationing of bread, said Nel. For example, if a monitor heard about bread rationing, this information went straight to the economic affairs ministry, and reports of potato disease went to the agriculture ministry. Though the Dutch official broadcasting station was censored by the Germans, Nel said,

> "I assume that (the information) about food and so on was reliable. But of course you also heard this gigantic propaganda. Mr Max Blokzijl was one of the lads I always had to listen to. Another was Anton Mussert. There could be clues everywhere: 'Die Deutsche Soldaten sind braun verbrannt heimgekehrt' (the German soldiers have returned home tanned) meant they'd been in the tropics."

Nel's annual salary at the BBC was £300 plus cost-of-living bonus, and she worked there for nearly two years. It was also possible on request to avail of 'Corporation bicycles' for free transport, but this carried a warning:

> "Users of Corporation bicycles are not permitted to use the bus service to and from Wood Norton (where the Monitoring Service of the Overseas Division was based) unless it is found there is room in the bus for such people when all passengers entitled to priority have been accommodated."

Quoting these regulations, Piet Wackie-Eysten remarked that the BBC did not leave much to chance.

iv. Like a Hair in the Soup

Nel's White Russian friend Lottie was still living in London in 1944, and a director of the Associated Press (AP) was living in the apartment next door. A girl-friend working for the AP told Nel she was doing similar work to Nel and making more money for it. The AP people were desperately looking for monitors in London at the time. It was a very different setup, as the BBC operation was vast, with 2,000 people listening in to every conceivable service. The AP had a tiny staff compared with this, and was "only for spot news."

> "The BBC did not pay so well, because it was government work. I met a journalist at a party about

then given by the White Russians (Lottie). He was an Associated Press director and he asked, just to keep the conversation going, who was I actually. So I told him that I was Dutch and what had happened to me, and then he said: 'What are you doing now?' I said: well, I'm monitoring, for the BBC. Then he said: 'We have no correspondent in occupied Europe and we also have a monitoring service, but with us all these details about bread and things are not important. We have to know what they're up to. Would you like to work with us? We pay better, but you do have to work at night a lot. But shorter hours and well paid.'"

As a result of this encounter with the AP director, whose name was Bob Bunnelle, Nel then did a test, and after obtaining the approval of the Ministry of Labour and National Service, joined the AP in Fleet Street, at a salary of 7 pounds. 7 shillings a week or about £382 a year.

Money was not the only consideration. Nel's letter accepting the appointment shows that she was looking for opportunities to get back to the Netherlands and calculated her chances of being sent to an occupied country were greater at an international press agency than at the BBC. She wrote to Bunnelle from Wargrave, Berkshire on 16 October 1944:

"I feel sure I shall be happy working for your organisation and look forward to the day when it will be possible for you to transfer me to your office in Holland,"

She began work on 25 October, initially on the day desk "until we get you worked into the organisation," said Bunnelle.

This did not take long, as a complimentary note from Bunnelle on 28 April, 1945 showed that Nel was already doing good reporting work by then:

Nice work on the link up today! As you see from New York's message, your report was about twenty minutes ahead of all others, which is very nice indeed, and which will go into your personal file as another evidence of the capabilities of Miss Nel Slis. RB

She referred to this as the beginning of her journalistic career:

"I sat in a closet with all sorts of other Europeans, who each had an occupied area to cover and write pieces about"

It also meant living in London again,

"where these V-1s and V-2s were descending. At that time, you found nothing scary, nor can I remember that anyone ever went into the cellars in Fleet Street when there was an air-raid warning'".

Fleet Street, then still the nation's press headquarters, was quite colourful at the time.

"God, and they drank, these young guys, I'll never forget that in my life."

Because they were scared, too, she finally admits:

"You heard the V-2s that flew over your head in Fleet Street. There was one that was really a big boozer. He was so queasy sometimes that he didn't know what to do. Then he opened the drawer and then, roetsch, he shut it again..."

Wondering whether to throw up in it, I surmised. Nel continued:

"'At the AP, it was all about news and not reports about potato disease. That was a good deal more interesting. I didn't do badly because I knew many people, you see, and I had my ears quite open. I often gave them a piece of news, for instance that Queen Wilhelmina was going to ride in a jeep through Walcheren (the peninsula in the southwest of Holland on which the port of Vlissingen or Flushing is located), or about the Dutch planes for Indonesia, or the Dutch plans for emigration. Because Holland was badly hit by the war, they were talking about emigration for the first time for many centuries. I had a couple of nice scoops there - I knew, for example, 20 minutes before the rest of the world that the Americans and Russians had met on the Elbe and that went straight into the papers."

This was the scoop for which Bunnelle had complimented her: Nel had picked up on French radio the news that the Russians and the Americans had made contact on 25 April at Torgau, not far from Berlin. The telegram from New York Bunnelle referred to read:

"Thanks, fine rapid work Paris radio on linkup, putting us approximately twenty minutes ahead both oppositions"

The opposition was the competing international press agencies Reuters and UPI. The telegram marked Nel's definitive arrival in the world of journalism, and gave a hint of her potential as a world-class journalist.

Nel summed up this period modestly:

> "Anyway I was trying hard to do that job when the war ended."

She went on:

> "By that time, the AP was saying listen, before the war only Reuters sold news in Europe, but now the AP will be in competition - we're going to sell the American news service, because it's become much more important now in Europe. Because I knew languages, I had been assigned to the job in London. At a certain point, I heard (and it was actually fairly secret) that they were going to Holland. I told that to Burne, Chief of Bureau, and he said: 'If that is true, will you go to Holland too?' I said: 'Well, I will go and see if that rich clay is still lying in Goeree and Overflakkee and if there are still a few cents there'. And then he said: 'We are going to set up a bureau there, will you work for us?' So then I said: 'Yes, I'll go back'.

So, as Nel was fond of saying, "I fell into journalism like a hair in the soup."

Halfway through a 1990s radio interview, when Nel was talking about how the English found her suspicious because she spoke two or three languages, the interviewer thoughtfully repeated "suspicious" and remarked that she had a colourful life as a girl. Were there others like her at that time, he asked. It was undoubtedly unusual then for a young woman to travel, study and work her way around Europe on her own, and even to be allowed to do so, as Nel duly conceded. She said a certain predisposition was necessary for this. She attributed her own predisposition to the fact that she had in a manner of speaking brought herself up.

Were other girls not jealous of what you had done at that time, the interviewer enquired. Nel snapped back, "I don't trouble myself much with other girls", possibly irritated by the repeated use of the term "girl." After all, by the time she had reached London, she was a seasoned traveller with a first-rate nursing diploma, experience of nursing the war-wounded in Finland and five languages under her belt. And she was 29. But she did "trouble herself with young men?" To this Nel replied frankly, despite or perhaps because of the series of rejected suitors she had already chalked up:

> "I was more involved with myself, how I could get from here to there, what would I do then, etc."

Then, relenting about her 'girls' jibe, she admitted:

> "No, I have always had very good women friends. Few, but very good."

Elaborating on the interviewer's point about few women travelling and studying independently at the time, Nel said:

> "Few Dutch women perhaps. Because look, Dutch girls did go abroad and so on, but they had everything nicely arranged for them, and I just had to wait and see. Yes, I was not *comme les autres*. An odd one out? Yes, but I was really not stuck up about it. I had to keep swimming."

In other European countries and no doubt in Holland, too, 'young ladies of good family' did travel then, even sometimes on their own. In Britain, for example, it was the inter-war era of bright young things á la Brideshead Revisited, with a degree of emancipation for some women at least. But there were still few who so serious-mindedly strove to "do something" in the world In Holland, it seems, there were none. It had not been particularly easy for Nel to 'keep swimming' and to find her way, even though her life had so far been an enormous adventure for the curious islander. This may explain why she often repeated the phrase about falling into journalism like a hair in the soup - at last, something that really engaged and challenged her, more than nursing.

However, nursing was an important part of Nel's life. Though she talked very little about it, she did say she enjoyed it and wouldn't have missed it for anything. Between her three years' training, Finland experience and about two years in Wolverhampton, it took up half of her adult life between leaving school and the end of the war. We cannot have Nel without her nursing. It, too is part of her, even though she went on to pursue a very different career.

Mulling Nel's early adventures, Tyna Wynaendts felt her attraction to languages was in itself unusual.

> "Usually people who are very good at languages already have one parent of a different nationality, or have been exposed at a very early age to a different language, but Nel wasn't at all. She never met foreigners; she'd never travelled abroad before she went to Paris, why did she want to go? For a Dutch girl to go to a Swiss (nursing) school was also outrageous - you would go to a Dutch school."

There were obvious forces propelling Nel out of the country - her unhappiness and her problematic father - but she also had good friends there. Tyna remarked that as well as her close friendship with Tyna's mother,

> "she had lots of boyfriends, even (when she was still) in Middelharnis."

The key to Nel, Tyna believes, is that

> "she really wanted to be independent, that's what she kept repeating: that it's a good thing for a girl to know that it's always better when you can be completely independent financially. That was very unusual. When I was sent to university in Leiden, it was never said of course, but it was more to find the right husband than to really do something academic. But Nel always insisted, make sure you can look after yourself."

Nel was awarded the Red Cross medal for Bravery, Skill and Dedication and a Finnish decoration from General Mannerheim for her work nursing the war-wounded in Finland. She also received a bronze plaque from the Princess Irene Brigade for her nursing in Wolverhampton. She once mentioned that one of the medals only finally reached her at the beginning of the 1990s, possibly the Red Cross one sent to Middelharnis.

Foreign Correspondent

(1945-1962)

4.
The AP's Slis

'Who are you, actually?

The first months back in the Netherlands passed in a whirlwind at the AP's new bureau at Nieuwe Zijds Achterburgwal 225 in the centre of Amsterdam. Nel, under the tutelage of Bureau Chief Henk Kersting, was learning the trade of journalism as well as acting as general factotum. Nel told me that AP and Reuters had shared an office in Amsterdam before the war.

> "But after the war, the AP set up its own offices in Amsterdam and I moved there in summer 1945, shortly after Holland was liberated. I was doing everything, selling photos, news, translating, getting news. Amsterdam and the AP bureau there was a witches' cauldron then,"

I never discovered what she meant by a witches' cauldron. At any rate, Kersting taught Nel the 'basic tricks of the trade', and was to be her supportive and appreciative bureau chief for the bulk of her career. He was already a well-known journalist, and had been in the resistance in the war.

Though relatively new to journalism, Nel did have the advantage of considerable experience of the world from her travels and adventures since leaving school. This prompted the rector of her old school, Dr. De Vletter, to invite her to tell a couple of groups from the higher classes something about these travels, De Vletter said:

> "If you like, in French or English, (tell them) about your impressions of Finland, your voyage from Finland to

America, the relations between Russians and Finns, and then tell something at around 12 in the teachers meeting, as you told it to me and my wife on Saturday."

i. Learning the trade

Among the early news events covered by the AP was a world cycle race, and the first Ecumenical World Congress. The latter was held in Amsterdam's Concertgebouw, home of the world- renowned Royal Concertgebouw Orchestra, in August and September. Nel was unimpressed by the American AP specialists parachuted in for such events.

> "Our American religious correspondent couldn't manage to say anything other than 'Concertgebouw' in a week. Another American colleague fainted in a tourist boat at the end of the festivities because of the large quantities of jonge jenever." (Dutch gin).

Nel gave me the impression that the Amsterdam-based period was quite brief.

> "After six months, there was an AP man making a tour of Europe to see how things were going and he said, we need someone in The Hague - the news had come that the International Court of Justice was being based there, and then, the Dutch were losing Indonesia."

Indonesia and the opening of the International Court of Justice, along with Marshall Aid and Dutch postwar reconstruction, were all big news for the Americans. The senior AP visitor was very surprised to find that there was a bureau in the capital of the Netherlands, but nobody was located in The Hague, the seat of government. Nel was in due course invited to be the AP's first correspondent in The Hague, and moved there to set up house and office in a flat in Javastraat 11. Kersting, who had recommended her for the post, had received a telegram from New York:

'We'll send Slis to The Hague'

This was an important post: all the big international papers had a correspondent in The Hague in those postwar days. Nel told me she initially went to The Hague on two months' trial, but the timing is something of a mystery. She said in more than one interview that she moved on 1 April, 1946, but according to her archives, it was much later, in July 1950. This is a huge difference, but less significant than it might seem, as she was certainly covering events in The Hague and anywhere else in the news long before 1950. Time does tend to telescope later on in life, and the Amsterdam period would perhaps have been overshadowed by the thrill of becoming the AP's first correspondent in The Hague. All the same, the specific and memorable earlier date she gave for the move in interviews is very odd.

I have taken my cue from Nel's own accounts of her early battles and followed them as if she did indeed make the move to The Hague earlier. But one detail about Amsterdam is worth mentioning. There, Tina Wynaendts told me she shared a flat with one Puk Gukov. Puk's father eventually married three times, and her mother was his second wife. The Gukovs were the richest family in Holland and owned the Catshuis, now the prime minister's official residence. Tyna said this female flat-sharing episode was unique for Nel. She speculated that because there was no loving relationship when she was growing up on Goeree-Overflakke,

> "maybe that was why she wasn't going to live with anybody after that - apart from this Puk. And they didn't stay friends."

It certainly was the last time Nel shared a flat with another woman.

Whatever about the timing of her move, politics was a new beat for Nel.

> "I had to make my way in the small world of The Hague and of parliament, which was beginning to operate again. Well, I'd never sat in parliament before, so I ran hell for leather - Slis in The Hague - and after two months, he (presumably Kersting) wrote to New York and said: 'Slis has done a workmanlike job'. That's how I started in the Netherlands with the AP, and I was with them until 1979."

'AP's Slis' was born.

ii. Battling against the Odds

Nel set up her office in the front of the flat, and the AP paid her rent of 50 guilders a month. She furnished it with a telex, a filing cabinet and a desk with a typewriter. This, along with piles of notebooks, remained her total journalistic equipment for her entire life, apart from the later addition of a fax machine. Material for much of this book was mined from the same filing cabinet, by then aged and battered. Fortunately for her, she did not have to face the switch to computers, which would probably have driven her crazy.

Nel described her initial difficulties in The Hague at length in many interviews. A few excerpts show her fighting her way into an unreceptive, often hostile male world and into another new reporting area.

"It wasn't easy. I had to work hard to get to know the unknown parliamentary and diplomatic world of The Hague. Right away I plunged into my books - especially political science - from the Kennemer Lyceum, which someone had luckily kept for me. I had been away for so long. I worked hard and undressed in the dark, because there were no curtains when I moved into Javastraat 11…I had nothing, how did you find a pillow, a towel - that alone was a problem already. I had no bicycle *(shades of the BBC's Corporation bicycles)*. I walked and walked; I walked the soles off my shoes. I sent my shoes to England to have them cobbled, it couldn't be done here. It was chaos in the Netherlands just after the war - anyone from Dachau got a job regardless."

Nel complained vociferously about the postwar period, especially

"hindrance by authorities and press information people who couldn't inform, never knew anything and only sat there because they had been so good in the war."

As she told one interviewer, she often had to carry on working mad with rage. There was no doubt in her mind that she encountered hindrance *because* she was a woman. She was after all virtually the only female around in those years. The interview goes on:

"There were bastards sitting there', she said. Sometimes she came home crying from rage and frustration. Then she went to the bathroom, rolled up her sleeves, showered her streaming eyes, looked at herself in the mirror and said: 'Slis, they will NOT make you small'. 'I was a tough one', she said. 'You must be very strong physically and mentally. Everywhere I went, I had to explain first who I was and then, what AP was. A female correspondent at that time was a freak of nature - I was the one and only in the Netherlands and there was no precedent for this. They didn't want to take you seriously. I could have stuffed them....' The civil servants, the politicians, and the spokesmen all got up her nose. 'In the beginning, a woman in this work was of course a novelty, but with all these spokesmen, just out of

Dachau or the resistance, it was difficult. Who is that broad, where does she come from? And I didn't find it necessary to say how important I really was. If there's one thing I never want to hear again, it's *"who are you actually."* That's what they always said, these godforsaken Dutch. It still rings in my ears."

This phrase particularly enraged Nel, and she often harked back to it.

"When I went to present myself at one or other ministry, I said that I worked for the Associated Press, and then they said - not all of them, some of them thought it was fun - then they said to me: 'Who are you, actually' Ha, who are you actually!! I will write a book about it one of these days, and this chapter will be called: 'Who are you, actually?' I'll never forget it my whole life! 'Who are you, actually?' Condescending? Yes..."

Luckily they weren't all like that. General Affairs Ministry secretary-general Cees Fock, whom she had nursed in Wolverhampton during the war helped her greatly and also gave her much-needed good advice. And through him, she met other people, gradually building up contacts that often became not only valuable sources but also good friends. Others were Ernst van der Beugel and Hans Boon, both foreign affairs ministry officials at the time.

Meanwhile, Nel was having little joy with her fellow-hacks. As one of her interviewers put it:

"All the male journalists and reporters were urbane and scrubbed clean. But they swaggered with indignation if they heard the word CAO (collective labour agreement). They all wore ties - preferably bow ties. At press conferences, they made a small bow and addressed ministers as 'excellentie'.

The journalists of the day were described elsewhere as

"Drab, grey three-piece suits who bowed and scraped to every minister like jack-knives and then asked obvious questions."

Not the AP's correspondent, her interviewer noted. After a few routine questions by other journalists, she habitually asked the minister, "But Mr.., tell us now, without beating about the bush, exactly how things stand

Nel said she got scoops because she dared to ask the authorities questions, unlike her male colleagues. "If it was about news, I trampled them all into the corner," she said modestly, adding

> "I was a woman, I was young, I was a lot more beautiful than I am now and I gave as good as I got. If I had something they didn't, they did not begrudge me that. It made me more aggressive than I was, and gave me a bigger gob, definitely. They found it really strange, actually. That broad that's walking around... who is that broad

Her approach was not always appreciated, especially her habit of phoning ministers after they had gone to bed. These late calls

> "were not (intended) to pester them, but because she herself had a somewhat unusual schedule: working hard in the daytime, and in the evening pounding away until deep into the night and then beginning again very early in the mornings."

This interviewer told the story of Nel being banned for three weeks from the foreign affairs ministry, because Foreign Minister Eelco van Kleffens found her too impertinent.

> "This is how it happened. Nel Slis was sitting in the press spokesman's office. When he went out for a minute to fetch a document, the minister came into the room just then, whereupon Nel Slis immediately shot at him: 'Well, Mr Van Kleffens, now you can tell me something directly...' So that ended badly. It was the period when the average journalist licked the backside of the minister and not yet the other way round, like now."

iii. Breaking the Mould

Quite apart from all the difficulties she was encountering in the Netherlands, Nel's ambitions still stretched beyond her native country. At an early stage, she tried to get a transfer to Paris, but there was no vacancy. Undeterred, Nel approached Paris Bureau Chief Preston Grover directly. He saw no opportunities for Nel there either, transparently confirming Nel's experience of prejudice against women in this male profession when he wrote to her, around Christmas 1951:

> "You know of course that you are rowing against a fast tide. You are practically the only woman reporter abroad

in the AP. The reason is of course that most jobs seem to call for men. I don't know why this is necessarily true, but that is the prevailing idea. Nevertheless, of all Europe, Paris is the most likely place for a woman reporter to find something to keep her busy"

Doubtless Grover meant writing about haute couture and the like.

Nel's boss Kersting also approached Wes Gallagher, AP's General Manager in New York, on her behalf to try to get her some training in the U.S. But Gallagher saw no post where Nel's many talents could be better used by the AP than in Holland. Even a visit by Kersting to New York failed to produce any results. One of the directors, Lloyd Stratton, remarked that *"she seems to be a fabulous woman"*, but concluded that this was all the more reason to keep her in The Hague. So Nel just had to find something to keep her busy back in the Netherlands, amid her dreary, nit-picking male fellow-journalists.

However, things were gradually improving, and Nel even found a few compatible souls in the press fraternity.

> "After all, in time I became a sort of copain and there were very good lads there who also helped you. You had Jaap Hoek of Trouw there, first class. And Dries Ekker of Het Parool, a deranged boy, sometimes a bit jealous if you got something before him, but very able and a good reporter, Louis Metzemakers of course (see later) and Marcus van Blankenstein, who also did not treat me like old rubbish. The nicest were Jaap Hoek and Metzemakers. Jaap Hoek was my first real friend among my colleagues, and later Marcus van Blankenstein. With Blankenstein, you could see very well that he had travelled the whole world before the war. That man was well-read."

Nel was quick to differentiate herself as a news agency reporter from newspapermen like Blankenstein

> "I'm no soul-searcher. I had no time for past, present and future dissertations. I was not getting into digging out why people behaved as they did. I was a simple agency reporter with a good nose for news, and I am paid for that nose."

She once said her nose got longer during her career as a journalist, which it did, literally as well as figuratively. Wryly, Nel remarked that despite the greyness of her male colleagues,

> "I still had more pleasure from these guys than from those women. There weren't any at all in my profession in the 1950s, you can say until well into the 1960s. And these other women, they were always so pitiful. They were hardly even grey. I can see them still, sitting behind their tea-tray, and SO happily married."

Oddly enough, towards the end of her long career at the AP, Nel said she felt

> "a certain homesickness for the 1945-50 period, the fighting with spokesmen, 'plucked out of the resistance' who didn't know what they should do with a journalist, looked askance at this skirted Argus and on top of this had never heard of the AP."

It is obvious from these descriptions that Nel was not simply breaking the mould of Dutch post-war journalism by her sex, but also by her direct, persistent and certainly aggressive approach, in contrast to the often mealy-mouthed, sycophantic reporters of the day. Friso Endt, Dutch journalist and foreign correspondent, recalled Slis among the press corps:

> "They were all big shots, the Dutch and the foreigners. And Nel came there among them as the only woman. She worked day and night, she never stopped. She went to every cocktail party. Not for her pleasure, but to hear and to feel what was going on."

At the beginning, the pressure to be ahead of the competition sometimes caused the odd slipup. Herman Bleich, a foreign correspondent in The Hague who knew her for years and along with Slis and Kersting was a key figure in building up the Foreign Press Association after the war, recalled:

> "As AP journalist, she was always in the front row, she had to be the first. As a result, she did not always have the chance to check up well. Sometimes she was too quick. During an important conference between Germany and Israel in the years after the war, in Oud-Wassenaar castle, the press were waiting below-stairs. We saw them come down the stairs. 'Dejected faces', said Nel, 'it has failed'. and away she went to the telephone (but she was wrong)."

Describing what is unique about working for a press agency, Nel said:

> "You always have to phone in your first paragraph, this is the great difference (from newspaper work). You must

always be the first one at the telephone. In the
Vredespaleis with those damned slippery floors and
stairs, I took off my shoes and stockings under the table
to get to the godforsaken telephone first without
slipping, and the phone was always damn well
downstairs'".

She was never tempted to switch to newspaper reporting.

"I found it much too interesting working for a press
agency, it was much more world-oriented. As well, I
learned so much with AP... I learned the five w's -- who,
what, where, why and when. That's what America
brought to Dutch journalism."

When she interviewed Colonial Minister Jan Jonkman about the
Indonesian crisis, New York immediately telexed that she must also have
the opinion of an Indonesian.

"I learned that early on: if there is an issue, then I have
to interview not only A, but also B."

Another aspect of being a good press agency reporter was pinning down
the facts.

"Facts. Facts I must have. Checking and then checking
again, you learn that at an agency. Otherwise, I get a
query... Ach, this whole business of journalism, there are
just three golden rules, and I question whether you learn
that anywhere at a school for journalism. I know for sure
not. These rules are: you must have done your
homework, you must have a tremendous interest in the
subject and finally, you must possess tenacious stamina.
And on top of this, I had the good luck that I also have a
nose for news."

Interviewing Jonkman in the last stages of the Dutch colonial era was
something of a breakthrough for Slis. The interview was widely picked
up, and she was taken more seriously, though it took a long time before
things really got better.

"They were polite, so was I. And that was that. I had to
fight harder than such a nice little chap from the NRC.
Distrust remained, and that was partly based on my
being a woman. Luckily I could fall back on Henk
Kersting in Amsterdam and on Dan Schorr. I learned a
lot from them, but I had to fight hard for it."

An anecdote about the early years surfaced in a 1963 interview in Het Parool, showing Slis at her most combative. She was sent to Margraten in 1948, and managed to hitch a lift in the car of the Polish charge d' affaires. On the way back, Nel asked him to stop at a pub called Tante Sophie so that she could go to the lavatory. Three drunken men and a drunken landlady were sitting together in the pub. When she was finished, one of the drunken men pushed into the booth, shouting "you are a spy." Slis reportedly "valiantly struck him away from her." A regular battle arose. The Pole, who had been waiting outside, appeared, shocked, in the doorway. "Call the police," shouted Nel. To her relief, the diplomat did so, and a Black Maria police van arrived and took everyone to the police station.

> "I was furious. I phoned Premier Beel and I said: 'What sort of country is this? A land of wild beasts. After that, I gave a press conference in bed, beaten all black and blue, and the NRC had a column on the front page, headlined 'Cherchez la femme'. I still haven't forgiven them yet for that. The fellows were up in court and given a two months' sentence; I got 27 guilders for my torn-to-pieces only black suit'".

Perhaps the incident reminded her of British suspicions that she might be a spy, when she landed in the UK in 1941.

To illustrate this period of her life, the most old-world and atmospheric photo of Nel that I found is the cover photo, showing her back in the AP office after the coronation of Queen Juliana. Still in party frock and hat, she is seated at an antediluvian typewriter, surrounded by male colleagues in top hats. One of the prettiest early photos of Nel catches her on her own at the Winter Olympics in 1949. But in virtually every photo throughout her life where she is in action as a journalist, it is striking that Nel always manages to be right next to the important person of the moment.

In 1955, after ten years with the AP in the Netherlands, Nel wrote a surprisingly polite and decorous article for the Foreign Press Association's 30th anniversary magazine, which still manages to give a vivid picture of her gruelling working life as a journalist. But the hustle and bustle of press agency reporting can be quite addictive as well, hence Nel's remark that

> "If things get too quiet, you would start missing them."

In her article, there are some covert digs at 'working' and cocktail-partying wives, carefully muffled so as not to alienate them or their husbands. She also talks about the need for women journalists to dress up and the extra expense they incur. This is less of a problem nowadays, at least in the Netherlands. But it can still be hard to get first names out of the Dutch. A company chief once told an exasperated agency reporter "I'll give you my first name if you promise not to use it."

St. Moritz, Winter Olympics, 1948

Indonesia Round Table Conference, 1949

International Court of Justice, The Hague c.1950 Slis interviews members
of Iranian delegation on oil consortium

Luxembourg Foreign Minister Joseph Begh, Benelux Foreign Ministers
Meeting, The Hague, 26 September 1954

iv. 'That Woman who stopped Molotov'

One story from the 1950s demonstrates Nel's determination and effectiveness when she got wind of something of which she did not approve. The weekly Vrij Nederland's reporter Igor Cornelissen, writing in 1982, remarks that Nel was known for years in The Hague as *'that difficult bitch'* but goes on to say:

> "It would be nicer and more appropriate if she went down in history as 'that woman who stopped Molotov. It must have been in 1957 that Nel Slis heard somewhere at a ministry or reception that the former comrade-in-arms of Joseph Stalin was to be fobbed off on the Netherlands as ambassador. On the same evening, she phoned Mr Fock, then secretary-general at the prime minister's office and very close to (premier) Drees. Nel Slis knew Fock from London in the war. 'I told him that these Russians wanted to appoint Molotov here and I said: "Cees, that really can't be allowed, goddamit." Cees asked if I knew it for sure and when I confirmed that, he said. 'No, of course we cannot have that man here." That was naturally, says Nel Slis, *front-page news*. If we remember correctly, then Molotov, foreign minister under Stalin, became ambassador to Outer Mongolia'.

v. Life outside the 'Office': Close and famous Friends and Enemies

Considering all the hours she worked, it seems almost impossible that Nel could have any life outside her work. But she always found time for her friends and for cultural events, which were often woven into her work as well. Conversely, many of her contacts also became good friends outside work.

An advantage of being posted to The Hague was that her childhood friend from the island, Jenneke, was now living there with her husband and three children, and Nel was a frequent visitor to her home. Jenneke's daughter Tyna Wynaerd found this long-lasting friendship remarkable considering they were so different.

> "My mother was really a femme au famille, who looked after her family and for whom her family always came first. And Nel, so ambitious, and a feminist also,

supporting women's rights; my mother was not interested in that. But they got on very well."

At the same time, Tyna felt it was not a very intimate friendship, perhaps because they were so different.

Tyna was aged around 10 when Nel started stopping by in The Hague, and felt herself fortunate to be speedily adopted by Nel as a sort of goddaughter.

> "She always looked after me and took me out to things. As a journalist, she got two tickets for nearly all the performances at the Holland Festival, and most of the time she took me with her, because she felt I had to learn about the good quality of ballet and so on. After the ballet, she would take me behind the scenes and introduce me - she knew everybody, violinist Isaac Stern and Nora Kay, prima ballerina of the New York City ballet and married for a period to Isaak Stern. Nel was friends with the whole Stern family, and I was then a ballet fan. We would be invited to cocktails after the performance - it was absolutely wonderful, especially meeting and knowing Isaac Stern."

Stern became another of Nel's good friends, writing her long letters every Christmas. He died shortly before Nel, in September 2001.

Nel also liked to take Tyna for a walk in the seaside resort of Scheveningen every Sunday, telling her that

> "for health and beauty, you have to get out of the house, and you need some wind."

Nel wanted somebody to walk with, and Tyna was always happy to go out with her. She would also sometimes visit Nel's flat on the first floor in Javastraat, and remembered her cat.

> "Just like mine, tabby, a normal cat. Nel was also very generous to me, taking me on little trips and holidays and buying me gifts."

Tyna remembered the faithful Aagje from the island, who cooked for Nel and looked after her.

> "She did everything for her; Aagje would have died for her."

Aagje worked for Nel until she went to Brussels, and later on, when she couldn't work any more, she went to Tyna's mother to polish the silver and do small jobs so that she could 'make her own living'. Ever Nel's loyal defender, Tyna told me that on one occasion Aagje even made sure Nel got some of her own family's silver

> "When one of Nel's aunts on her mother's side died, Nel went there to give a helping hand and Aagje went with her on her own initiative to defend her interests. They went through the house and Aagje said you must take this and you must take that - and you can take the silver, nobody wants it. And Nel said afterwards she was very grateful, because at that moment she had not thought about it."

Nel would often drop into Tyna's home at around 'borrel time', the Dutch cocktail hour between 6 and 7, fascinating Tyna by her un-ladylike habit of drinking jenever.

> "She was one of the first women ever to drink jeneva: at that time women were supposed to drink sherry or port, but not jenever, that wasn't done. And my mother frowned on it."

Throughout the period when Tyna was at secondary school, Nel was around several times a week. She gave a lot of advice, for instance telling Tyna she didn't keep her shoulders straight and should see a specialist, and naturally knowing exactly the right person to see, or telling her she must stop ballet because her feet were getting knobbly.

> "She interfered a lot, but I liked that, because she mainly had a different opinion than my mother's and it often happened that this would be more what I wanted to do."

Surprisingly, Tyna said her mother only occasionally seemed to mind Nel's interference. "I think she rather liked this friendship." Perhaps for a woman immersed in home and family, it was refreshing to have such an exotic friend as Nel.

A bonus for Nel was that she could get things off her chest with her surrogate family when life infuriated her too much.

> "She would also come in when she was upset about things, also when somebody didn't want to talk to her - and she had enemies too, people who couldn't stand her. She would come for a borrel, fuming, and would talk to my parents, who didn't quite understand the whole atmosphere and what she was talking about, but just knew she had to let off steam."

Nel was also close to Tyna's brother Piet.

"But she spent less time with him than with me because, well, it wasn't so easy to take a boy into town to go shopping - I don't think he did so many things just with her, more with the whole family. Nel came for Christmas, for instance, because my mother would say well, on these days, she's on her own and it would be nice, but it was also an obvious thing that she would be invited, she was more or less one of the family."

Nel did however also take Piet to concerts. He was equally fascinated by her. In the beginning, he said, they called her Auntie, but that annoyed her. He remembered her Renault 4:

"to our secret amazement, completely ignoring traffic signs, she would park on any random street corner. Her unrestrained use of language, the foreign cigarettes she smoked, the jenever she drank made an indelible impression on my brother, my sister and myself. She often took me, a young music-lover, to concerts in the Kurhaus or K&W with her free press cards."

Like Tyna, he was introduced by Nel to many famous people, including Leonard Bernstein:

"With whom she withdrew to the Kurhaus bar after the concert, where Bernstein then after some time took Sandor Vidak's place behind the piano."

Many of Nel's contacts with famous musicians resulted from her friendship with Johanna Beek, like her husband an impresario who represented many of these musicians in the Netherlands. Piet remembered Nel telling stories of a weekend with Mistislav Rostropovitch in the Beeks' weekend cottage. Surviving photos of Nel with such international figures show her with Rubenstein and Stravinsky.

Interview with pianist Arthur Rubenstein, c.1950

With Douglas Fairbank Jr., American actor, decorated WWII officer, 1949

As a child, Johanna's daughter Yolanda was similarly impressed by Nel.

"She was so much not a conventional person. I was brought up very properly and loved her out of the-ordinary swearing and screaming, and my parents were great friends."

But Nel could also be extremely unreasonable, and there are a number of stories of violent rows with people, even close friends. Nor was she in the least prepared to make up with someone once they had fallen out. Yolanda told one of these stories.

"My parents had a little cottage in Brabant, my father didn't like company, but he loved Nel very much. She was one of my parents' few friends. I would see her there sometimes during the holidays. One day she had a row with a mutual lady friend – she never wanted to talk about it, but from that moment, my parents couldn't have them in the house together. My father died long ago, when I was 27, but my poor mother on her deathbed wanted Nel to make peace with her. I tried desperately, but Nel is so stubborn. That was an example of her total stubbornness. Why could she not even pretend, for the last wish of my mother. But there was no way, it was against her principles."

Nel talked about disliking people with gusto, but sometimes this seems far too mild a term. Tyna suggested this was one reason why Nel was by no means universally liked.

"That horrible woman' – I'm sure there are people who really disliked her, because she could be so violent when she talked about someone she disliked."

Once, Tyna herself faced an explosion from Nel, though on this occasion, she felt it was justified.

"I had to meet her in front of the Holland Festival for a concert, and I was late; she had left the ticket for me. At the end, she said, why were you late? That's the last time, you can forget it. She was FURIOUS. She was right, of course. As a girl (I was 13), if you're invited, you're not late. And it was partly because my mother wasn't around, as she would always tell me it was time to go, and I was much too dependent on that. So it was my own responsibility to get there, and I was late. And she was really shouting at me and I was very, very upset and went two or three days later to apologise. She said, you know, in life, when you do that, when you're not respectful, that's one of the first rules, and you'd better learn it. And she was right, of course."

Nel also got on well with Tyna's father, though they would have fights from time to time because he considered she interfered too much with the family. She had less contact with Tyna's elder brother.

> "He was a less adaptable person than Piet and me, I think, and Nel has rules and if you don't go by them... I remember once, we were invited to Nel's place and he unscrewed his pipe and blew through it to clean it, and it went all over Nel's carpet. She wouldn't put up with that. But he was nice to her too, he helped her a lot later on. He liked her, but they were never very close."

When Tyna was about thirteen, Nel started getting her to do her filing.

> "That was wonderful, because she paid me, for an hour or two of filing. She had a pile of newspapers, and she gave me subjects and told me to make cuttings - she had all the newspapers. All those cuttings in her drawers, many of them I cut out for her. She would say, for instance, make cuttings of Wilhelmina, and I said why? Because when she dies, the AP will want a story, and I want it right there, now, I want to go through my own drawers and pull out what's important. It all had to be classified chronologically as well. I would cut them out and write the date on them. It was a way to get out in the evening where my parents would allow me to go."

In later years, Tyna was impressed by one of Nel's holiday jaunts with Johanna Beek.

> "Nel went on a holiday with Yolanda's mother, and they started from Paris where I lived at the time, and I did the first stretch with them. They had no plan at all, they were just in Nel's car - she was a terrible driver - going south somewhere, and we had dinner in front of this hotel near Paris, and the next day they put me on a train. I thought it was so nice to go on a holiday like that without any plans, and just stop at a nice restaurant if you see one. And they were really enjoying themselves. I was about 17, and Nel would have been about 40. Johanna was complaining that she'd just discovered Nel in The Hague, and 'there are so few women I really get on with who have cultural interests and who have a little

creativity in their way of living. Now I have a real friend, and now she's going to Brussels.'"

Meanwhile, back in the early years in The Hague, Slis continued her journalistic learning process, and she undoubtedly learned fast - especially, she told me, from foreign reporters.

> "More and more people used to come here reporting for American and British papers on what was happening in Holland after the war. I learned a lot about journalism from the Americans, working for the AP. I had to, it was my education. There was a Jewish American journalist who worked for the Christian Science Monitor, Dan Schorr, he taught me a lot about journalism."

And she fell in love with him.

Footnote: Nel's salary when she started working for the AP is not known, but by 1953, her gross monthly salary was 671.65 guilders, which translates into 304.78 euros.

5.
European stories, an American love

Slis with Schorr and after

The story of the Dutch losing their huge Indonesian colony brought Slis and Schorr together. American journalist Daniel Schorr is said to have turned up in The Hague and enquired:

> "Who is Nel Slis? Because through her interviews about Indonesia, Aneta (*news service*) is continually being beaten by AP..... Are you Slis? We must have a drink."

i. The Schorr affair

Nel herself was depreciating about her Indonesian stories.

> "My reporting did not influence opinion in America so much, it was primarily the reports from the correspondent in Jakarta that did. I have always reported factual news. This is also the job of an agency. Nor have I ever been tempted to influence opinion in America...The Americans and the British wanted the Dutch out of Indonesia. We had completely crazy diehards here. We held the sceptre for three hundred years over a country that is a thousand times bigger than

Holland, and we got rich as shit from it. Look at Wassenaar *(a super-rich leafy suburb of The Hague full of big colonial villas)*, a product of the old planters."

Dan Schorr told me his version of this period over the phone from Washington in 2000, when he was just finishing his own autobiography Schorr had previously been working in New York for Aneta, the news agency of the Dutch East Indies (former Indonesia). During the war, Aneta took over the representation from the Dutch ANP news service because the ANP was German-controlled. The ANP was and is a Dutch press agency for, and until recently owned by, the Dutch newspapers. Schorr said:

> "I wound up in the Netherlands because I had been with Aneta before going into the army in the war. Back from the war, I decided I wanted to go into mainstream journalism, but the ANP said, can you do one thing for us before you leave - go to Holland and reorganize our service."

After Schorr arrived in the Netherlands in 1946, the reorganisation turned out to be very difficult.

> "Dutch journalism was emerging from the war and five years of Nazism: it was not any good; they had lost their sense of what was news and what was propaganda, and they had no independence from government. In New York, agencies like the AP and UPS were using the ANP and it was often pretty bad, useless. I had to try to reorganise the service, but there was a lot of opposition from the ANP, particularly a guy called Lambooy, who had played a questionable role during the occupation. So it was very, very tense, with me coming along with my free American ideas - back to free journalism. But there was one guy in the ANP that I did respect, he had a much broader vision, Louis Metzemakers, and we became good friends."

Lambooy certainly sounded a nasty piece of work and Nel had also run up against him. She was pleased to irritate his curiosity when she found herself sitting opposite him the only time she wore her Red Cross silver medal and Finnish decoration.

> "I knew that I would provoke him with that. He couldn't contain himself, and said: 'Miss Slis, what is that?' I got what I wanted. That man had actually told press chiefs earlier: 'You must not say anything to Miss Slis, she is

not serious'. And that sort of thing, Slis does not take, you see."

In Schorr's struggles with the ANP, he said:

> "The whole arrangement didn't work very well, I was not able to do it single-handed. It was that year I first met Nel, I believe - I knew her professionally and socially. I went back to the US at end-1947, having fulfilled my promise for a year. I concluded I no longer wanted to work for a Dutch or any other news service, but I did want to work in Holland. There was not any good job around, so I went back as a stringer, first for the Christian Science Monitor, and later for Life and then Time. After that I worked for ABC Radio which became CBS which eventually led to a career with CBS."

Talking about working with Nel in Holland at this time, Schorr said

> "Nel and I had the idea that we could help each other. She had a profound acquaintance with things in Holland, while I could help her with my knowledge of American journalism. We shared an office. Part of it was her apartment, I even remember the address, Javastraat 11. I had a separate room with a desk and a telephone. That was from 1948, for three or four years. I will not disguise the fact that our relationship was not just professional.

> "I did help her, too, there were lots of very big stories she was able to break to the AP with my help. One I remember, things were going badly in Indonesia, the Dutch resumed police action against Sukarno, and I heard from someone in the US embassy that the Truman government took a dim view of the Dutch behaviour and they were ready to threaten them. If the Dutch didn't show more accommodation to the nationalist parties, that they would suspend the Marshall Plan aid. I realized I could do this for Nel - the news would be out in a couple of hours for one of my clients. I gave the story to Nel and there was an AP bulletin, also for their clients in the Netherlands - they learned of the threat to suspend aid because of the refractory attitude of the Dutch in Indonesia.

> "Also, aside from whole stories, I could look at Nel's copy and show her how to simplify it. She was a great, great journalist, she knew a news story, she knew how to

interview people. But writing for an American news service, she needed help, which I could give her.

"She helped me, because in the early years I didn't know Dutch, and she would help me read the newspapers. It was a fruitful cooperation, most fruitful. Nel had enormous enthusiasm, looking into whatever she was looking into. She was better at 'did you notice what he said there' - she had a better feeling of what was under the surface, I don't mean to be sexist but, as a woman, she had more sensitivity, intuition. I was more on the surface. She frequently gave a sense of nuance I didn't have.

"She also had a great temper. She had a great sense of justice and if her sense of justice was offended, she got very angry, storming around, Godverdomme... (Goddamit). A temper, but attached to her sense of justice, not just angry. For example, in the early days, there was still rationing, and when we went to see some government official for lunch, the officials were able to work their way round the rationing and she didn't think that was fair. She was very truly a democratic, egalitarian person and that sort of thing made her very angry. Mostly angry at the establishment, at pretentious establishment people.

"She was very proud, by the way, of her beginnings, coming from the island, she would talk quite often about that Goeree.... Holland's so small, but there are still differences... between Friesland, North Holland, the Hoge Veluwe... The Dutch manage to find ways of disapproving of everyone else. Nowadays not any more but earlier, the Catholic south was not highly regarded.

"We vacationed together. In 1948, we went on a trip to Brittany and on another occasion, we took a trip to Austria. We were very close. I don't recall her speaking of her father - she was reticent. I do recall that before she met me she had an affair with a Russian that turned out badly. I found it remarkable even at her age, with her good looks and talent, that she had never been married.

"(*Perhaps she wanted to marry you*) I suppose so. I have to admit I did not treat her fairly. It was all wonderful, free together. Then in 1953 there was the great flood and, after that, I got lots of work and lots of attention back in the States and CBS offered a job working in the States so I left Holland. In the way people can do, selfish, egotistical. Back in the States, she was out of my life. Then I felt ashamed, I didn't write, didn't contact her.

"Later, I did go back with a delegation of journalists in 1955. There was a reception at Hotel des Indes and Nel was there. Typical, she walked over and said you bastard, you never tried to get in touch. I came back again once in the early 1980s, married with two children, really a question of taking my wife around Amsterdam. I didn't get in touch with Nel but I did with Henk Kersting, who said gently you'd like to know how Nel is, she's doing fine."

Schorr sounded choked at the end of the phone conversation, perhaps affected by his memories.

There was a bit more to the end of the affair. Nel, who had met Schorr's mother, said to me that the mother told him if he married a goy, she'd kill him. On other occasions, Nel admitted the mother threatened suicide if Schorr married a goy, a more virulent-sounding threat. According to fellow-journalist Friso Endt, Schorr also left the letter lying around and Nel found it and was convinced he did this on purpose. She said dismissively:

"He didn't want to marry me, but there were other friends... I've always been a loner, so it didn't matter to me - I've always had a lot of friends",

It's true that Nel always had a lot of friends but she also made it clear that Dan was the only man she actually *did* want to marry, and it was painful when it didn't work out. That remark was a transparent cover-up. 'I've always been a loner, so it didn't matter to me' only reveals how much it did matter to her.

Some while later, at the beginning of the 1960s, Nel had her handwriting analysed. Among elements in the analysis, freely translated by me, it found.

"Good logical intelligence present with a sharp understanding. Via strong sensory perception and an adequate processing of impressions, an extensive experience has been built up."

The analysis continued in the same professional vein:

"Dealings are characterised by exceptional vitality, diligence and perseverance. A plan, once adopted, will be brought to fruition at any price. Often, an impulsive motive is at the bottom of this, which however, if considered important, pushes aside all other matters. The writer is by nature pretty hasty and sometimes too unbridled…

"The way of operating is very accurate; committed and carried out with dogged tenacity… Due to experience, great confidence in (the subject's) own capacity has been developed in relation to specific matters.

"There is however a remarkable feeling of dissatisfaction in relation to life in general, which can lead to painful severity both against the own self and the environment. The self feels besieged by the oblivious outside world and is always ready to spring to defence. Often a counter-attack is launched before there is any question of a real attack

"Character: strong, honest, faithful to conviction and very decisive. Great pugnacity is coupled with this, which is passionately indulged..

"A great drive to expression gives form to the unbridled energy, whereby the manner of behaviour can often be very "original" (*putting it mildly*).

"Accommodation is not innate and only present if the writer herself considers this necessary. She takes little account of the interests and feelings of others, and can also easily hurt someone without consciously intending to do so. Right is however right and there is no person in the world who can convince the writer otherwise. She readily takes on another in conscious opposition, and is then aggressive and quite uncontrolled..

"It does not cause the writer the least difficulty to make her way into a community, she is often able to push through into pretty closed circles. There is a strong desire for love, but the writer is very idiosyncratic in this. She rejects the ordinary and is actually disappointed by the community in her affection."

The last sentence made me think of the affair with Schorr. Possibly nobody else measured up to him in Nel's eyes so she was disappointed in love and, to an extent, also in life. Piet Wackie Eysten, who selected the handwriting excerpts above, also remarked that Nel did not easily share her innermost feelings, even with her most intimate friend, Piet's mother. Only rarely did she entrust a sentence or two about her feelings to a black day-book:

> "It looks as if a great part of my life is being spent by feeling persecuted"

> "God help me to be humble, brave, wise"

These few words from Nel's vulnerable core reduced me to tears, especially after reading that startlingly perceptive handwriting analysis.

Piet concluded that Nel was perhaps unsuitable for a long-term relationship. Her temperament, he felt, would have put such a relationship to a severe test from time to time. Perhaps this is so but one thing is certain. Nel did not want anyone to think that she really cared much about breaking up with Schorr. And perhaps Schorr never truly had any idea of the depth of her need for affection. Superficially, this seems such an un-Nel-like characteristic but one that makes so much sense looking back at her lonely childhood. Or perhaps he did perceive it, and this scared him off.

Nel's friend Louis Metzemakers said 'Danny' Schorr broke off the affair when he went back to America, as did others, including Dan himself by inference. But I don't really believe that; I feel that Flora Lewis, the writer and columnist who became another lifelong friend of Nel's, told the true story:

> "It was Nel who broke it off, as I understand it, because there came a point where she said, make up your mind, I'm not going to hang around. Either we get married or we break up, because she was beginning to feel too much hurt by this. And then he left Holland in any case."

> "She wanted to marry Dan. But for a very, very long time, not only with Nel but long after, Dan simply absolutely refused to consider marrying anybody. The reason he always gave was that he was afraid he would upset his mother. Whatever Nel may have said (*about the letter*), I think that Dan for his own reasons just didn't want to marry. He was afraid of marriage, why I don't know. Nel really loved him and they got on very well."

> "But then when he left Holland and took up with other women, it was the same behaviour. I think he exaggerated and, to a certain extent, invented in his own mind his fear of offending his mother as his own shield.

> So he could say oh, sorry dear, I adore you but I can't possibly marry you, my mother... I gave him lectures later, long after Nel, in other countries, saying it's all very well, you're having a great time as a bachelor but there'll come a time when it's Thanksgiving or Christmas and you'll be all alone, you won't like that. He did marry a Jew in the end but a long time later and apparently the mother was enchanted."

Tyna was surprised by Flora's account as Nel had always given her to understand that Dan did want to marry her but was prevented by his mother. Perhaps Nel simply found this less wounding. The end of the affair could be passed off more lightly that way.

Tyna also pointed out that it was still considered quite outrageous in Holland in those days for an unmarried woman to be openly living with her boyfriend.

> "They were very close but we didn't talk about that at home, because they were living together and they were not married and my mother didn't really approve. So that is typically Dutch, everybody knows it but we just don't mention it. I only learned later that there had been this period in Nel's life because, in my family, it was ignored."

Tyna knew Flora quite well

> "She was a wonderful person, in a way like Nel but more brilliant. I mean, Flora is one of the most brilliant minds I've met."

My first attempt to interview Flora Lewis was a dismal failure. While I was visiting Dublin in April 1999, I was tipped off by Yolanda that Flora was in Holland to do a television interview. I phoned her at her Amsterdam hotel and she sounded friendly and invited me to have dinner with her there on my return. Flora had to change this as the television people wanted to take her out to dinner. I joined them at a restaurant called Zuid Zeeland near Amsterdam's pretty Flower Market. I had met Flora once before in Nel's flat some years earlier and I found her quite alarming then, even meeting her as a newcomer to journalism under Nel's wing. I hardly expected her to remember me. This time around, she was in an extremely bad temper and neither the young Dutchman who had interviewed her nor the young woman, presumably a TV executive, seemed to be having much luck in putting her into a better mood. Worse still, the restaurant was cramped and bourgeois and produced indifferent pretentious food it imagined to be 'French cuisine'.

Flora talked grumpily with the television people. They discussed Iris Murdoch, how extremely difficult Altzheimer's disease makes people and what a hard time was had by Iris' husband. Nel was never diagnosed as having Altzheimer's but her loss of memory and sometimes raging moods were similar to those who do have it. Suddenly Flora turned to me and said, you can ask your questions now. But I passed on this uncomfortable offer and wrote down her details in Paris to arrange a meeting there later.

Unfortunately Flora didn't reply to letters. I complained to another journalist, Alan Tillier in Paris, that I found her intimidating and he mailed back:

> Yes, Flora is intimidating. I shall never forget inviting her when I went to live in Paris in the 1970s. She grabbed a bottle of Scotch and proceeded to down it. She can also be snooty - later when I needed a job and asked her about the chances at the NY Times she replied haughtily, 'We cannot all be stars, Alan'. She looked like Bette Davis crossed with Joan Crawford that day.

This was a perfect description of her as she appeared to me that awkward day in Amsterdam.

Eventually I phoned Flora up as I had to go to Paris for a wedding the following Saturday and she kindly agreed to see me between the wedding and the reception. She talked to me about Nel in her charming flat in Paris overlooking the Seine, full of antique furniture collected from around the world. This was in January 2001, nearly two years after the previous debacle. She was subdued and patient - in fact, like a lamb, as Nel once improbably described herself. Flora mentioned that she had been quite ill that year, accounting for the non-communication.

Flora, who certainly understood how much Nel cared about Dan Schorr, told me she actually first met Nel through Schorr. Flora arrived in the Netherlands from Berlin in 1949 when she was working for the New York Times:

> "I came to live in The Hague, Nel was the girl friend, she was more or less shacked up with Dan Shorr, who was an old friend from New York. Because of Dan, we met Nel and saw quite a lot of her. She came up into the house and I became very fond of her. When they broke up, after we moved away, whenever I was in the area, I

always went to see her. And she visited me once in a while."

A twist to the tale of Shorr's departure came from Friso Endt. According to Friso, Paris bureau chief Frank White told Henk Kersting he had to fire Dan Schorr. Friso told me:

> "Nobody knew that except Nel. He had to do a story for Life about the first Marshall Aid goods arriving in Holland and when he was told Life postponed it for one or two weeks, he sold it behind their backs to the Daily Mail. Nel used to say: 'Oh, he was so eager for money.. I warned him not to do it for a couple of pounds'. But she never told anyone and he went away with the Oranje Nassau order (*a Dutch decoration*) and a big party.'

> "Dan said Nel told him he was a bastard? He was but Nel learned the trade of journalism from him. It was Dan Shorr who made her. You say he said he learned a lot from Nel? On well, that's nice. Of course, she always said, he had no manners, he was a boy from Brooklyn and she taught him how handle a knife and fork... I always saw him when I was in Washington and he always asked about Nel. So that's a fact. But it was Dan Schorr who taught her the American way of asking questions. That was very unusual in this country. I was the young reporter from Het Parool and I was interested in English and American journalism because I thought that their way of putting a story together was quite different and much more interesting. So I became a stringer for London dailies."

> "Nel used to live here on the Javastraat. On the first floor, near the corner. She had a big terrace at the back. I went there. I was a young boy and I looked on Nel as a mighty journalist. She was the only woman and they were all afraid of her because she had a big mouth. In the days of Nel and before, in the days of Henk Kerstens and Herman Bleich, the Foreign Press Association was powerful. Oh yes, they built up the FPA."

Friso, who was living in Javastraat at the time of this writing, also had a long career in journalism and was president of the FPA after Nel.

Though their personal and professional partnership was doomed, the Slis and Shorr combine made a huge impression in those years. As Het Parool newspaper observed:

"Those were the years that Schorr and Slis had the news from The Hague in their hands, seconded by people like Ekke of Het Parool and Hoek of Trouw.

The touching, blurry photos of Nel and Dan in relaxed and intimate mood show their closeness, counter-pointed by the rather fierce photo of them looking like two peas in a pod in full professional mode at some press conference or reception. As a footnote, nestling next to each other in the Foreign Press Association archives, I found Nel and Dan's acceptance of an invitation to meet Juliana, Queen of the Netherlands on 19 March, 1952.

Nel and Dan Schorr

Nel and Dan Schorr

Nel and Dan Schorr

THE ASSOCIATED PRESS

denHaagMaart 13   19 52
Javastraat 11.

Beste Pal,

    Ik zal graag van de partij zijn op Soestdijk a.s.
Woensdag 19 Maart.

                    Met hartelijke groeten,

                                Pal Slis

Daily Mail

ASSOCIATED NEWSPAPERS, LTD.   Daniel L. Schorr   Editorial Department,
TELEPHONE - CENTRAL 6000.   Correspondent for   NORTHCLIFFE HOUSE,
TELEGRAM - DAILY MAIL, LONDON   the Low Countries   LONDON, E. C. 4.
Herengracht 58   The Hague
                    Telephone 180089

                                13 March 1952

Dear Pal:

    I shall be happy to accept the
invitation to attend the meeting with the
Queen on Wednesday, 19 March, at 11:15 a.m.

                With best regards,

                                Dan

Accepting invitation to meet the Queen

FPA meeting with Queen Juliana, 19 March 1952

Schorr went on to become a top reporter for CBS, said Flora Lewis,

> "until he got into a big fight with them for broadcasting something they didn't approve of; that's when he left and went to CNN. He was one of the first at CNN."

Piet Wackie Eysten said when Schorr was involved in a court case in the US years later because he refused to name a source who had given him a secret report on the CIA, Nel followed reports about this affair closely. And, on her 75th birthday, he wrote to her, saying

> "Lives drift apart in these decades. You might not recognize me as a family man with a son at Yale and a daughter at Harvard. Yet, the Dutch years are not to be forgotten. Nor you at the centre of them."

ii. Life after Schorr

After Schorr left, Slis continued her reporting in the Netherlands. While Flora was in Holland, they had both followed the story of the Netherlands losing its Indonesian colony, including the Round Table conference in 1949 and the subsequent settlement and Flora gave me some details and an assessment of this process.

> "We were living in Holland that year so we spent a lot of time with the Indonesians. It was a very interesting negotiation. The Dutch hated the Americans, because the Americans were pushing very hard for Holland to de-colonise, and the Dutch weren't about to dissolve the empire. The Dutch, at first, had the same reaction as the French.

> "But they finally came around. And then, once they accepted, eventually decided on independence, I must say they handled it very gracefully and very well. They were extremely generous both with the people from Indonesia and the Surinamese in solving issues like allowing people to chose between remaining in what had been the colony as a citizen of the country or remaining Dutch and going back to Holland.

> "Actually, at first, the Dutch took the same attitude as the other European colonial countries, but once they made up their minds that they were going to accept it and they made a deal at the Round Table, they handled it very decently, very thoughtfully. This was something that

was hard for everybody, after that long a period of colonialism. De-colonizing necessarily broke a lot of patterns, everybody had some kind of problem. Like coming off communism, whenever you have a big social change.

"At first, there was a great deal of resistance. There was going to be a war like the British had in Malaysia like Algeria and Vietnam later. So it was very important that they didn't carry it that far. They gave up before getting to the confrontation and said ok, we'll make an agreement, we'll make a deal. Some things were wrong... but it wasn't a choice of having a perfect cast of characters and they did, - with a great deal of push from the United States which was resented – nonetheless, come to the conclusion to make an agreement, otherwise there really would have been a war. It was coming quite near to that. And, you can imagine, with maybe 150 million in Indonesia in those days and 10 million in Holland - if they had had a war like the French and Indochina, I wonder whether they would have survived at all."

As one of Nel's interviewers recalled,

"Indonesia was world news. A small country that was losing its empire and had Britain, America and the Eastern Bloc against it. 'And still,' said Nel, 'and still, I believe that we have withered since then. Not that I believe we should or could have held onto Indonesia but you had more people before with a broader spirit, people that had looked over the border. Because what are we now all-in-all, in the Netherlands? Fifteen million nit-pickers. We don't have anything else apart from that gas to sell and that is diminishing. The French are right when they say that we must be the 'transporteurs' of Europe'."

A 1963 report in Het Parool largely focused on saluting Nel on her departure to Brussels, but also hinted at how raw, slightly uncomfortable and sometimes hypocritical the new relationship still was with Indonesia and Indonesians 14 years after the Round Table Conference. The end of the excerpt is vintage Slis.

"Who wasn't present at the reception given by the Indonesian Charge d'Affaires, Mohammed Sjarif that Monday evening in Oud Wassenaar castle to celebrate the Indonesian Independence Day? Everyone was there... Out in the chilly autumn evening, people stood for twenty minutes in the queue that swung from the driveway via the hall to the reception hall. There a broadly smiling Sjarif shook hands. The Dutch Prime Minister was in the queue and the Spanish ambassador, the Duke of Buena in the queue ('He has surely left long ago, he has already said his goodbyes?' 'That's true, but he was so curious that he couldn't resist coming.')

"There were lots of businessmen. ('Are we the Chinese of Europe or aren't we?') There were a great many people that only one or two years ago had said that there was 'nothing to talk about with these peloppers'. Now they had friendly and (yes) flattering smiles for the Indonesian diplomats.

"A journalist sipped at a drink (a stick equipped with a red-and-white flag in his hand) who had written 'exclusively' from New Guinea - fighting slogans about the fatherland's forces against these miserable and nasty Indonesian paratroopers.. This was the same man who wrote a year later from the palace of Sukarno (and again, very exclusively) about how completely charming the Indonesian president actually could be.

"A great day for the Dutch and the Indonesians indeed," said Sir Andrew Noble, the British ambassador.

"'And do you think you will be able to supply Friendships in Indonesia?' a question from a journalist to a board member of Fokker Aircraft. Answer: 'No comment'. People in the Netherlands love to say that though.

"Ekker of the Regional Daily Press enquired of the press attaché to the Indonesian embassy, 'And when will we have an exchange of ambassadors?' 'Perhaps it will be this year, I believe,' was the answer.

"Then a savvy photographer stepped up to Premier Marijnen, talked quickly with him, took a glass of sherry and a glass of fruit juice from a tray and, still talking, led the Dutch Premier to the Indonesian Excellency. A glass of sherry for Marijnen, a glass of orange juice for Sjarif and zip went the flashbulbs.

"It was at the Indonesian reception that people could also (perhaps for the last time here) see Nel Slis, Associated Press' correspondent in The Hague, at work. As the guests were departing, we were standing next to AP bureau chief Henk Kersting. Nel Slis stepped over to Sjarif to say goodbye. Kersting said: "It wouldn't surprise me if Nel is 'on kissing terms'". And yes indeed, she laid a hand most warmly on the shoulder of the Charge d'Affaires and kissed him goodbye on both cheeks, saluting him on the success of this reception."

Nel also continued to write about the effects of Marshall Aid and how the Netherlands got off the ground again and became industrialized. As she said.

"That was a story! Don't forget that before the war, the Netherlands was a country of farmers and fishermen. There were no industries, only agriculture. We lived off Indonesia. And then the discovery of gas. That has been our biggest salvation."

In a Slis feature from a later date on Sicco Mansholt, who was to become the architect of the EEC's Common Agricultural Policy and head the Common Market Executive Commission, she reminded her readers of his key role in Dutch postwar reconstruction:

"At the age of 37, Mansholt was picked by socialist Premier Willem Schermerhorn as Holland's first agricultural Minister to reorganize Holland's ruined agriculture and the food distribution for a starving population. Mansholt made Dutch agricultural produce competitive again on the world market while improving the structure of agriculture and raising farm incomes. Farming is in his blood. On a clear sunny day, he is apt to sniff the air and say, 'Good day to plough.'

"His former political aide, Alfred Mozer, recounts how, when Mansholt was visiting the late Pope John XVI in Rome, he found the two 'talking like two farmers, with Pope John slapping his thighs and shouting 'bravo, bravo'."

Another important story Flora Lewis mentioned was about the proposed Benelux union, between Belgium, the Netherlands and Luxembourg

"There was a plan for a Benelux union, which eventually got overtaken. That was a big story, way before the

Common Market and it was the first big integration plan. In the end, it never took shape because the Common Market took over and all three went in to that together instead. Well, I wrote about it a lot in those days because that was where European affairs were moving, it was part of the buildup."

In May 1948, Nel had been greatly impressed by a meeting between Schumann, Churchill and Adenauer, hosted by Dutch premier De Gaspary in The Hague, which called for a United Europe, further exciting her interest in European affairs. That was another early pointer in the buildup to the establishment of the EEC, which was eventually to result in Nel's secondment to Brussels.

During the postwar period in The Hague, Nel also began doing what the Dutch call "schnabbeltjes" and the Irish, "nixers", freelance assignments on the side for newspapers and other publications. These included the Religious News Service in New York and Ladies' Home Journal as well as the more prestigious New York Times and Newsweek. She used pseudonyms transparent enough to those who knew her, like Adriana Dykes or Len Koert (Adriana was her second Christian name and Lena Koert her mother's name). She also provided summaries of reports in the Dutch press important for the EEC information service in The Hague. In 1960, shortly before her move to Brussels, a freelance relationship was formed which was to endure virtually as long as she could still write. Through Dries Ekker of Het Parool, she had contacted the EEC daily news bulletin Europe, headed by the Italian journalist Emmanuel Grasso. She always got on well with Italians.

Newsweek took news stories from Nel on the loss of Holland's New Guinea colony and the death of Princess Wilhelmina, the old queen, who had abdicated in favour of her daughter, Juliana, plus features on a variety of other subjects. These included the 50th birthday of George Szell, at the time a regular conductor of the Concertgebouw Orchestra; a Leiden professor's experiments on how dogs and mice breathe underwater ('the mice died upon return to the air but the dogs survived'); and Princess Marijke's name-change to Christina.

But her most important work was her feature writing for the AP which wanted a 'human touch' and 'feel and flavour'. 'Humanized story-telling is needed day to day', New York instructed the foreign bureaus. This was undoubtedly one of Nel's strengths. The AP, for example, praised her reporting on a gathering of royalty in Amsterdam for the silver wedding celebrations of Queen Juliana and Prince Bernhard. Nel also provided her service with a memorable tale—of adultery and its mediaeval treatment in the small Dutch village of Staphorst.

iii. Randoll Coate's story: Staphorst

The Staphorst story reported by Nel is a minor classic of extreme Calvinism and superstition in a country village, which will probably live on forever, much to the chagrin of the village dignitaries. Nel's investigation of Staphorst's marital customs also made a big impression on one of her numerous fascinating friends, Randoll Coate, a former British diplomat specialising in the design of garden mazes.

It is not hard to imagine that Nel herself was underwhelmed by the behaviour of the Staporstians but still relished making a good story out of it. The main incident - the parading of an adulterous couple through the town in a pig-pen on a cart by the young men of the village amid much shouting and singing - is creepy enough, but the reference to the public humiliation of yet another poor unfortunate girl who failed to get pregnant has special poignancy. The Staphorst women were still wearing national costume at the turn of the century and as in some other areas in the Netherlands, the heavy Calvinist atmosphere was palpable.

Distinguished maze-maker Randoll Coate, a former diplomat, wrote to tell me the story of how he met and became friends with Nel and the impression the Staphorst marital customs made on him. He also talks about Nel's awesome reputation in The Hague and later in Brussels.

> "I arrived to take up my post at the British Embassy in The Hague in the autumn of 1953. I soon heard from colleagues that the most renowned and feared journalist in the whole of the Press Corps was the AP correspondent Nel Slis. When I met her I enjoyed her frankness, her plain speaking and her sense of humour and we became firm friends.

> "Nel gave me a copy of her humorous and satirical book on Holland called "Dykes and Bykes" which contained a chapter on the marital customs of the village of Staphorst. The mayor took exception to her colourful account of the proceedings and invited her to show her that the old custom no longer applied. As I was very interested in the folklore of Holland, Nel invited me to accompany her and I accepted with alacrity.

> "We arrived in Staphorst on a Sunday and were invited to join the Sunday service. Once all the congregation was in church, the doors were locked for two hours and the Verger tapped with his staff anyone who fell asleep during the very long sermon.

"The main argument between Nel and the Mayor was her description of the Opkamertje still being used for its original purpose: when a daughter reached marriageable age, a golden heart was placed over the lock of the front door and this signified that the suitor might climb through the diamond shaped window of the Opkamertje and press his suit. The Mayor asserted that this practice had long been discontinued and invited us into one of the houses decorated with a golden heart on the door. During the visit Nel managed to slip away into the Opkamertje and on her return she winked at me and whispered that the bed was quite rumpled and had obviously been slept in that night. This fact coupled with the presence of the golden heart made her feel that she had won her point!

"Nearly ten years later when en poste in Brussels, we renewed our friendship and it always amused me that when I mentioned that Nel Slis was a good friend of mine, journalists would blanch and exclaim: 'But she is the most feared journalist in Brussels!' Nel was always so kind and interested in our two daughters and my wife and I will forever remember her as a loyal and hospitable friend with whom we always had a great deal of fun."

Later, Randoll and his delightful wife, Pamy, were kind enough to invite myself and my daughter to lunch in London. Their house was in one of the loveliest corners of London, The Boltons, and framed by magnolia trees in full bloom. Pamy produced a delicious soup and prawn dish and a wondrous dessert. We talked about Randoll's classically erudite, intellectually challenging and very beautiful mazes. Of course we also talked about Nel and the Holland they had known in those days. Pamy remembered that the Staphorst natives were so hostile to visitors from 'outside' that they actually threw stones at them. They also found other nooks and crannies of the quiet and rural country fascinating. They had a treasured copy of 'Dykes and Bikes', the little book of short, pithy pieces that Nel wrote about her country which includes the Staphorst story.

6.
Covering Royalty

Queens of the Netherlands and Libya: Juliana's Hofmans affair

i. Three generations of Dutch Queens: Wilhelmina, Juliana, Beatrix

Queen Wilhelmina wrote a book, 'Eenzaam maar niet alleen', meaning 'lonely, but not alone.' 'a bit like me,' Nel once said. Wilhelmina disliked and got rid of much of the pomp and ceremony of the court, deciding she should be addressed simply as Mevrouw van Oranje (Mrs van Orange). Oddly enough, though her granddaughter Beatrix was a modern and informal queen, protocol was to address her more formally as 'Your Majesty' first off and subsequently as 'ma'am', as with the British queen.

Nel had already reported on Wilhelmina for the AP during the war when the Dutch monarchy was in exile in London. Remembering this period, Nel said:

> "There Wilhemina undoubtedly went through her most human period. One thing I remember from that time... She had asked then Premier Gerbrandy to take her to a quiet, strict protestant church. She lived outside London and went to a number of churches with Gerbrandy, all of which she found too 'roman' *(catholic)*. Eventually it

seemed as though she had found the church but then it turned out that there was only standing room or only footstools that you could kneel on." This was too much even for the down to earth Mrs van Orange, whose response was, 'Kneeling I do not do."

Nel said she began covering Queen Wilhelmina

"in what you could call her democratic period. But not where the press were concerned - the press was kept at a safe distance."

There were no interviews or talks with chief editors or drinking coffee with members of parliament as Juliana, her successor did later. But Wilhelmina was far easier when it came to photos. In her time, they were mad about dressing up and the royal family was much photographed, often in national and historic costumes. Nel went on.

"That was different with Juliana, who always had a great aversion to photographers" When Wilhelmina abdicated in 1948, I remember vividly that all my American colleagues hired top hats and tails but at the last minute, they decided not to go to the church in Amsterdam. I myself, in party dress, hat and gloves, refused to stick around staring at the pillars in the church for three hours. So we got through those three hours together, all dressed up like that, in a cafe on NieuwezijdsVoorburgwal.

"The really fun and spontaneous moment came when Juliana and Wilhelmina appeared on the balcony of the palace on Dam Square. The old queen clapped Juliana hard on the shoulder and shouted loudly, 'Long live the queen,' then promptly disappeared for good. Some people said her teeth fell out when she shouted.

"There were no riots in those September days, nor were any expected. I can still see two communist MPs with small children on their shoulders, waving flags. But I still ran foul of a policeman, who tried to keep me behind a barrier until he saw my press card."

In 1980, when Wilhelmina's granddaughter Beatrix was crowned queen, there were indeed riots in traditionally socialist Amsterdam, much to my surprise as a newly arrived resident. I and my then husband were on Rozengracht, around the corner from the Nieuwe Kerk on Dam Square where she was being crowned, and a street party was in full swing with food and drink stalls, music and festive decorations. Suddenly, a series of Black Maria police vans whistled ominously past, heading towards 'disturbances' in Dam Square. In the evening, we tried to find a fireworks display by Central Station but only saw a busload of soldiers in dress uniforms and wearing cockatoos. The rest of the evening was spent running away from tear gas, water cannons and hordes of riot police, who eventually totally surrounded us. We took refuge in a cafe until things quietened down. We never found the demonstrations.

In 1966, the wedding of Beatrix and Claus had sparked more serious riots, partly because Claus was German and was said to have been in the Hitler Youth. People were also affronted by Beatrix's lavish spending plans for her residence. After the wedding ceremony, smoke bombs sent black plumes into the sky as they paraded through Amsterdam in the Golden Coach.

When the then Crown Prince Willem Alexander, Beatrix's eldest son, married the Argentine Maxima thirty-six years later on 2 February 2002, footage was shown of that earlier wedding with the dark smoke clouds billowing away over the Golden Coach. Her father had been junior agriculture minister in the notorious Videla Junta and there was therefore considerable political concern about the marriage. Eventually a solution was found. Her parents were not invited to the wedding, and watched it on television in Brussels. (Maxima's parents also remained absent on the occasion of Beatrix's abdication and Willem-Alexander's investiture as the first king for over a century on 30 April, 2013). Willem Alexander and Maxima's wedding turned out to be a popular affair despite a tricky start.

Meanwhile, Maxima, an attractive young woman with long blonde hair, had won the hearts of the Dutch following a television programmes which featured an interview with the couple and their subsequent perambulations through the country. Her popularity was largely thanks to her pleasant personality and successful efforts to learn Dutch. The Dutch even seemed to forgive her somewhat naive remark that she believed her father when he said he knew nothing of all the disappearances in Argentina saying, 'Why should he lie to me?' Many were probably touched by her tears at the wedding when 'Adios Menino' was played on a bandoneon (a type of concertina).

ii. Juliana and the Dutch Rasputin: the Greet Hofmans Affair (1956)

In the early years of Juliana's reign, Nel recalled the queen's first state visit to France. The press were told at the last minute that they were expected at an Elysee reception. Thanks to her connections, Nel looked suitably glamourous for the occasion.

> "Thanks to our fashion reporter in Paris, Pierre Balmain then lent me an impressive evening gown which, a bit musty, had already been shown many times by one of his top mannequins."

Elysée Reception, Queen Juliana's State visit to France, 1950

In Paris

Later, there was the birth of Marijke, Juliana's fourth and last daughter, who later changed her name to Christina. Nel describes the frenetically expectant atmosphere, as it was thought that it might be a boy:

> "We camped for a week or more with about 100 journalists in a hotel in Baarn, in a cold and snowy January. We bivouacked daily in front of the gates of the palace in Soestdijk, very cold. Finally, it happened. It was a girl.
>
> The AP competed with the ANP in those days in the national papers, so the ANP telex room was practically sealed up. I remember the competition was terrific - it might be a prince. An American colleague working for Aneta at the time was sacked on the spot by the late Van der Pol of the ANP because he thought he'd passed on news to me, the AP."

A few years after Marijke was born, news began to leak out about Juliana having scarlet fever while pregnant and the first rumours circulated about Greet Hofmans. She was a faith healer of dubious provenance who became a kind of female Rasputin figure. In the view of the queen's husband Bernard, Dutch MPs and many others, Hofmans exercised an undue and undesirable influence on Queen Juliana, As a result, Nel said,

> "A small number of journalists, among them Henk Kersting and myself, were put in the picture by worried MPs. It was a code of honour at that time not to publish this, something that would be found impossible now."

Both Dan Schorr and Friso Endt said they talked with Prince Bernhard about Hofmans, he was understandably worried about her, and it seems likely Nel did too. But nobody revealed their sources. In fact, Nel said her major informant on the Hofmans affair was her old friend Cees Fock, then Prime Minister Drees' chief aide. One of her interviewers described this relationship with the PM's top aide in Nel's own words:

> "He told me everything about the history of Greet Hofmans," Nel whispered. "They found me an important link because I was from AP. No, they never took advantage of me," she said confidently. "They never gave me misleading information. I was after all too slippery for that."

Nel did discuss publishing the Hofmans story with her editor Kersting but he felt it was too sensitive for the AP to break the story. However, they discovered that Der Spiegel was about to publish which would allow them to follow so they got ready to run with the story on the heels of Der Spiegel.

> "AP in Amsterdam was asked for a photo of Greet Hofmans by Der Spiegel, a photo client of our bureau in Bonn. Our story was ready and we knew which day Der Spiegel would publish. For days, we were busy getting the story completely ready to put it on the telex the moment Der Spiegel hit the streets. I remember vividly how I, scarcely recovered from this publication, was phoned in bed in the morning before daybreak and dew. AP New York had sent a short message: **Slis must have seance with Hofmans.**

> "At the crack of dawn, I set off for Nassaukade in Amsterdam, where Greet received her clients. I sat in the waiting room on a beautiful warm summer morning among a colourful crowd, with people from all walks of life - women with dogs and men as well. They lapped up everything she said, they were really taking it seriously. They animatedly swapped their experiences with Greet. I must have looked rather bewildered because they cheered me on with: 'she is terrific', or 'I have benefited a lot from it'.

> "In between, I racked my brains about what I could actually ask her. I was as fit as a fiddle and did not suffer from depressions. Then my turn came to go from the waiting room, behind a curtain, into a little room, to face Greet - a sort of severe, tall, thin and dark schoolmistress - black skirt and high-necked white blouse.

> "She had piercing eyes. At the last minute, I thought: 'You're not going to get me'. I told a story about a friend whose husband was sick, a true story. She buried her face in her hands. After what seemed a very long time, she said: 'I see that this man is going through a very long, dark tunnel and it does not end well'. She was right, too. He did die, as a matter of fact, of cancer."

What did Nel make of her? "Hoffman believed in herself. But on the other hand: a fake, a real fake. I found her a totally creepy person, completely gruesome. She also had connections with communist figures here and there, I believe. I don't know.... I found it creepy. She then eventually vanished like snow in the sun."

Nel explained how Hofmans gained her Rasputin-like influence over the queen.

> "Juliana had caught scarlet fever when she was pregnant with Marijke. She was warned by the doctor that she should not go to see the sick soldiers that had come back from Indonesia. But Juliana wanted to 'do good'. She wanted to see all those sick soldiers. So then she caught scarlet fever or something like it. People said that this caused the damage to the eyes of the child she was expecting. That was of course a tragedy."

In her anxiety about the blindness of Princess Marijke, Queen Juliana sought help from Greet Hofmans.

> "There were things that we didn't write about in those days, and now we would."

For example, Nel said that during the Hofmans period, Juliana was due to go on a state visit to America and was to address Congress, at a time when Holland was trying to get weapons out of America to defend New Guinea. Under Greet's influence, Juliana, who wanted to write her speech herself said in it that all weapons should be thrown into the sea. The then foreign minister, who was to accompany her, tried to dissuade her from including this statement. Juliana became angry and then made a truly bizarre remark: "What I would like to write is *beer is best again*." Yolanda explained that the Dutch brewers jointly ran an advertising campaign in 1950 to promote the drinking of beer, under the slogan, "Het bier is weer best" (beer is best again). Only much later was this story used by journalists, said Nel. Juliana did make a state visit to the U.S. in 1952 and it is likely that Nel either mixed up the dates or the foreign ministers here, as Stikker was Foreign Minister earlier, from 1948 to 1951. In fact, he resigned over the New Guinea question, later becoming NATO Secretary-General (1961-64) after Paul-Henri Spaak. Dutch New Guinea became independent in 1961 and joined Indonesia soon afterwards. Nel's reference here to defending New Guinea is also obscure.

In a Newsweek article on Juliana's daughter Beatrix, Nel notes that the less than regal publicity about Juliana resulting from her mystical attachment to Hofmans had a sequel in her attachment to a Polish-American, Adamski:

> "Who claims to have talked with creatures from the planet Venus."

As Nel hints elsewhere, Juliana's mother Wilhelmina had been pretty much out of touch with reality well before she abdicated and Juliana and her strange vagaries became more and more worrying to Dutch MPs. So the down-to-earth and emphatically normal Beatrix's arrival on the public stage must have come as a relief to many politicians in Holland.

All the same, Juliana enjoyed wide popularity among ordinary Dutch citizens similar to that of Elizabeth, the Queen Mother, in Britain. Whereas the British 'Queen Mum' managed to keep her public charm intact even when she was over 100, Juliana seemed to win Dutch hearts by being seen as 'everybody's favourite auntie'. After all, it doesn't matter so much if your favourite auntie goes a little batty.

In 1973, Juliana again provided Nel with huge international press coverage with the celebrations of the quarter-century of her reign. Many German newspapers picked up Nel's story. Among these, the Schwarzwaelder Bote, Oberndorf had a touchingly bland headline: Juliana is a nice woman.

An intriguing, but frustratingly incomplete, fragment by Nel on Juliana, her husband Prince Bernhard and Princess Beatrix was written around the end of the 1970s. This was soon after the Lockheed scandal involving Juliana's husband:

> "Juliana's husband Bernhard knows his wife is strong-minded. 'If my wife says no, there is nothing doing', he is reported as saying. She has an iron constitution and outdoes her retinue when on state travels.

> "An example of this is when during the 1953 fatal floods in the Netherlands when some 2,000 people lost their lives as the dykes broke, she had been photographed in big boots wading through the water all day long. When photographers asked for one more as she stood alone with a background of waves: she said no, that is enough. Her aide said, 'you are right'. She replied, 'the queen is always right'.

> "Juliana is a tireless worker, while her husband, Prince Bernhard, loves to travel. His business skills have impressed Dutch exporters.

> "The Dutch appear to have forgiven the prince his official disgrace in the Lockheed scandal. It must be noted however that Prince Bernhard has not visited the United States since.

> "Whereas Prince Bernhard often travels alone, German-born Prince Claus and the heiress to the throne Princess Beatrix, have travelled to the Soviet Union, China, Africa and the Middle East, always together.

> "Queen Juliana, who had a lonely youth as an only child, is now the happy grandmother of 10 boys and two girls between the ages of 1 to 12.

> They all gathered at her 70th birthday at the rambling white mansion of Soesdijk where the queen lives.
>
> "She is very popular and lives down to the people. Beatrix is a different generation - more a realist. As in the average modern family, there is a notable generation gap between the two, one of ten European royal houses.

"Eventually Juliana fell prey to Alzheimer's disease, which was probably also what was destined to rob Nel of her excellent memory though the cause was never diagnosed."

iii. Princess Beatrix: "Among my Own People" (1959)

When Beatrix was to make her first visit to America in 1959, Nel set about moving heaven and earth to get an interview with the princess:

> "When the Hofmans period was on the wane, Princess Beatrix was sent to America. I also worked for Newsweek then and made every effort to get an interview with Beatrix. First there was no answer to a letter from Kersting. Later, I got a tip from Willem van den Berge that there was an American lady staying at Soesdijk who belonged to a sort of sect a la Hofmans and that she had been chosen to write a story about Beatrix for an American publication. After that, I had a lunch with Renée Roell (Beatrix's best friend) of early season asparagus and strawberries.
>
> "I moved the chair in front of her and said down my nose: 'Of course I respect the fact that the princess is not giving any interviews yet. But,' I added threateningly, 'when she does do that, it should be with the person who first requested it in this country'. Not convinced that Mrs Roell would accomplish anything, I went with great courage to Luns (then foreign minister). I explained to him that, after having reported the Hofmans affair to the people in the most humane way, the minimal reward we were entitled to was an interview with Beatrix. Three days later, the message came that Beatrix wanted to give an interview. But UPI and The New York Times had to be there too. Disappointing, but better than nothing."

Beatrix had recently been on a trip with most of the European royalty of the day. This was a cruise organised by Queen Frederika of Greece on the Agemenmon. In the course of the interview over tea in Soestdijk palace, Nel asked how Beatrix had found the trip.

> "Wonderful," said the princess, "because I was among my own people."

Actually a very natural remark, said Nel.

> "After all, journalists would also rather sail with other journalists than with, for example, construction workers. But it sounded bad and must have been a lesson for life for Beatrix."

Nel made world news with Beatrix's remark, and in the Netherlands

> "There was no newspaper that did not pick it up."

Dutch journalist Ageeth Scherphuis' version of Nel's story has The New York Times popping the fatal question:

> "Quite casually, we came to the cruise with European royalty that Beatrix had then recently been on at the invitation of Queen Frederika of Greece. "Did you enjoy that?" asked Gilroy of The New York Times, 'With just royalty?' 'Well of course', she said, 'I enjoyed it'. And then, completely innocently, without her meaning any harm by it, she said: 'I liked it, because I was among my own people.'"

It was the realisation that The New York Times would lead with this remark that compelled Nel to run with this part of the interview.

> "Sitting next to me in the car on the way back, Gilroy said: 'That was interesting, the remark she made about her own people, very interesting." Ahhh, I thought, he is going to make that his lead. If I don't put it in, I will get trouble. And for that she has never forgiven me. I am sure. Much later, I explained it to her, but that didn't make it any better."

Scherphuis said of the incident:

> "To my question as to whether she would also have put it in if the New York Times and UPI had not been there, she didn't need to think for long. 'No, then I would not have put it in. I can imagine it was actually a very natural remark. I think I would not have wanted to do that to her.'"

This was an important incident. It is clear that Nel felt unhappy about using this lead, but considered she was forced into it by the competition. Possibly she was also anxious not to kow-tow to royalty. In another interview, she was more critical.

> "She stood there with *beaucoup de presence*, very self possessed... I thought: what a nasty remark! The interview appeared in De Volkskrant with the same headline and that she never forgave me. A little present in the form of a sixteenth century print of Drakesteyn Castle didn't manage to make things up. As president of the Foreign Press Association, I asked if her majesty would take part in a *table ronde* one time but she never responded to that."

But she went on to praise her:

> "She is enormously self-assured, she also did a good job in Japan. That was lapped up by all those Indonesian fellows. She also works day and night, that one. That is a tremendously ambitious woman with an enormously inquisitive spirit. If she wants to know something, she calls up six professors from Leiden. She is a good queen. She also does not want to be unpopular so she wanted to soothe that group of former Indonesian prisoners of war during her state visit to Japan and yet it was not over the top."

Nel was less impressed by Beatrix's relationship with the press. She said disapprovingly

> "The only audience that she holds with the press is the meeting with a bunch of chief editors who are not allowed to publish anything about it."

Beatrix may not have completely forgiven Nel for her headline but she did appreciate the print of Drakesteyn Castle, the little castle in Lage Vuursche where Princess Beatrix lived before becoming queen and to which she returned following her abdication. Nel found it on a visit to Brussels. Among Nel's papers was a short letter on light-blue paper with a crowned B in the upper left-hand corner. In almost untranslatable courtly Dutch, it was undoubtedly a friendly note:

Drakesteyn, 21 May 1963

Dear Miss Slis,

Hereby I extend to you heartfelt thanks for the most charming, attractive old print of "Drakesteyn" that you recently found in Brussels. I greatly appreciate your friendly gesture of buying it for me.

With best wishes, Beatrix

Here is what Nel wrote about Beatrix's visit to the US for the AP soon after the '*with my own people*' incident:

```
BEATRIX

THE HAGUE. August 28 - The Netherlands is
sending a winning young woman on a solid
business mission to the United States. Due in
New York on September 11, Princess Beatrix (21)
will spend eleven days in the new world,
tracing the steps of the first Dutch colonists
on Manhattan island.

Attending the Henry Hudson celebrations, the
heiress to the Dutch throne will tick off major
Dutch interests. Arriving on Holland's newest
flagship, the Holland America liner, SS
Rotterdam, she will plant the first tulip bulbs
in Sterling Forest in the Hudson valley and
return on a jet plane of the Royal Dutch
Airlines on September 22nd.

The sturdy, athletic Princess will hobnob with
the powerful including President Eisenhower,
Mrs Eleanor Roosevelt and Mrs Nelson
Rockefeller as well as attend a cosy luncheon
with students of her own age at Vassar college.

About a week before her departure, the princess
demonstrated that she can handle a news
conference like a pro. As a kind of warm up for
the press conference scheduled in the Waldorf
Astoria on the day of her arrival, she told
three American reporters at the Royal Palace
that she was still enjoying her freedom and
that there were no suitors yet.

In fact, she made it clear she thought freedom
was great and that, in another two years from
now, she hoped to move into her newly acquired
seventeenth century castle, "Groot
Drakenstein", about six miles from the palace
of her parents in Baarn.
```

Constitutionally, Beatrix came of age on her eighteenth birthday which admitted her to the Council of State, the advisory body to the crown. From now on, she received an annual 80,000 dollar allowance from the treasury.

It did not give her all the freedom and rights of a twenty-one year old. But soon after Beatrix celebrated her 21st birthday, early this year, it became known that Beatrix had become the owner of the moated castle, hidden in a leafy, tree-shrouded area, 'where I can invite my friends'.

Presently Beatrix shares an apartment with a girlfriend in the University city of Leiden, but spends most weekends on her sailing boat or else at home at the Soestdijk country palace.

Some of the Dutch press rapped the young princess because she indicated that with regard to the choice of a husband, perhaps a royal mate would be a natural.

Some Dutch newspapers-partly outraged because the interview had only been for American reporters-also resented that the princess, when discussing her royal task, mentioned her trip on the Greek ship Agamemnon as one occasion where she had become aware of the problems of reigning royalty. (In 1956, the princess accompanied her parents on a cruise to which the king and queen of Greece invited European royalty. The guests were mostly exiled royalty and the British and Scandinavian royalty turned down the invitation - at that time there had been some criticism of Dutch royalty accepting the invitation).

"Poor advisors," the official labor paper, Het Vrije Volk, commented bitterly on Beatrix's remark to the press that on this trip she had been able to be herself as she was among her own people.

Beatrix has a ready wit and quick answers and learns fast. She will not make a mistake for the second time.

Government officials who have dealt with her say she has qualities of leadership that raise her above the ordinary. She is a linguist and she speaks English particularly fluently.

She shows a remarkable poise and control for her age, and is gracious when fulfilling public functions. She admitted in her first interview that the trip to the United States scares her "a little", but that being herself will help.

The auburn-blond, blue-eyed princess is popular among her student friends, who say she is excellent company, a great pace maker and immensely cheerful. Dashing around in her little green Fiat, the princess has plunged herself with zest into her law studies as well as into the extra-curricular activities at Leiden University.

Early this summer she passed her bachelor of arts in preparation for her law degree, "as well any good student," according to Leiden professors.

She is extremely conscientious in her law studies which she hopes to finish in another two years.

Not being the fairy princess type, Beatrix is a sportswoman, who loves to sail - in her own boat - ride a horse and go skiing. She is good at all of them.

In daytime, she dresses plainly without frills. But come evening, Beatrix goes all out with a gala gown and plenty of jewellery.

From the early looks of it, Beatrix may well grow into the first modern business queen and perhaps partly as a reaction to her more mystically inclined mother, Queen Juliana, who has a very delicate intelligence of her own.

But when surveying the future, the Princess must sometimes wonder what brought her mother the tremendous popularity and devotion of the man in the street in Holland.

As queen, Beatrix was reasonably popular most of the time but sometimes attracted criticism for being somewhat high-handed and interfering in affairs of state. It is true she has not warmed the hearts of the Dutch in the same way as Juliana. But I found her trademark beehive-like hairstyle and rather ugly big hats endearing. I also liked a story about her at the time of the European Union summit in Maastricht in 1991. This was recounted to a group from the Foreign Press Association, invited for a visit a few years later. A restaurant-owner had laid on a classy luncheon for the European Union leaders attending the summit in his vast restaurant in a beautiful old castle. Maastricht is known for its excellent food though, ironically, it managed to give its visitors food poisoning at an earlier EEC summit in the late 1970s. In the Calvinistic north of the country, all comers including top-ranking politicians or corporate leaders are generally given "broodjes" (rolls) for lunch. But in southern Maastricht, thanks its proximity to Belgium and its influences, even the companies provide slap-up meals for visitors right down to journalists. Proud of his cuisine, the Maastricht restaurant owner wanted all the EU leaders to sign their names on a wall in the restaurant but the bureaucrats involved insisted this would not be appropriate. However, Beatrix spotted the wall and cried: "Come on, Europe," I imagine in her jolly-hockey-sticks kind of way and they all signed his wall.

Nel firmly quashed any idea that she had some kind of easy access to the Dutch monarchy, apart from Bernhard. "Oh, no. Prince Bernhard was of course the easiest. You could really talk to him. Perhaps if you are a dame de compagnie (court lady companion or lady-in-waiting), they would now and then open their hearts to you. But Bernhard was very easy. You had no difficulty with him."

In a 1990 interview when Nel was looking at photos of herself dancing with Claus when she was president of the Foreign Press Association, she dismissed rumours that had been current then about Claus having an affair with a politician's wife. She also criticised some snide remarks made by foreign minister Josef Luns in a Belgian paper. Nel said of the prince, who became subject to serious depressions and a series of illnesses in the 1980s:

> "He was still his normal self then, that poor devil. But it is a good marriage all the same. *Enfin.* Some dirty paper or another wrote that she (Beatrix) had an affair again with that awful Laurens Jan Brinkhorst. I don't believe a damn thing about it. But Jan, of all people." *Again this roar of laughter.*

> *"What does she think of this muckraking by Luns in the Flemish paper De Morgen?* Completely indecent. Because I know for sure that it (depression) is genetic. Pa appears to have shot himself in the head in Kenya. If Claus suffers from the same thing, that is sad. Luns, I believe, has slightly lost his head."

The daughter of this same Brinkman married Prince Constantijn, brother of the present Dutch King, Willem-Alexander, who is the youngest son of Beatrix. Luns presumably suggested in De Morgen that Claus was a suicidal depressive. Poignantly, just before he died in 2002 after a long illness, Claus himself actually won a libel case against a Dutch magazine for suggesting that his father committed suicide. However, the death of Claus revealed that from a difficult beginning, the prince had quietly achieved widespread popularity, both with the Dutch and internationally. Nel went on to say in that 1990 interview that she shared other commentators' criticisms of the Government Information Service (RVD), which released practically no news about his illness.

"Taking the long view, they must come clean as far as information about Claus goes, otherwise there will be too many rumours."

Otherwise she had no complaints about the RVD at that time.

"I have an excellent relationship with Bax (*then head of the RVD*). He is very open with me. He feels very sorry for (*Beatrix's eldest son, then Crown Prince*) Willem-Alexander. Apparently he has the greatest difficulty in getting to grips with history and political science, while his brothers take to this like a duck to water. That Friso (*middle son*) appears to be really brilliant."

Elaborating on her relationship with the government information service, Nel said

"The RVD has nothing to fear from me. I do not poach on their territory. *Je suis discrete.* They have told me a lot. I have used it, but *between the lines.* I do not publish everything. I have the reputation of total trustworthiness. I am somehow a bit straightforward. The protestant is still in me, though after all the prots could go to hell. I have a certain propriety. I do not bring out the most sensational things but I can write it in such a way that you still smell it a bit."

Returning to Willem-Alexander, who became the Netherlands' first king since Willem III in 2013, Nel was complementary about his other qualities aside from those early academic struggles.

"Willem-Alexander has a lot of his grandfather in him: *il a du charme,* he has an easy manner, likes good food and pretty girls. *Il aime la vie.* I believe that he is good at dealing with people, but he is no big thinker."

Beatrix announced her abdication in favour of Willem-Alexander in a television address on 28 January 2013, three days before her 75th birthday. This made her the country's oldest reigning monarch ever. She said she would formally stand down on 30 April, which thus became the last traditional 'Queen's Birthday' festival since her reign began. Beatrix had instituted her mother Juliana's birthday on 30 April as the official Queen's Birthday holiday after Juliana abdicated in her daughter's favour on her 71st birthday in 1980. This was because Beatrix's own birthday was on 31 January, rather a chilly time of year for this festive occasion. Since Willem-Alexander has taken over, it has become the 'King's Birthday' holiday. Beatrix reigned for 33 years, just beating her mother Juliana's 32-

year reign. Her abdication was the third in a row: Wilhelmina had abdicated in 1948 after the longest reign of the three, an imposing 58 years. She had become queen in 1890 at the age of 10, under the regency of her mother, Queen Emma.

A sad note at the time of the royal 'changing of the guard' from Beatrix to her son was that Willem-Alexander's brother Friso was still in a coma after a skiing accident at an Austrian ski resort in February the previous year. Friso died back home in Holland after a year and a half in a coma.

Willem-Alexander and his wife, who is titular queen, plan to be more informal than Beatrix, saying in a joint television interview just before he ascended the throne that it does not matter to them how they are addressed by their citizens after they become king and queen. Willem-Alexander said:

> "I am no protocol fetishist. People can address me as they like, because they can then be at their ease…"

Maxima backed him up:

> "Everyone calls me Maxima. Ultimately, queen or princess, it does not matter. It is more what we represent than the title."

In a final glance back at the older generation in her article on the monarchy, Nel wrote:

> "My last royal tour de force was the White Funeral of Queen, or rather Princess, Wilhelmina which I found in a way pathetic. Wilhelmina towards the end of her reign had already frequently been 'out of the picture' while Juliana temporarily took over. The most pathetic thing in this bitter winter was the atmosphere in the little palace on the Lange Voorhout, where Wilhemina lay in state. It had something strangely lonely that made you ponder about her perhaps interesting but rather arid life."

The funeral, in 1962, was known as the White Funeral not because of the weather, but because much white was used instead of black as Wilhelmina had requested. An old newsreel shows a white coffin, the hearse carriage draped in white and the horses drawing the carriage in long white covers, making them look like a cross between heraldic jousting horses and ghosts. Juliana and the other women mourners were also dressed in white.

iv. The Last Queen of Libya (1954)

"All done up in wonderful Dior dresses"

Nel probably saw more of Libya in 1954 than I did when I was actually living there twenty years later. She told me of

> "Trips to Sabrata, Leptis Magna with the Turkish Ambassador and Benghazi with the Italian consul to Surinaika. And there we stayed in a hotel run by the Brits!"

The Turkish ambassador and Italian consul were perhaps more culturally inclined than our Libyan friends who whisked myself and my husband rather too rapidly through the impressive Roman site of Leptis Magna.

I found out about the Libya episode in my 1981 interview with Nel, when she was musing about Africa.

"There's a whole new Africa, very important I think for Europe to keep pace with developments in Africa - with characters like Ghadaffi around," said Nel presciently. She went on:

> "A Persian friend of mine was married to an American diplomat, and I was in Tripoli visiting them in the winter of 1954. Yes, I saw King Idris. I interviewed Fatima: she was all done up in wonderful Dior dresses...Yes, it was very different then because it was pre-oil and they were as poor as rats. I've a great admiration for what Italy did for the Roman ruins. The Libyans had a very nice, thin upper crowd, a delightful and handsome people. But now rather Muslim, Ghadaffi, anyway I think religion is rather poisoning the atmosphere - it has done more harm than good... Religious wars..."

Libya is certainly very different these days, in contrast to 1954 when Nel visited the country and to 1973-74 when I lived in the eastern town of Tobruk, near the Egyptian border. At the beginning of 2011, I watched Libya's popular demonstrations on TV with amazement. Tobruk was unrecognisable from the overgrown village I remember where goats were munching cardboard boxes on the corner by our apartment at night and donkeys pulling carts everywhere by day. My husband was working at the Higher Petroleum Institute. The students all had friends on the revolutionary committee or were on it themselves, but felt quite free to criticise Ghadaffi. Tobruk was an Idris stronghold, which may have helped people feel more independent. In fact, Gaddafi even got some praise. The students told us that if you had a problem, you could get to see him, and he would also actually do something about it. The medical system was completely free with no bureaucracy, though after getting pregnant I did sometimes wonder if I was getting the right pills. It didn't seem so bad then, even though Ghadaffi was clearly a little potty. But those were early years and I suppose his absolute power had not yet had time to corrupt him absolutely.

Libya was formerly an Italian colony and an old Italian tourist book I found from the Mussolini era described the sole tourist 'sight' in Tobruk as a thousand-metre long barbed wire fence. After the war, this curious sight-seeing object was replaced by the German, French and British cemeteries resulting from the many World War II battles fought in the area. The country gained its independence in 1951 and was ruled by Idris until 1969. He was overthrown in a Gaddafi-led bloodless coup while he was visiting Turkey. Thanks to Libya being in the news so much in 2011 because of the uprising against Ghadaffi, I discovered that Fatima lived on as late as 2009, when she died at the age of 97 or 98. She was a very beautiful woman and given to good works. From her obituaries, it seems that Nasser was quite nice to the couple, though they lost all their possessions. A year or two before her death, a small palace was restored to her. Idris died many years before her. Ghadaffi was killed by his captors and paraded before a mob in his home town of Sirte, two years after Fatima died, in October 2011.

While in Tobruk, I tried to teach English to the daughter of Idris' former chauffeur. But the only time I really got her to make an effort was when I had tea with her mother, who spoke no word of English. We sat on the floor in a bare-walled, carpeted room on rose-patterned cushions, and the mother poured tea from a great height and smiled and nodded, waiting for her daughter to interpret. Rose-patterned cushions and curtains were everywhere, inexplicably bequeathed to Tobruk in the war by the UK's Royal Air Force.

When I was living in Tobruk, young men about town visited our apartment frequently to do their raki drinking with us so that their parents didn't know. But their parents were almost certainly doing the same somewhere else so that their children didn't know. Clearly it didn't matter what you did as long as you didn't do it on the street and frighten the horses or rather the donkeys. The harbourmaster of Tobruk told us that before prohibition, 30% of Libyans drank alcohol but after prohibition, this went up to 90%.

The completely swathed women with just one eye visible described by Nel in her interview with the queen hadn't changed a bit when we were there. Students said they would be different and let people meet their wives. But they admitted others they knew had said the same but still reverted and kept their wives hidden after they married. Ghadaffi himself had a kind of bodyguard of dashing if somewhat fierce-looking women in modern dress and the schoolgirls of Tobruk also had those snappy navy blue trouser suits. But these girls all still disappeared into the blanket after they left school. In Benghazi and Tripoli, women were certainly out and about in western-style clothes, going to university and holding jobs so Fatima was right up to a point in her optimism on emancipation. Obviously the population has grown enormously since I was there, when it was only about two million. Today I watch the struggling country after its Arab spring and hope that things will turn out well for my Libyan friends. I still find Nel's interview with Fatima a fascinating piece of time travel as I write this, in the 21st century era of the 'Arab spring'.

The Queen of Libya

(by Nel Slis, Associated Press correspondent, who became the first western journalist to be received by the queen in her palace)

-----Benghazi, Libya (Ass.Press)-----

Fatima-al-Sjifa, queen of Libya, is one of the most elegant queens but perhaps the least known.

She is married to Idris, the first king of Libya, who is 20 years older and a first cousin of hers. Both belong to the tribe of the Senoessi, a religious sect which has followers in every country in North Africa.

The 43-year-old Queen Fatima was brought up in Arabic-speaking countries, mostly in Egypt. She does not speak any foreign languages, but understands a little English.

Before her marriage, she had a role dealing informally with men and scores of British officers remember how she played tennis in shorts. Since she became queen of Libya, however, she has led the life of the typical Libyan woman, strictly separated from all men.

"It will be a slow and gradual process before Libyan women attain emancipation", she told me, "But the Libyan girls are very much longing to learn and to win their freedom."

Queen Fatima, small and elegant in her black clothes, which were made for her by Christian Dior, spoke Arabic which was translated by her lady-in-waiting, the beautiful 24-year-old Mrs Selma Dajani, a Palestinian, whose husband was one of king Idris' advisors.

Queen Fatima spends the greatest part of her
time in the small palace just outside the war-
battered city of Benghazi and one of the two
capitals of Libya. King Idris, who himself
comes from the province of Cyrenica, prefers to
live here than in the more cosmopolitan co-
capital, Tripoli.

Queen Fatima, who was receiving a journalist
from the west for the first time, said she was
pleased that there was interest abroad for her
poor country, which had suffered so much from
the war.

It is hard for one to imagine that the elegant
queen, who would attract attention in any
society and would command respect, is a
descendant of raw Arabs who, like the
forefathers of her consort, whose fourth spouse
she is, were in the habit of roaming through
the desert.

Tranquil and smiling, Queen Fatima told via her
lady-in-waiting of the journey she had recently
made through Europe and during which she
visited Germany, France and Spain. Her eyes
began to shine when she spoke of her visit to
southern Spain, Andalusia, where she found the
Arab influence very striking.

She spoke of the future possibilities for the
emancipation of Libyan women. Instead of
playing tennis in shorts, she is currently
obliged by her royal rank to go back many
centuries and live the life of seclusion... of
99 percent of Libyan women.

The women of Libya live a more concealed life
than their sisters in

other Arab countries. They are dressed in the
barracan, a hand-woven wool or silk cloth- the
material depends on their circumstances- in
which they wrap themselves up in such a way
that only one eye is visible.

Only when she goes abroad does the queen live
like a western woman, dressed in European
clothes, and then a visit to a fashion show or
to the Folies Bergeres in Paris - where she has
indeed been - fascinates her just as much as
any other woman in the world.

Having to dress in the barracan is perhaps
harder for her than for all her Libyan sisters,
in view of the fact that she knows the freedom
of the west.

The wife of the leading statesman in Libya, premier Mahmoed Moentasser, for example, never comes in contact with the world.

But this is simply the Mohammeden law which in its most orthodox form forbids the woman to be seen by a man other than her husband. A woman sees her husband for the first time after the elaborate marriage ceremony, which lasts a week.

Queen Fatima, however, believes that Libyan women will make important progress in a subsequent generation on the road to freedom. They will be able to study and go abroad.

While a Sudanese man dressed like a European butler served exquisite, sweet and creamy cakes, she said, "we have many good American friends and one of my greatest wishes is to visit the US one day."

"If I were to go to the United States," Queen Fatima went on, "I would dearly like to fly, but the king won't fly."

King Idris does not like either flying or sailing, but he has still accepted an official invitation to himself and the queen to make a visit to Turkey this spring, a country with which Libya is linked by many historic, religious and emotional bonds.

It must have been quite an adventure getting to and around Libya in 1954, especially as Nel, like Idris, was allergic to flying and must have got to North Africa by boat. Three years later, Nel's itchy feet sent her off on another memorable boat trip, beating Beatrix to America by a couple of years.

7.
Slis goes to America (1957)

i. A Collision at Sea

On a windy Monday, three hundred and twelve Hungarian refugees and five hundred Dutch emigrants were among the 1,050 passengers and crew crowded on board the 9,117-tonne transport ship S.S. Waterman. She sailed from Rotterdam on 11 March 1957, bound for Halifax and New York. Nel was on board, on her way to a four-month stint in the AP's New York bureau and a trip around America. Her aversion to flying was about to provide her with another scoop - and a narrow escape from disaster.

Three days after sailing, the Waterman collided in mid-Atlantic with an Italian freighter. Nel the reporter instantly sprang into action. The initial telegram after the incident shows how quickly she managed to get access to the ship's facilities to contact her AP office. Her eyewitness account was in all the Dutch newspapers the next day and winging its way into newspapers around the world. I can imagine her racing around pestering the ship's officers for information and for some way to send her telegram and reports, and buttonholing stewardesses and passengers for their reactions and stories. Here is the first instalment of her report:

MIDATLANTIC COLLISION, 14 MARCH

In the early hours of Thursday 14 March, stewardesses Anneke van Riel from Hilversum and Riet Muller from Amerongen were taking a morning walk on the deck when the Waterman collided with the 7,174-tonne Italian freighter SS Merit. There was a dense fog, preventing them from seeing the Merit until it struck. The impact and clanging alarm bells a few seconds later jarred most Waterman passengers from their sleep and lifeboard stations were manned.

In assorted attire, some 850 life-belted emigrants - including two hundred and fifty small children and babies - with the 200 crew including about one hundred Indonesians, gathered at the lifeboat stations in superb order when the alarm sounded. There was no panic during the 45 minutes passengers waited at the lifeboat stations, under a light cloudy sky. At 9.20 GMT, the lifeboats were swung free but not lowered. Most of the passengers were unaware just what had happened, except for the two stewardesses. The collision had ripped a hole in the Waterman's hull plating 15 feet above the waterline, but passengers were assured there was no danger.

When 54 year old Captain J.C. Flag calmly called off the alarm and shipboard life returned to normal, normal routine meals resumed in four shifts and several people appeared at the breakfast table still wondering what had happened. Canada-bound 51 year old Dutchman, Reverend Willem Wilman from Friesland sat quietly at breakfast unaware of the alarm, listening to the tales of his fellow diners about how they went to the lifeboats in hastily picked up garments, some with shaving soap still on their cheeks. There had also been a remarkably quick reaction to the alarm among the 100 Indonesian djongossen/djonges, who quit laying the tables in a flash and stood by the lifeboats trying to take photos to use at the first port of call.

About noon GMT, loudspeakers told the passengers that the Waterman was returning to Europe. The migrants, especially the 300 Canada-bound Hungarians, appeared confused and disappointed. Most Hungarians had never seen the sea before. They heard the news in Hungarian from an interpreter. The 500 Dutch emigrants, of whom 200 were going to Canada and 300 to the US, under the Refugee Relief Act (1), were deeply depressed at the idea they were returning because they had 'burned their boats' behind them.

Having delivered her first reports, Nel started looking into the condition the boat was in, and finding out what was going to happen next. The operating company, Royal Rotterdam Lloyd, ordered Captain Flach to head for the French port of Brest for repairs to its hull plating which had been ripped open. Luckily, the ship's drinking-water system remained intact, a crew member told Nel. Another Dutch government ship, the Zuiderkruis, was to meet the Waterman at Brest to take the passengers on to their destination. Some of the Dutch passengers told emigration officer Berend Kosters they would refuse a further sea trip and insist on air transport. Others cracked jokes about going back: 'Now we can pick up our forgotten umbrellas'.

The Waterman was now sailing in a moderate wind, following a fairly rough night. In the evening,

> "Dutch and Hungarian emigrants started fraternising: international card and chess games were popular. The Hungarians had danced aboard the ship the previous night when the ship was rolling in rough seas. Some passengers stayed on deck on Thursday to watch the Merit, still in the vicinity. The Italian vessel, owned by Lofario di Giovanni of Genoa, had been hit on her bow but was able to resume her journey to Hamburg after radioing that she was in no difficulty. The 6,067-tonne German freighter Eibe Oldendorff, which was en route for Amsterdam, was meanwhile making for the Waterman to stand by.

These Hungarian refugees, like the children who ended up with Nel's surrogate family on Goeree Overflakkee, had doubtless fled Hungary after the bloody crushing of the 1956 uprising by Soviet troops.

Continuing her story, Nel at first speaks of:

> "The good atmosphere which has prevailed from the beginning of the trip since the Waterman's departure from Rotterdam - possibly helped by the camaraderie of together surviving a potentially dangerous incident. Passengers are drowsy after the emotion of the morning and many are retiring to their cabin to sleep. Dutch emigrants are urgently trying to send reassuring cables to their relatives."

Later, she does see a reaction setting in.

> "The state of alarm has had a delayed effect on the emigrants. By nightfall on Thursday, a kind of snake-pit atmosphere prevailed on the ship. Afraid to go to their

cabins, many emigrants bundled up in the lounges and on the various decks. Scores of Hungarian refugees huddled together on the chilly upper deck. Rumours were rife among the Hungarians, who failed to understand the proceedings. They had only recently been brought to Dutch transit camps from Austria. Despite brief announcements by an interpreter in their own language, they felt unhappy at the idea of returning to Europe."

The Dutch emigrants were not too happy either. After several days of seasickness, some wanted to go back to Holland and fly to the USA or Canada. One couple with three grownup children was determined to leave the ship, and let the children go on alone. Immigration officer Kosters spent all night persuading them to stay with the ship.

Investigating the largely male Hungarian group, Nel discovered that about 70% were young labourers and about 30% intellectuals or artists. Among them was Budapest's most famous photographer with his wife and three daughters

"His son, an active member of the revolutionary group, had to stay behind. As a photographer, he was connected with the Budapest opera during recent years."

Among the intellectuals were engineers with their families, a bookkeeper and a printer with his wife and sons.

"Many of these have friends or relations in Canada, whom they expect to help them along. There is also an orthodox Jewish group including some six children and a rabbi. They are the only people that conducted and attended their religious service. Although the Hungarians have behaved in a perfectly orderly way, they have at times showed a hostile and suspicious attitude to everything that reeked of authority. Only the intellectual group has any knowledge of the English language. But the Hungarians spent a good deal of their time aboard studying in the little grammar books provided to them by the Canadian authorities in Holland. The Dutch group of migrants, mostly going to Western Canada, seem to rely on their often inadequate smattering of English."

The last sentence sounds like a sly dig at her compatriots by our linguistically adept reporter.

ii. Brest - Halifax - New York

On Saturday 16 March, five days after leaving Rotterdam, the Waterman limped into Brest with its cargo of dejected Dutch emigrants and Hungarian refugees. The passengers were to be taken onto the Dutch ship SS Zuiderkruis, due to arrive from Rotterdam that night. The Dutch consul in Brest, Robert de la Menardiere, arrived early in the morning with boxes of sweets for the 250 small children and babies aboard the Dutch ship.

A surveyor from Lloyds of London boarded the ship to assess the damage from the collision. Nel then discovered how much the crew had to do to keep the ship going and how disastrous the collision might have been but for some nifty steering of the Waterman at the crucial moment. Representatives of the Dutch government shipping department were also due to arrive in the evening. Nel continued:

> "After the collision, the Waterman was sailing at 9 miles an hour instead of its normal 17 miles, as crew members worked feverishly for over 24 hours to partition off the undamaged wheel-house and screw-axle. The Merit's anchor ripped open the carpenters' and plumbers' room, right behind the vulnerable wheelhouse. Wooden and iron plates and sailing cloths were used to shield the wheelhouse to prevent water from entering it. Water and oil were pumped out in order to lift the poop deck and reduce the risk of water running into it. If a last-minute steering manoeuvre had not swept the Waterman around, the Merit could have ripped the Dutch emigrant ship open right in the middle, with fatal results."

On the following Friday, 25 March, the Zuiderkruis sailed into the Canadian port of Halifax and the first 311 Hungarian refugees who had sailed from the Netherlands on 11 March went on shore to start a new life.

> "With a sigh of relief to quit the rough Atlantic... But their feelings are mixed with apprehension about what is to come. The Hungarian group is the first to be transported by sea to Canada, out of some two thousand awaiting departure in Dutch transit camps. Their first encounter with the sea has been agonising to many of them. Especially after the collision, many Hungarians have huddled on the chilly and wet decks during the bleak nights, rather than returning to their cabins. Each

day, they carefully measured the distance separating them from terra firma on the ship's maps."

Under an agreement between Canada and the Netherlands, the Dutch provided food and accommodation for the Hungarians in the Dutch transit camps and the Canadians paid their passage. At the camps, they were exhaustively prepared for their new life. Nel reported that there were seventeen Canadian teachers and two social workers to give them intensive courses in basic English and orient them for their life in Canada. They even had dressed dolls to show the women how they and their children would dress and miniature supermarkets to demonstrate their future shopping.

Nel found the transportation of Dutch migrants and Hungarian refugees extremely well organised, putting this down to over a decade of experience

> "The Netherlands, blessed with an extraordinarily high birth-rate and one of the lowest death-rates anywhere, has adopted a fixed policy of full employment, which means stimulating industrialisation and emigration."

Between 1945 and 1957, about 120,000 Dutch migrants moved to Canada out of a total of 277,000 emigrants. Most went to Ontario, Alberta, Manitoba and British Columbia. The Waterman was the first joint shipment of Dutch and Hungarians.

Nel was pleasantly surprised by immigration procedures in Halifax, "contradicting tales of gruff and abrupt immigration officers." Halifax had handled some 28,000 immigrants over the past 11 weeks. Immigration superintendant H.M. Grant told Nel he and his staff of 100 had received immigrants from Greece, Italy, Germany, Holland and Hungary over the last weekend alone.

After the migrants disembarked, they entered a large assembly hall from where they pass through a medical examination if necessary. Nel reported:

> "They can screen one a minute, and in the adjoining hall there is the civil examination of the migrants and in the case of the Hungarians, they receive railway tickets and money."

She went on:

> "In the next hall, they are met by representatives of churches, the Salvation Army and social services. Parents can go and see to their luggage in the baggage room, while a Red Cross nursery receives the children. They finally enter the last hall, where they can have a hot meal

before boarding a waiting train, and purchase food - meat, chocolate, milk and fruit and vegetables - in a special government-run food store where prices are low. Most Dutch migrants took in large stocks, because many faced a four-day train journey."

For sick migrants, a small hospital including several wards and a small surgery were located in the same building complex. For migrants whose papers were unsatisfactory and who had to wait, there was a dormitory and a recreation hall with television and a cafeteria.

The Canadian immigration officials were businesslike, efficient and very humane, Nel concludes. Still, to me, all of this emigration process that Nel describes has a strong wartime flavour of people being shifted around in bulk like troops. Nel herself was in fact unhappy about the emigration drive, concluding that "emigration" was a product of government policy rather than a genuine individual decision. She did think large families were perhaps more self-motivated, emigrating because their children would have more opportunities than they had at home.

As the Zuiderkruis pulled into New York harbour on 27 March to unload her last 260 migrants for the New World, Nel sounded off in her report about the effect of government policy on the crew.

"The Dutch government, in its zeal to ship as many migrants as fast as possible to far distant lands, draws up the shipping schedule at the expense of a harassed crew. Crew members' unanimous complaint is that 'we are never home'. Many of them have not spent more than 14 days with their families per year. In the opinion of the crew, the three Dutch ships were originally meant to ply tropical waters with a heavy cargo. Without the stability of such a cargo, a commander responsible for some one thousand lives is unable to keep up a regular schedule when crossing the raging Atlantic. Not being able to keep up with the schedule as laid down by the Dutch directorate-general for shipping, it is the crew that is the loser by running out of home leave on practically every crossing."

The Dutch government owned three such Victory ships refurbished for shipping people instead of cargo: the Grote Beer as well as the Waterman and the Zuiderkruis and it chartered a fourth, the MS Johan van Oldenbarneveldt. Nonetheless, she said, morale on the ship was good:

"The ships are so much Dutch territory that the Dutch Reverend Willem Wilman said that differences between Nederlandse Hervormd (Reformed), Gereformeerd (the more Calvanistic branch) and another offshoot known as Article 31 persisted even through the collision and frightening storms. Dominee Wilman is Netherlands Reformed and a member of the Labour Party, as he himself proudly proclaims...

"Despite delicate encouragement by Van Gilse and Wilman, the Hungarians did not go in for worshipping, except for the orthodox Jewish group. The rabbi did on one occasion act as interpreter when Dominee Wilman expressed the desire to talk with the seven Hungarian protestants.

"It was also the rabbi who made a moving farewell speech at their last dinner aboard, toasting the health of Queen Juliana and the Dutch people, 'who gave us such a warm and friendly reception in Dutch transit camps'."

iii. In the AP Heartland

The trip to America had followed another bout of persistent lobbying of the AP by Nel, this time successful. Nel had been working for the AP for over a decade and felt it owed her something. So after giving up on getting to the Paris bureau, she came up with the idea of visiting America to work there for a few months. Once again, her efforts did not succeed at first, but later she contacted Lloyd Stratton in New York and asked him to press her case within the AP. This he did, suggesting that:

"Nel could produce her worth at both the world desks in New York and Washington."

But he also asked Kersting whether the Amsterdam bureau could cough up the costs of her stay.

Following some haggling, a complicated compromise was reached on a four-month stay. Nel would have to pay for her travel and accommodation. Part of her salary could be charged to "Foreign News Collection" and part to "AP World Service" while the costs of her replacement in The Hague would be paid by AP Amsterdam. Nel also gave up her holiday, on condition that she could make a trip around the U.S. after finishing her stints in New York and Washington.

The working part of Nel's trip proved successful. On her return to the Netherlands at the end of July, she found a short personal note from Stanley Swinton, General News Editor of AP World Service:

"Just a welcome home note to say how much we appreciated having you here."

Kersting was pleased, too, pronouncing Nel's visit:

> "Very useful, looking at it from this end, both to herself and the Amsterdam bureau operations."

All of Nel's stories from America were picked up by AP subscribers, her style and English improved and her knowledge of US relations would undoubtedly benefit the work in Amsterdam and The Hague. Stratton was equally positive, writing:

> "Nel left her mark on the AP staff, both at Washington and New York. She gave a very good account of herself as a workman (sic) and also as a person."

Stratton attributed the improvement in her English to

> "the hardboiled training and criticism she got and admirably took from the Washington news desk and from Swinton in New York."

Nel herself also referred to this in a letter to Stratton after her return to Holland.

> "Even the criticism was welcome and refreshing as well as useful, of course. I figure I learned about as much during my four months in the U.S. as I have in the last four years in The Hague. Let's hope it will result in a heavier flow of feature material from The Hague."

Wes Gallagher was impressed, too, telling Nel:

> "We were delighted to have you and you made a real contribution to the service and a personality hit in the Feature department. "

Among a few bread-and-butter AP reports I found by Nel datelined New York, one quoted below intimates that Nel did not think much of the American ambassador's wife, who must have been less than thrilled by how she was described. But Nel had had enough of diplomatic wives back in the Netherlands. The ambassador also sounds pretty odious to me, but perhaps that just reflects my prejudice against 'jutting, forceful jaws'.

> "The new American ambassador to the Netherlands, Philip Young, 47, is tall, dark and handsome. He radiates energy, while his jutting, forceful lower jaw speaks of considerable willpower. Ambassador Young and his lively, prematurely grey (sic), blue-eyed wife, together with their dachshund Kontiki, are due in the Netherlands June 21. Short and plump (sic) Mrs Young has been

active in the American Red Cross and the Girl Scouts movement and has also been an active campaigner for the Republican Party.

Later they will be joined by their 24-year-old unmarried daughter, Faith, who has been teaching English literature. The young family will sail on the +United States+ liner on June 14 for Le Havre, France and proceed from there to The Hague by car. The youngest daughter, Shirley, 21, is married to an American army officer and was a schoolmate of Ellen Stone, daughter of the dean of The Hague diplomatic corps Canadian Ambassador and Mrs Thomas Stone.

Ambassador Young, who has been working in the American government since the age of 30, said in an interview, 'I am very much looking forward to my first diplomatic post'. He imagines 'it will give me sufficient leisure time to roam around the country in order to learn all about the Netherlands. That will be more instructive than sitting behind my desk'.

The new American ambassador dresses simply. He is 6 feet, 2 inches tall, weighs 190 pounds and his dark hair is parted in the middle. His athletic appearance is deceiving because, he says, 'I am totally disinterested in sports and not good at any'. His hobby is woodworking; he makes some of his own furniture and pipes. He is a chain-smoker and his pipe rarely leaves him, even when he talks.

Ambassador Young said he was very appreciative of 'the role the Netherlands plays as a promoter of West European unity and of NATO', but he refused to commit himself on such touchy issues as West New Guinea or landing rights on the U.S. western seaboard for Royal Dutch Airlines. He visited Europe in 1951, but has never been in the Netherlands. Young said he is a great admirer of Queen Juliana. He met the Dutch queen, as a princess, at a family supper given by the late President and Mrs Roosevelt during World War II."

A second report, on the construction of nuclear shelters, is a grim reminder of the cold war days. For me, it evoked memories of a massive bomb shelter I saw under a mansion-sized 'cottage' in New Hampshire a dozen or so years later. It had been built by a rich matriarch who had spent the last 20 years of her life corresponding with the Pentagon about bomb shelters. A well-concealed entrance led to a complex of small rooms underneath the cottage, completely sealed off by a protective layer of lead. One room had 12 camp beds, while others were stuffed with every conceivable form of provisions, including a cupboard full of silver polish and another with prunes in brandy.

About the time Nel was writing this item in America, one in three English schools were given talks on what to do in case of a nuclear attack. The advice included whitewashing the windows and filling up the bath (if you had one) before the bomb fell, which sounded difficult in the likely time available. There was also a demonstration of making a singularly useless looking primitive heater with a flower pot and a candle. Those were paranoid days, when the threat of a nuclear holocaust hung palpably over the world.

Nel's nuke report featured an interview with West German interior minister Dr Gerhard Schroeder, who had come to study the US civil defence system and graciously concluded that it was 'adequate'. After a day looking at the civil defence system of Greater New York, he told her

> "So far, I have only seen it on paper and it is interesting to see the actual plans and people responsible for it, because we are collecting data on the financing of the construction of shelters... We have similar requirements in our Ruhr area which is also densely populated and heavily industrialised."

Schroeder said he expected little opposition later that month when the first German civil defence bill would be read by parliament. There was agreement on the organisation but not on the future construction of shelters

> "Some of our people want to defer construction in view of later and possibly different requirements based on new data relating to radioactive fallout."

Schroeder was due to visit Britain, Sweden and Switzerland later to study their systems, after a weekend sightseeing in New York and a visit to the US civil defence headquarters in Battle Creek, Michigan.

Another vignette, of a South African bishop, recalls the early years of the anti-apartheid struggle. The Anglican bishop of Johannesburg, Richard Ambrose Reeves, described in Nel's report as an outspoken foe of segregation laws, was in the US on a fundraising tour to aid the dependants of 156 South Africans on trial for opposing the government. Speaking in St Ann's Church in Brooklyn, New York, Bishop Reeves said optimistically that if the racial struggle in South Africa ever led to open conflict between the church and the state, the whole of the Anglican communion would be ranged behind the church in South Africa.

> "As a church, we have no choice but to resist to the end, at whatever cost, any attempt to divide us from our brethren in Christ."

It would have been nice if all Anglicans had indeed done so, but at any rate this particular branch of Christianity also produced Bishop Tutu, who promoted reconciliation after the end of apartheid

iv. Nel's Grand US Train Tour

In May, Nel set off on her tour around America. The Dutch version of her journal for the folks back home in Holland is a little unsatisfactory. It whets the appetite for more and leaves me wondering what Nel thought but did not write to paraphrase Brecht. It seems a dutiful rather than enthusiastic record but still worth including for its historical interest. Even the AP modestly calls it 'daily notes'.

Headlined 'Vacation journey through America', underneath it says in brackets:

```
Miss Nel Slis, Associated Press correspondent
in The Hague, who is working for a few months
in New York, has made a three-week vacation
trip through America. Here are some of her
daily notes.
```

Nel begins with some statistics on money, an ever-fascinating subject for her Dutch readership.

> "It is possible to visit 21 states in America in three weeks, stretching over more than 12,000 kilometres, for less than 1,900 guilders (500 dollars). I did everything by train. That cost about 750 guilders. Per day, I spent on average slightly less than 40 guilders for hotels and meals."

She also advises travelling in May rather than the holiday months when hotels raise their rates.

Then come some comparisons with Europe.

> "Depending on personal tastes, travelling through Europe offers the charm or inconvenience of the continual changes in language, money and habits. In America, this is different. The time does change in nearly every state and one has to put one's watch one hour back or forward. The laws also change. In some states, one

cannot get any alcoholic drink on the train; in others again, one can. That can be annoying for those who are fond of alcoholic drinks (*Nel liked her whisky*), especially if one considers that the train sometimes travels through three states in one day."

Nel rated the journey along the Hudson between New York and Chicago:

"as beautiful as a trip along the Rhine. Though the Americans can't say that this is where Charles the Great stayed and there Napoleon, one hears people saying 'here is the Ford family's castle' and 'Roosevelt lived there'."

Chicago she found:

"an impressive city with an enormous mixture of races and the biggest abattoirs (slaughterhouses) in the United States."

Meeting the Vice-President of chemical company Union-Carbide, she reports:

"To my surprise, this man, whose name is Lloyd Cooke and was a Negro, told me that he would not hold this job if he had not been ten times more brilliant than his white competitor. He was a man in his forties, recently divorced from his Canadian wife and engaged to one of his employees. She was a young American engineer, born in Germany. He also told me that he is president of the Chemical Society in Chicago but that he will never succeed in becoming a member of Chicago's golf and country club."

A comment that made it into Nel's widely published later report of her tour

As well as a magnificent collection of modern contemporary European paintings in the Museum of Art, Nel noted that Chicago was famous for its beefsteak.

"Which one can best eat in Stockyard Inn, a very snobbish and luxurious restaurant, next to the abattoirs and near the building where the Democrats hold their conventions. All the furniture is upholstered with splendid shiny cowhides, and the drawings on the wall look dubiously much like those of the French grottoes of Lascaux."

Via Nebraska, Nel arrived in Colorado's 'mile high city' of Denver, where an unusual 20-centimetre snowfall cost her a pair of galoshes. Here she first notices the feeling of the frontier,

> "continually shifted to the west by the American pioneers which makes travelling through America so fascinating for Europeans. One begins to realise better what courage these pioneers had in those days... Today, even in the modest hotels with rooms for five dollars, one finds all the comforts which people in the better hotels in the Netherlands look for in vain, like Kleenex in all the bathrooms, always a telephone, enough lights, the facility of having your clothes pressed *a la minute* and in most cases, radios and televisions."

The journey from Denver to Salt Lake City was spectacular, though the robotic stewardess was a disappointment to Nel.

> "Sitting in a special train on the upper deck in the 'vista dome', with a completely transparent roof, one can marvel at the Rocky Mountains, this year still completely covered with snow. The stewardess on the train uses the loudspeaker to give a continuous commentary on the landscape and the history of the construction of the railway. This history is an epic in itself. But when I met the same stewardess later in the bar, I discovered to my great surprise that she herself scarcely understood the text she read and could not give any further supplementary information at all. Apart from this, she looked very attractive and elegant and had a perfect broadcasting voice."

In Salt Lake City, in the Mormon state of Utah, Nel found a city of broad streets and much greenery, unique for its prevailing Mormon atmosphere as well as the biggest American open copper-mine, Kennecott, and the Great Salt Lake itself. On a trip to the lake, Nel sat in the water next to a middle-aged Parisian who was taking a vacation in America with his wife. Piqued, he said to her:

> "One thing I do not understand. Taxi-drivers in Paris have a very good wage. But here, every taxi-driver actually has his own car. France is a rich country, after all. How is it that America is so prosperous?"

Nel found the most beautiful train journey in America was after Salt Lake City, along the ravine of the Feather river,

> "offering with its virgin forests fantastic natural beauty for a whole day, nearly all the way to San Francisco."

Along the way, Nel noticed she was arriving in a completely different part of America.

> "After Denver, 'the west' begins, and the subject of conversation of the ever-garrulous Americans changes. Before Denver, there was much more talk of stomach ulcers and psychiatrists; after Denver you come across a great naive interest in everything that is foreign and nobody appears to have an ulcer."

By chance, in 1971, I myself stayed for a few days at a ranch in North Dakota run by a cowboy with an ulcer but he was probably the exception that proves the rule.

I found only one solitary mention of the 'beautiful cosmopolitan city of San Francisco'. I imagine Nel would have loved it, but no account of it appeared in the file of her US trip. Then on she goes south to Los Angeles, with Hollywood and Beverly Hills:

> "the residence of the rich film stars, which is reminiscent of Bloemendaal before the war."

Bloemendaal is now a plush, leafy and expensive but otherwise unremarkable little town in a pretty seaside area west of Amsterdam.

Nel was quick to report that not everyone in Los Angeles was rich.

> "The Fairfax 'farmers market' (expensive) and the downtown 'central market' (cheap) give visitors an impression of the enormous wealth of the film world and the modest existence of the toiling other inhabitants. There is also a large Dutch colony. The Dutch told me that as long as one is not American, it is difficult to get a firm foothold, unless one is specialised."

I am told that both markets still exist to this day,

From Los Angeles, Nel travelled to Phoenix in Arizona, in fashion at the time as a 'health state'.

> "Since this (status) has been generally accepted, the value of the land has multiplied tenfold. It is indeed very pleasant here, warm and dry and, recently, superb hotels have mushroomed."

Nel's visit was recorded, along with one of her favourite photos of herself with two cats, in the June 6 edition of a local Arizona news rag called SAGE:

> "VISITOR. Recent visitor to Cactus, friend of Mrs Rosella Oelke, was Nel Slis, the only female Associated Press Correspondent overseas. Miss Slis, author and newspaper woman in her own country, is a native of Holland and lives at The Hague. She is touring America on vacation and is seriously considering buying a residence."

I feel sure that Nel was hinting of 'buying a residence' tongue-in-cheek, unable to resist hospitable but naive acceptance of such an unlikely and financially impossible thing for her to do.

The pocket-sized publication has a splendid front-page slogan:

"EVERYBODY IS READING SAGE

The only newspaper you can open up in a high wind - or read on a horse."

Next came New Mexico, also with a reputation for health, and El Paso in Texas with its bridge over the Rio Grande into Mexico.

> "In Ciudad Juarez, the biggest town on the border, people can eat beefsteak for one-third of the price in America if they pay in dollars. Juarez, with its many shops, is completely built up on American tourism.."

Nel also discovered that Texans had a strong vein of patriotism about their state.

> "People returning from Mexico over the Rio Grande have to give their nationality. There, one hears as well as 'American', people saying 'Texan', mightily irritating customs and immigration."

Heading through the desert from El Paso to San Antonio, still in Texas, Nel said,

> "it got pitch-dark at three o'clock in the afternoon when a huge rain, hail and thunderstorm broke out. The area through which we were travelling is completely empty desert where one virtually does not see a single living soul. Once or twice there was a hamlet where I saw stranded drivers standing around."

In San Antonio, Nel discovered the town had a well-preserved history,

> "including the 'Alamo' building which is the symbol of the liberation of Texas from the Mexicans and the house where the Spanish governor lived, who was Philip V's representative. Here you can see the weapons of the

House of Habsburg, unique in America. There is a very Spanish-American atmosphere in San Antonio with its many former missionary houses now visited as museums."

Nel reported that the train from San Antonio to New Orleans in Louisiana ran through

"a swampy area with thick forests and a very humid and sultry atmosphere. New Orleans is 'French' and 'touristic'. Everyone goes to visit 'le vieux carre' where the French-Canadian Bienville once kept house and held orgies with Creole beauties. 'Creole' is a complimentary term in New Orleans. It has nothing to do with mulattos or half-breeds, but rather with the Americans of French-Spanish origin. Thirty percent of the population here are Negroes and for the first time since New York I encountered racial discrimination here, which continued throughout the entire South to Washington."

Then she got hijacked by a 'larger-than-life' rich woman,

"an oil trader, widowed and divorced, with all force insisting that I should see her indeed beautiful house in Laurel, Mississippi."

The woman was just divorced from her second husband, whose family practically owned the little town, Nel discovered:

"They were lumberjacks who had made their fortune two generations earlier from the wood from the forests in Mississippi. The woman found Laurel boring, but she was energetically planning to create her own environment and to make sure that the environment did not overwhelm her. She has a good library, a splendid collection of gramophone records, two beautiful dogs, a lovely house and her own forest. She advised me to visit one of the plantations which have been described so many times by Tennessee Williams. I would then see that nothing is further from the truth than that everyone living there is depraved and degenerate. The plantation owners, who sometimes own three or four aircraft with which they fly to New York to go to the theatre of an evening, she called 'very entertaining' and 'good chess-players'."

It is easy to imagine that Nel was not altogether taken by this bored rich woman and definitely disapproved of all that ostentatious wealth and flitting off to New York, quite apart from the underlying current of racism. Though she may have admired her American energy.

A large number of local American newspapers picked up Nel's post-vacation report of her tour of America. A version in the Tampa Sunday Tribune which featured the charming photo of Nel interviewing a young black lift-boy appears in Appendix D.

By the time of her visit to America, Nel had been reporting from Holland for the AP for some twelve years with another six to come before her move to Brussels. She was an AP 'name' in America and, according to some, even better-known in New York than in Holland. But Yolanda Frenkel-Frank said Nel did not like America or the Americans and this seeps through here and there in her travel notes.

Pondering Nel's feelings about Americans, Tyna Wynaendts added:

> "I think it was a love-hate relationship at first – no, I think she hated them more than she liked them. She appreciated many things, especially people like Isaac Stern. And she realised that they could be the people they were because of America with all the opportunities of that country. But I think deep down, she never had a very good relationship with her bosses in the States and they were not very nice to her. No, I think she did not really like Americans."

Nel's negative feelings were particularly aroused by her big battle to extract a pension from the AP. Tyna recalled that

> "she had a period when she was fighting about her pension rights, when she was shouting about the Americans every time we met her. Because they wouldn't give her anything after all those years. And then she went to America, she didn't really want to go, not so much that she didn't like the country, but because of the voyage; she wouldn't fly so she had to take a boat. But she felt she had to go, to talk about her pension. In the end, they promised her a pension. She said it wasn't good enough, but she got something. Certainly there was a period of her life when she could have wrung the necks of every single one of them."

One of the few cultural items I found in Nel's archives only made me realise how many more there must have been. Nel loved music and ballet and was a personal friend of violinist Isaac Stern and conductor/composer Leonard Bernstein and she also counted Igor Stravinsky and Arthur Rubinstein among her interviewees. Perhaps these items will resurface one day. The New York report I did find was about an international experimental film competition proposed by a Belgian film librarian who certainly didn't lack ambition about the people he wanted to get on his jury, including 'such people as Hemmingway, Faulkner and Picasso'.

'LA SLIS' IN BRUSSELS

(1963-73)

8.
Emerging Europe

If the CAP fits: Manshold, Luns, De Gaulle et al

Nel had always been enthused by the concept of a united Europe. While covering the Dutch began to pall, a new age and a new reporting opportunity was dawning with the emerging EEC. As she recalled:

> "At the end of the 1950s. Holland became quite boring: the time of (Prime Minister) Biesheuvel, de Jong. I thought: I must get away. Economics became more and more important and the union in Europe began to take shape. I have always had a huge interest in a united Europe. From the beginning, I wrote about it. The AP did not believe that it would ever happen but I went on writing about it even if they didn't use it. I have always thought that a united Europe would come and that it couldn't be otherwise… "

In May 1948, Churchill, Schuman and Adenaur had called for a united Europe in the Ridderzaal (Knight's Hall) in The Hague. Nel said:

> "And I still know exactly how I began my piece: *in green and leafy The Hague.* Europe has always impassioned me. I really wanted to get my nose into it... Holland was a nation of ten million nit-pickers... who, even worse, do not even know their languages. French, German and English and that in loud, full and convincing tone. That is surely the basic requirement."

Nel spoke all the languages of the EEC's founding six, including Italian. *"We'll send Slis*, because she speaks five languages," the AP was eventually to decide.

The European Economic Community was set up in 1958, a year after the Treaty of Rome was signed. Founder members were France, Italy, West Germany, The Netherlands, Belgium and Luxembourg. The UK, Ireland and Denmark joined in 1973, Greece in 1981, Spain and Portugal in 1986, Austria, Finland and Sweden in 1995. Ten joined in 2004: the 'Visegrád Four'- the Central Europe states of Poland, Czech Republic, Slovakia and Hungary; the Baltic states of Estonia, Latvia and Lithuania, also tiny Malta, the Greek half of Cyprus and Slovenia which was the first member from former Yugoslavia. As part of the same wave, Bulgaria and Romania joined in 2007. (The 'Visegrád' name comes from a meeting of the Bohemian, Polish and Hungarian rulers in Visegrád in 1335 when Charles I of Hungary, Casimir III of Poland and John of Bohemia agreed to create new commercial routes to bypass the staple port Vienna and obtain easier access to other European market).

Nel with Aagje and cat

i. Prising Open the Door in Brussels

As the European movement began to gather momentum in the early 1960s, its importance finally dawned on the AP and the American business community. Nel told me their interest was further encouraged when the British began initial negotiations with the EEC:

> "The AP's Fred Cheval (*Brussels bureau chief*) said Britain wants to come into this business. They suddenly realised that it was serious, they ought to have someone in Brussels and they knew I was interested and well in with the idea."

A short secondment to Brussels for a European Defence Community conference gave her a chance to get a toehold there and she made the most of it. Cheval told Kersting that:

> "Nel's work on the EDC conference deserves the highest praise. She contributed greatly to the stories through her excellent contacts with the Dutch delegation and her constant spirit of enterprise and initiative. She was of tremendous assistance in the successful carrying out of tough coverage."

Thanks to this, things began to move, at least after Nel returned from a holiday in Italy in August 1962. This trip, incidentally, caused a friend in the American embassy to complain that The Hague seemed even duller with Nel on holiday, adding:

> "Even the Dutch don't seem to hate us with any interesting intensity."

Soon after her holiday, Henk Kersting sent a confidential letter to Nel, dated 19 September, giving her strict instructions to throw it away after reading it. This she did not do. Kersting quoted a reply from Lloyd Stratton to his letter raising the question of a full-time AP staffer to cover the Common Market (EEC) in Brussels. The reply was positive, despite the ominous and prophetic note about Germany:

> "I would not object to assigning Nel to the job. She is an excellent reporter and possibly under the tutelage of the London desk her writing would improve to suit. I believe Cheval would not complain, although possibly Germany might not be too happy. However, no other solution to the Market staffing problem has been found and Nel has worked hard and well."

> "I frankly feel that the AP can use me to greater advantage in Brussels than in The Hague. My assets - speaking French, Dutch, German, Italian and English - would benefit the AP... I virtually single-handedly disposed of New Guinea and old Wilhelmina. Successive

weekends went into Wilhelmina's obit, her death and finally her white funeral. The EEC, however, needs someone who likes the work, which includes also a careful filing, updating and lots of meticulous doings which I happen to like and am used to, having pottered on my own for almost 20 years."

So it was that Nel gradually prised the door to Brussels wide open. As she put it, she was sent to Brussels

"to see how postwar Europe was doing. For a couple of months, I was up and down to Holland disposing of Wilhelmina, and then they appointed me."

A letter from the AP in New York dated June 25 1963 finally confirmed approval of Nel's appointment as full-time Common Market correspondent. Amsterdam Bureau Chief John Gale put it at 10 years, presumably from that official appointment, while Nel often talked of 12 years, no doubt including all the commuting back and forth at the beginning and end.

ii Going away with a Bang

Nel's departure received remarkable media coverage. She was given not one but two well-attended receptions by way of send-off. On Thursday 22 August 1963, the Foreign Press Association had a chance to say farewell to her in the Nieuwspoort press centre in The Hague. They gave her the card reproduced in the Appendix. On 2 September, at a reception given by Kersting and his wife, politicians in The Hague did the same. These included Foreign Minister Joseph Luns, "the only minister who frankly sometimes called her 'Nel' (instead of Miss Slis) during press conferences," one reporter remarked. "At any rate, if he was really excited," she told the reporter.

The last official event Nel covered was a reception given by the Indonesian Charge d'Affaires on 23 August. This actually produced a newspaper report headlined 'Hearty leave-taking of Nel Slis' rather than anything about the Indonesians. Part of this story has already been quoted in Chapter 5 but the author had yet more to say about the Slis phenomenon:

"With her (departure), we are losing a unique figure of whom people can say at her leave-taking that she is already legendary now. Tough and thoroughly indefatigable and at the same time loudly grousing that she is knackered, never dull, knowing everyone, appearing at all receptions and sometimes saying things to Dutch heavyweight men which make her fellow-journalists exchange shocked looks with each other. Later saying: 'But Nel, you really can't do that!' And she would respond: 'Why not? Surely he can have manners'. Like at the last press conference that Frits Philips *(founder of the Dutch flagship multinational Royal Philips)* gave in The Hague, 'Gentlemen', said Philips. And Slis, spoke over everyone, saying, "Gentlemen? Are ladies forgotten here?" She was the only woman.

The writer concludes:

And now Nel Slis is leaving us. Too bad!

Another article by G. Toussaint in *De vrouw en haar huis* (Woman and Home), October 1963, wrote:

"The Hague, and actually the entire country, is the poorer from the loss of an important woman. The journalist Nel Slis, loved and feared by many who have had dealings with her, these press officers, ministers, ambassadors and press chiefs have taken leave of her in an exceptionally warm way. She was always and still is a cock-of-the-run, somebody that never minces her words and also does not need to do so because she turns out to be well-informed about all topics which she has come across in her profession. A cheeky hussy maybe, but a sympathetic hussy...

"She joined the AP in 1944 and left for The Hague in 1945. For all these years she has put everyone whom she suspected could have news through hell. But she got it out of them. Modesty becomes a person, they say, but 'pressing on' and getting on top of the news is also a characteristic that apparently attracts people. There will seldom have been a reception as well attended, as animated and as varied as that which was offered to Nel Slis on her departure from the Netherlands. It is too bad that she is going away, but it is a delight to have known her."

Other newspaper cuttings from the period reveal that as well as ministers Luns and Bot, the ambassadors of Belgium, the US, Britain and Poland were among those that turned up in Nieuwspoort to say farewell to Nel. One story, headlined "Gemist" (Missed), records that warm words were spoken but complains that Nel was not given a decoration by the government,

> "Because Miss Slis has disseminated much good about the Netherlands around the world, via this American press agency in commentary and news. And there are those who are honoured for very much less."

The writer goes on:

> "In a few days she will be gone. The Hague will miss her then. A woman who held her own ground. No small performance, as it is not so easy to work for Associated Press. American journalism is different to ours. This is sometimes too easily forgotten in judging her performance or simply not even understood. And how often did she not set the ball rolling at international press conferences for Dutch colleagues who could not get their questions out so quickly. People will miss that too, as well as the warm personality that she has."

Under a photo with Ministers Luns and Bot is another bouquet for Nel, citing the reception:

> "offered for a woman that has indeed brought the name of Associated Press in The Hague very much alive and has represented this press agency exceptionally colourfully."

All this publicity also led to the unexpected contact from the past of one Lies Prins, a fellow-nurse from Nel's Wolverhampton days a couple of decades earlier. She also learned of a grandniece in Amsterdam hitherto unknown to her.

Undated portrait

Nieuwspoort reception for Nel's departure to Brussels, October 1963 With AP Bureau chief Henk Kersting, Foreign Minister Joseph Luns

iii. Brussels! La mer a boire

Nel moved with characteristic speed to change her address to Avenue Moliere 168 in Brussels. Tyna Wynaendts, then aged about 14, helped her to move and stayed for a few days to paint a wardrobe. Tyna told me about the trip and about Nel and the removal men.

> "She had bought this wardrobe, just plain wood, and she wanted it darker brown to go better with her antique furniture. A nice memory of that move was what happened with the four or five Dutch removal men. They were very simple and, in the beginning, they showed a sort of mistrust because she was this eccentric woman who bossed them around so they were a little bit grumpy.

> "Then, when it was all done, they asked whether they could leave but Nel said, 'Oh, no, it's much too late, we are now going to the best place in Brussels to eat mussels, near the Grande Place'. 'No, madam,' they said, 'no, no, no,' but Nel wouldn't listen to them. She said,

156

'No, we should go'. So, very reluctantly, they just followed and it turned out to be a delightful evening because, with the help of some beer, they had such a good time that they just slept in their truck because they couldn't drive after all that beer. I'm sure they're still talking about it now."

To do her work in Brussels, Nel found she had to begin all over again. It was difficult and exhausting. Right from the start, there was a hassle about her accreditation: Was she a Dutch journalist or an American because of her press agency? Luns eventually helped her out again. He was a recurring theme in Nel's journalistic life and stars in this chapter as Foreign Minister and later, NATO chief.

Once again, Nel was working from early morning to late at night, reading up on new subjects, going to cocktail parties and meeting as many people as possible. As one of her interviewers wrote:

"Once again she had to fight her way in as the only woman among hundreds of men. In Brussels, it was even more difficult than in The Hague. 'I was still a woman and I was now also a direct competitor because the AP was published in Dutch papers. As a result, the gentlemen had to run harder. I still have a nasty taste in my mouth from that'. The Dutch newspapermen, now her competitors, closed ranks against her. 'I could not get in because I did not work for a Dutch newspaper', she recalled angrily. 'The Dutch boys took care of that. This man from Het Vrije Volk was a very bad one. Luckily I don't remember his name any more, that is an advantage of getting old'."

There were some two hundred journalists accredited in Brussels at the time, destined to grow to a vast press corps of a thousand by the end of the century. Three were women, with Nel being the only press agency woman.

"In Brussels, I dared not ever turn up unprepared, did my homework down to the last iota, more than the men did. Above of all, I did this so that they could not undermine me. You also had to look smart and be well-dressed, that was watched for out there."

During an early EEC briefing, Nel was swamped with trigger prices, threshold prices and other peculiarities relating to European economic policies. She described her Dutch colleagues as 'wet blankets'.

Metzemaekers, then working for Het Parool, was the only one that was friendly.

She told her interviewer how he rescued her.

> " 'Metz,' I said, 'I'm dying, I don't understand a bloody thing'. 'Well then, we'll have lunch', he said and then he wised me up. But mark my words: in those first couple of years, I didn't go to the theatre or a concert on a single evening. For two years, I read up about European politics every evening. Yes, sure, Slis always did her homework. I didn't go anywhere except receptions where I could 'pick the worms out of their noses'. But Metzemakers was always a very decent colleague, *pas un petit bonhomme*. Whenever he saw that I didn't understand something, he said that he would take me with him and explain it to me later."

On top of this was the difficulty of actually reporting on these esoteric Common Market goings-on in a palatable form for AP's customers. I remember myself that it was still difficult in the 1990s to arouse the interest of a regular financial news service in reports on the EEC, as it was such a specialised subject with so much technical jargon. I always felt the EEC specialist in our team was greatly undervalued for that reason. And such difficulties are quite apart from the sheer exhaustion of all these lengthy EEC meetings. As Nel put it,

> "Brussels was a *mer a boire* (insurmountable task): I was in the thick of potatoes, gas, ecus. I did learn a lot there but writing short pieces which could be understood by people was very difficult sometimes… It was a killer job."

Still, she added with satisfaction,

> "I was often the only one that wasn't completely wiped out by all these meetings. If I didn't have this Zeeland iron constitution, I wouldn't have made it."

By way of compensation was the excitement and camaraderie of those early days, she told me.

> "Very many journalists were still really inspired by Europe then. Sometimes we clapped if something was achieved after long negotiations… They were hellish, those council meetings, but I was younger then. Professionally, it was a most interesting time working with a wonderful press fraternity who were excellent;

keen, interested and hard working. With 200 journalists from all over the world, there was no such thing as jealousy and pettiness. (*Well, apart from some of her Dutch colleagues, I thought*).

"At that time, it was new, it had a great idealistic side to it. Nowadays, it has become more routine. At the start, it was a sort of starry-eyed business. I thoroughly enjoyed it, nothing was too much. I worked day and night and did plenty of homework at weekends on agricultural and monetary affairs and I didn't mind. It was like a popular university, you learned a lot with a wonderful crowd."

Still, it was exhausting, and eventually Nel found herself craving a holiday. She actually asked her half-sister Jaan and the faithful housekeeper Aagje to look after the cat,

"because I so madly want to get out at last for a month's holiday as I am dead tired after two years' hard work and scarcely a decent weekend."

A solution was found for the cat and Nel enjoyed a summer break in Turkey.

iv. Metzemakers explains: De Gaulle and the CAP

Louis Metzemaekers said Nel's biggest problem was that she was parachuted into Brussels by the AP with no preparation whatsoever. Metzemaekers was in Brussels from 1957 to 1968 and Nel arrived in 1962, and leaned heavily on him - "Loutje, give me a lead," she would wail. Metzemaekers told me that

"Nel gave the impression that she was terribly dependent on fellow journalists, because she didn't know anything about the whole business when she arrived, especially all these specialist matters. I was the one that had to guide her, so to speak. She didn't have so much self confidence."

Nel's fellow-journalist Friso Endt had gone on at great length about how much Metzemaekers helped her in Brussels. In spring 2000, I arranged a meeting with Metzemaekers. Friso told me Metzemaekers was completely blind but that he was still writing by dictating to his wife. After his stint in Brussels, Metzemaekers later became the highly respected chief editor of Dutch financial newspaper Het Financieele Dagblad from 1967-77, a paper I worked for in the 1980s. He was also a specialist in Arab affairs.

He sounded clear as a bell on the telephone and said he would be glad to tell me what he could about those Brussels years. I arrived at the address to find the house was a building site, with new owners doing it up. Fortunately, he had only moved to the next village, keeping the same phone number. He was living in a plush crimson-carpeted old people's residence, his wife having died. A big man with a deep voice, he was sitting in his room smoking and listening to a tiny radio.

Metzemaekers said that when Nel arrived in Brussels, the main common market agenda item was the customs union. Under the Treaty of Rome, this was to be achieved in 12 years. A certain percentage of internal and external tariffs were to be harmonised annually. In fact, it was achieved two years early, in 1968. Amazingly fast, said Metzemaekers. All of this was a completely new subject for Nel and a highly technical one. In wading into these new subjects, Metzemaekers considered Nel's best qualities were that she was extremely active and diligent.

> "She had no family; she had the whole day and night to be active. I always had problems with that because she always came to me. Was she driven? Yes, she was."

The European Commission provided information via press conferences and there was one every week with the commission spokesman on what had already been decided. But the most important source of information was the meetings of European ministers, which had to approve all proposals. There was a meeting with the ministers of all six countries nearly every month. Conversely, the ministers were largely taking decisions based on proposals by the commission, which had much more influence then than it does today, according to Metzemakers.

In July 1965, French President Charles De Gaulle broke off French negotiations on the Common Agricultural Policy and inaugurated the 'empty chair' policy. This meant France was still a member, but was not present at meetings. Seven months later, in January 1966, France 'rejoined' under the Luxembourg compromise, in return for retaining unanimous voting when major interests were at stake.

Many of France's early disputes with the EEC were related to the financing of agriculture and agricultural policy. Agriculture was most important for France and the aim at the time was to achieve free trade between the six member states, plus a common external tariff. The Americans had big problems with wheat. Achieving free trade in wheat within the EEC was particularly important for France as the biggest producer of soft wheat whereas the US exported durum (hard) wheat. The French therefore only wanted to allow the American grain in over a high tariff wall, in order to protect soft wheat within the EEC.

Metzemaekers said the "pig-headed" French president General De Gaulle had already caused a furore earlier by using France's veto, against the wishes of the other five members, to block Britain's application to the EEC in 1963. He did so again in 1967. There were fears that the whole community would break up because of De Gaulle, who "threatened everything."

Georges Pompidou eventually succeeded De Gaulle as French president in 1969. This was an improvement, said Metzemaekers, though he groused about Pompidou's foreign minister:

> "Pompidou put in place a different policy for France; it was easier with Pompidou. But these men never gave press conferences. It was the foreign affairs ministers that gave them. French foreign minister Couve de Merville was difficult, very difficult; he never gave press conferences for us, but he did give them for the French journalists."

Metzemaekers said relations between Dutch foreign minister Luns and the French were always sour and he had an anti-French attitude. Nel, as we know, got on well with Luns but from her early sojourn in Paris, she was also a confirmed Francophile. She herself said that despite his squabbles with the French, Luns insisted he liked France and the French personality. In any case, Metzemaekers said,

> "France was an important EEC partner and for that reason, the news from the French side was naturally important for us."

Luns, together with Sicco Mansholt, architect of the EEC's agricultural policy, were the key Dutch figures on the European stage of the day. They were both major forces within the EEC. Nel's reports paint a vivid picture of the two apparently very different men. But both were big men, physically and politically.

v. CAP Architect Mansholt

The EEC's Common Agricultural Policy (CAP) was created by Sicco Leendert Mansholt, the Dutch member of the Common Market Executive Commission, forerunner of the European Commission. Mansholt was put in charge of agriculture when the Common Market was set up in 1958 and was the only one who remained through most of her stay in Brussels. Metzemaekers said that thanks to Mansholt's efforts, agriculture was actually the most integrated sector after about five years, far more so than industry. The purpose of the CAP was the establishment of a single market for agricultural products and for financial solidarity through a European Agricultural Guidance and Guarantee Fund (EAGGF) set up on January 14, 1962.

Mansholt himself had a good press, according to Metzemaekers.

> "He was a convinced socialist; he was actually, in the
> Netherlands, the most important player at that moment,
> as the maker of agricultural policy."

I found several photos of Nel and Mansholt. She already knew him well from her AP years in The Hague, on account of his role in rebuilding Dutch agricultural policy. During his 13 years as the Netherlands' first postwar Agriculture Minister, his international career had already begun to take shape, as he played a major part in the Food and Agriculture Organisation. On several occasions, the FAO also invited him to visit 'underdeveloped' countries like Pakistan.

Nel's stories on Mansholt show that he too, like Luns, had quite a few spats with the French. In February 1964, she reported that the "dynamic, six-foot vice-president of the EEC Commission" lost no time in his position on the EEC's nine-man executive body in denouncing France's refusal of Britain as a member. He warned that the rejection of the UK was a threat to the EEC's continued existence and went on to give his credo:

> "I want a truly economically and politically integrated
> Europe, based on the Rome Treaty, working in close
> partnership with the United States. I want a Europe
> open to all democratic European countries that can
> accept the Rome Treaty. A test for such a Europe is the
> preparedness to accept Britain as a member."

Mansholt was, said Nel, the most outspoken member of the Common Market's executive. He was also firmest in the defence of its principles, including Atlantic unity in the shape of the North Atlantic Treaty Organisation (NATO). Mansholt, she said, was the main protagonist of Atlantic unity in the commission:

> "Those who know Mansholt feel that the fifty-five year
> old blunt and burly European statesman will defend the
> principles of Atlantic Unity with the same toughness as
> that with which he defended Dutch farmers' interests
> during his thirteen-year period as Agriculture Minister in
> Holland…Mansholt, who sees (European) integration as
> a cornerstone of Atlantic unity, has infinite patience in
> reaching what he considers his aim."

He was not always calm, though.

"Mansholt is an extrovert, and apt to lose his temper. People who have known him for a long time, however, say that he has calmed down considerably although it does happen that he bangs his fist at commission meetings. Through the years, they say, he has developed into a true diplomat. He speaks in plain language, to the relief of many for whom the complex agricultural jargon of the Common Market (sluice-gate prices, target prices, threshold prices) is meaningless."

Among his strengths was his solid expertise in agriculture, along with his determination that the EEC should succeed. He helped pilot it through a 1962 crisis when a rift threatened over final regulations for a CAP for cereals, eggs and poultry:

"Often during the two months of uninterrupted conferences with little sleep and constant haggling, Mansholt patiently chalked up his facts and figures on a blackboard to remind the six agricultural ministers of what was good for the community."

Mansholt was greatly influenced by his remarkable socialist mother, Nel reported.

"As a boy, he was unruly, only to be tamed by his mother, Wabien Andreae, daughter of a bourgeois judge in the provincial city of Leeuwarden. She had run away from her ancestral home in the late nineteenth century to propagate socialism among the poor peat farmers in the area. That was how she met Sicco's father, Leendert Mansholt, a wealthy farmer's son who was inspired by her evening lectures on socialism. Coming by his socialism through both sides of his family, Mansholt remembers how he and his brothers used to sing the 'Internationale' in bed at night while his parents indoctrinated poor farmers and their wives.

Wabien spoke to farmers' wives throughout the provinces by mounting tables, chairs and farm carts, translating political demands by giving them practical examples like: 'Think of it, how much nicer it will be not having to go out to pump your water but to get it straight from a faucet in your home.' In her 90's, on the way to visiting her married daughter, Aleid, in Australia, she taught Dutch emigrants English as she sailed on a small emigrant ship to Sydney."

Mansholt's early working experience gave him a solid grounding in agriculture. When he finished his junior college, Nel recorded that his father, a gentleman farmer, sent him to take a three-year course in tropical agriculture so that he could then help his uncle on a tea plantation in Java, Indonesia, formerly the Dutch East Indies. He told Nel:

> "I never worked as hard as in Java and there I learned to work with people."

In Java, Mansholt supervised hundreds of farm workers. When he returned to the Netherlands, his father decided he could run the family farm, provided he worked as a farmhand first. The farm was on land reclaimed from the Zuyderzee (South Sea), now the IJsselmeer (Ijssel Lake). Mansholt then settled on a farm of his own in this area. He married former schoolteacher 'gentle Henny Postel'. His farm was partly destroyed at the start of the war and flooded again at the end of it.

At home, Mansholt was apparently rather absent-minded.

> "To his wife, he is a man with few close personal friends, fiercely absent-minded, not an intellectual. She tells of the time she came home to find he had eaten the dog's food out of the ice box, unaware of the dish she had prepared for him."

Mansholt's organisational skills had first emerged in the war.

> "During the German occupation of Holland in World War II, Mansholt played a leading role in the resistance movement, supplying food, shelter and forged ration cards for Jews and the politically persecuted. When liberation came, he managed the lowering of the water level in Dutch canals so barges heavily loaded with food and weapons could pass under the bridges."

When the war ended, when he was 37, Mansholt was picked by socialist Premier Willem Schermerhorn as Holland's first Agriculture Minister and was tasked with the job of reorganising Holland's agriculture and managing food distribution for a starving population.

> "He spent 12 years in the job, making Dutch farming competitive again on the world market, raising their incomes and improving the structure of farming. Farming is in his blood. On a clear sunny day, he is apt to sniff the air, and say: 'Good day to plough'."

Nel also remarked that though Mansholt learned to speak fluent English and French, he spoke his foreign languages 'with verve rather than perfect grammar', and had difficulty with 'le' and 'la'. After Mansholt gave a lecture on agriculture in Paris, the suave Dutch ambassador of the day, Johan Willem Beyen, reported to the foreign minister:

> "Sicco made a fine speech on agricultural integration in Europe. But not since Sodom and Gomorrah has there been so much sinning against the sexes."

Nel also gave a blow-by-blow account of a spat Mansholt had in 1968 with French foreign minister Michel Debre and with his own commission president, also French. She reported that relations within the common market executive commission were soured in November that year by this clash between Mansholt and Debre. In July, Debre had written to the executive commission president Jean Rey complaining that Mansholt had a 'biased' attitude towards De Gaulle's government. Debre cited Mansholt's remark at a news conference in The Hague that Gaullism was an obstacle to the community's political progress. He asked Rey by virtue of what mandate did Mansholt condemn the millions of French voters who had expressed their confidence in De Gaulle. To Mansholt's intense annoyance, Rey apologised to Debre in his reply, telling him that Mansholt had often caused much concern to him, to the executive commission, and to his predecessor, Walter Hallstein. He blamed Mansholt's 'politically dynamic personality' and 'fighting spirit' but said the community had benefited from these qualities and that, therefore, some patience should perhaps be shown towards him. To smooth things over, Rey pointed out that Mansholt's remarks were made in his private capacity, protesting against Debre's allegations that the commission was biased.

Obviously stung, Mansholt wrote acidly to Rey that 'your reply has disappointed me' and it was regrettable that it had not been submitted beforehand for the approval of the entire commission. He insisted that:

> "My criticism of the French government's policy has never prevented me from taking an entirely impartial attitude where French interests in the community are concerned."

Mansholt blamed Rey for agreeing with Debre on 'so-called interference in internal policy'.

> "By doing so, you are reducing the executive commission members to a level to which the French government would like to reduce them… You evidently had the right to have a different opinion on the political task of the commission members but this does not authorise you to condemn one of your colleagues."

If ever he had had differences of opinion with Walter Hallstein, Mansholt said, he never differed over a commission member's right to have a political opinion. In a riposte to Debre's specific complaint, Mansholt said that at his news conference he had reviewed the many differences between France and its five partners: over Britain's membership; council decisions by majority vote; the democratic future of Europe and the role of a European parliament therein. As long as these and other important political differences had not been cleared up, European political unity would remain an illusion, he predicted. Acknowledging that he told journalists that De Gaulle's triumph in the elections would not help this situation, Mansholt said blandly he had too much respect for the President of the French Republic to suppose he would review his policy after his overwhelming victory in the elections.

> "What I have said is that differences among the member
> states will make a European policy impossible."

He added that he thought it of the greatest importance that the people of Europe should be well informed and have no false hopes. Mansholt concluded that the commission's task was to carry out European policy, and

> "being perfectly independent, the executive commission
> would judge itself how to interpret 'a political opinion'."

Shucks to you, Debre and Rey, seemed to be his message.

A shorter report gives Mansholt's predictions for the EEC from his first press conference after he took over from Italy's Franco Maria Malfatti as president of the commission. He predicted that:

- the EEC would become more democratic;
- farm policy would shift away from high support prices to direct subsidies;
- Sweden might become a member within four years and join Britain in pressing for a European parliament with powers of its own;
- members would realise the need for stronger community institutions.

Mansholt also endorsed the idea of a political secretariat to deal with general foreign policy questions and said this should be located in Brussels.

Mansholt was a little premature on Sweden but proved right in his assessment of Switzerland as a case apart. He dubbed it 'an island for some capitalist activities'. Speaking while the dictator Franco was still in power in Spain, he said encouragingly:

"I will be very happy to welcome a free Spanish people in the EEC."

Mansholt also correctly forecast that the majority of the socialist party in Britain would soon be convinced of their 'stupidity' in opposing membership.

People were already starting to worry about pollution and Manshold planned to sponsor a programme

> "to give the community the necessary political strength to lead the world to overcome pollution, overpopulation and the exhaustion of raw materials."

In a letter to his predecessor Franco Maria Malfatti, who resigned to stand for the Italian parliament, Mansholt had called for a planned economy, non-polluting production and increased recycling of waste. He suggested that the community's research centres set to work on these problems instead of their unfinished program of nuclear energy. Taking a position which was later found an echoed in the Club of Rome's advocacy of zero growth, he called preoccupation with gross national product 'diabolical' and instead urged concentration on a goal of 'gross national happiness'. Mansholt said the community should set an example in seeking to make the world liveable for his grandchildren's generation.

Interestingly, asked whether he would steer the community in a socialist direction, Mansholt said his aim was democracy and that Christian Democrats were often more progressive than some socialists. He welcomed the trend towards internationalization of trade unions. For example, he said, when Dutch and West German firms merge, it is important for Dutch workers to have the right to talk with their German employers. Nel herself concluded Mansholt was really a leftist liberal, despite his family background of socialism.

Mansholt also said that the US, with its huge social problems and international burdens, was no longer capable of carrying the burden of leadership. Despite this, he also stressed the importanc of collaboration with the United States. More surprisingly, he suggested that Europe might have to be protectionist about its economy, not with hostile intent, but to lead others in the direction the world should go.

It is interesting to see how so many of the same issues remained hot topics or become even hotter in the 21st century, especially with the accession of the 12 mostly former East Bloc EU member countries in 2004 and 2007.

In 1971, Mansholt served briefly as executive commission president, stepping down in January 1972 to be succeeded by the Frenchman Francois Xavier Ortoli. Nel's portrait of Mansholt in April 1971 showed his openness to new ideas on the ever-vexed question of agriculture, no matter how shocking these might be found. Mansholt, who had built up the whole edifice of support to farmers, nonetheless saw the dangers of overproduction and dared to suggest reducing farming numbers and taking farmland out of production.

> "Another bombshell thrown into the European Economic Comunity (EEC) is not excluded as Sicco Laendert Mansholt takes over the top leadership. As Vice-President of the six-member European edifice, the blue-eyed tall and balding Dutchman, whose strong physical condition belies his 61 years of age, shook the community to its core in 1968. He proposed that before 1980 some five million farmers should leave their land and 5 million hectares of marginal farming land should be taken out of production.

> "Bavarian farmers shouted 'farmer killer', when the revolutionary Mansholt Plan for agriculture was published and the West German parliament called for Mansholt to leave instead of 5 million farmers. Only last month a third, watered-down, version of his plan was approved by the EEC Council of Ministers, who haggled over it for four years. A year ago, bloody and violent demonstrations in the streets of Brussels led the council to accept a resolution laying down the principles for spending more on farm modernisation than on support prices for inefficient farming.

> "But his great charm and personal warmth disarm most. Walking into meeting halls with hostile farmers, he usually walks out amid thundering applause, and has earned the sympathy of all young farmers organisations in Europe."

On U.S. complaints about EEC protectionism, Mansholt gave as good as he got:

> "Mansholt has never been bashful about talking back to anyone. He argued with American state secretaries for agriculture, who came here to complain about the EEC protective farm policy, telling them US policy, too, was protectionist and that the US should abandon its agricultural waiver in the General Agreement for Tariffs and Trade (GATT). Mansholt reproached them for being unwilling to agree terms for global agreements on

major farm commodities, which he tried to push for years."

Mansholt was clearly a wonderful source for journalists, and Nel made the most of this. She explained that he had his reasons for talking so openly to the press:

> "Mansholt can be extremely blunt, when angered by the six ministers at a council meeting over pig-meat prices or other details, while more important issues are at stake. Getting impatient at council meeting. he is known to have put up a warning finger, telling them: 'I will inform the press of your behaviour'. He feels that since there is no close parliamentary supervision of the Common Market, there should be vigorous criticism in the press."

Nel also investigated Mansholt's staff, who considered him

> "a terrific organizer, never losing sight of the big picture... He has carefully picked his staff, whom he gives a great deal of personal freedom to draft, defend and execute EEC farm policy."

She went on to describe the 'devoted trio' who had supported him from the beginning:

> "His immediate collaborators include his director-general, a non-conformist Frenchman, Georges Rabot, born a farmer's son from Savoy in France. Mansholt has known him ever since he began campaigning for a European Green Pool in 1952. Rabot is a quick-minded, quiet person, somewhat mysterious, who shuns all publicity. So much so that a new secretary, when receiving orders, later ran after him, saying: 'may I ask you who you are?'

> "Number 2 is Berend Heringa, a warm-hearted Dutchman, who is responsible for all the technicalities of the farm market organizations. In contrast to Mansholt, who is a liberal socialist, he devotes his spare time to Dutch reformed church activities in Brussels. Responsible for farm structure, the farm fund and competition is Adolfo Pizzuti, an Italian from Rome. He is a fast thinker with a great sense of humour. Born in Rome's backyards and a self-made man, one time at a meeting in a posh Roman restaurant the proprietress embraced him. He explained that as a poor schoolboy,

she had given him leftovers of minestrone when he was hungry.

"All three men have a solid background in agriculture, both nationally and internationally. His staff praises him for his immense loyalty, never letting them down when they have made errors. He takes them very seriously, 'Sometimes, you would think he does not hear or he forgets what you said,' one of his staff said, 'but no, it's like a bottle thrown in the ocean, that pops up the other side of the globe.... you will suddenly hear Mansholt using your ideas in one of his many speeches... But he has a sixth sense for what is possible,' said Heringa. 'He will ask much because he knows that he will get much less. His great art is that he always knows that end and can go on being acutely aware of the various ministers' internal political difficulties.'

"Pizzuti said Mansholt has been instrumental in helping Italy's poor south by finding markets at home for the South's products like durum wheat, wine and olive oil. The common market organization sponsored more efficient distribution in Italy, 'Mansholt himself is a lone wolf; knowing more people than most, he has few close personal friends. He is fiercely distracted, loses mail, glasses and documents,' Heringa said. When his former aide Alfred Mozer resigned after Mansholt had worked with Mozer for some 10 years, he told the former trade union leader, 'I have never been able to make a farmer out of you', to which Mozer replied, 'I never succeeded in making a socialist of you.'"

At the time of Mansholt's impending retirement, Nel wrote:

"There is no knowing what Mansholt will turn to after he retires from his post next January. He promised his wife not to return to Dutch politics as his robust health recently suffered a little due to high blood pressure. In the back of Mansholt's mind are two ideas. One is setting up a European Socialist Party or, as he calls it, a kind of neo-Marxist party. He will no doubt devote much of his thinking and activities to bettering the lot of the underdeveloped once he retires when he will shuttle back and forth from a farm he bought in Holland and another one in Sardinia. But what he needs most is to work with his hands so he will be sailing and improving his 40-foot, clean-rigged fishing boat he converted into a yacht."

A last word from Nel on Mansholt was picked up by a number of German papers. One from the Spandaven Volksblatt, 6 January 1972, was headlined 'Utopian for Europe', reflecting Manshold's idealistic leanings.

With EEC Commission Vice-Chairman Sicco Manshot, early 1970s

vi. Lewis on Europe

Nel once claimed, to my faint incredulity, that she never argued with her great friend Flora Lewis, because they were like-minded. It was certainly true that they shared a great interest in Europe and it turned out that Flora agreed about not arguing.

"I don't remember any disagreements with Nel. Yes, perhaps because we were like-minded. In public affairs, the kind of things we were writing about. I've always been very pro-European and interested in the so-called building of Europe, the stages of developing the European plan."

Flora herself was most impressed by Jean Monnet.

> "Monnet I consider the most important person. And we both agreed with his views. I never lived in Brussels, but Nel spent a long time there, and was very much involved in the evolution of the Common Market. Those were all developments that I approved of so I didn't have any reason to argue about it."

Monnet, one of the fathers of the European Union movement, was a French economist who put forward the Monnet Plan (1947-53) for the modernization and re-equipment of French industry. Monnet became the first president of the European Coal and Steel Community (1952-55), forerunner of the EEC. In 1956, he founded the Action Committee for the United States of Europe, the ideals of which were opposed to those of De Gaulle. He subsequently became a strong critic of De Gaulle's foreign policy.

Talking about the EU's later problems when we met in January 2001, Flora said:

> "It's not that Monnet wouldn't approve of the way the EU is going now, though he would not be satisfied obviously because it's not going well. But the reason Monnet succeeded as well as he did is that he was a man of tremendous persistence. He had a number of very serious setbacks, much worse than what's going on now, particularly from De Gaulle. He always clashed head on against De Gaulle."

It was evidently impossible for virtually any leading proponent of European unity to avoid clashing with De Gaulle. Elaborating on Monnet's persistence, Flora added:

> "Even when there were very long periods, a year or two at a time, when things weren't going anywhere, he wouldn't give up. When he couldn't get anywhere with government, he would go after businessmen or go after labour leaders. He was always working on somebody somewhere. Whenever he met an obstacle, he would go around it. So that's what he would be doing now. I interviewed him many times, though I don't know whether Nel did too."

For some reason, this reminded Flora of Nel's fear of flying.

"Nel had one huge handicap, which was that she would never fly and she would never take an elevator. It wasn't that big a handicap in Monnet's day, but it would have been in Brussels in the later years, when they got that big building. In New York, she couldn't possibly have covered the United Nations. I mean, she'd climb, she was tremendously energetic physically, swimming, she walked a lot as well. But because she refused to fly anywhere, she could only go places she could drive, or take the train."

Or she had to go by boat, as with the Waterman and other epic voyages.

vii. Luns

The other leading Dutch player on the European stage in this period was Joseph Luns, Dutch foreign minister from 1956 until 1971 when he became Secretary-General of NATO. He, too, was physically large, and Mansholt and Luns look quite alike in some of their photos. Politically, the socialist Mansholt and conservative Catholic Luns were near opposites but both were pragmatists in the pursuit of their goals.

Flora Lewis had a somewhat more negative opinion of Luns than Nel. She also rejected Friso Endt's suggestion that Nel may have gone to bed with Luns to get stories. This was based on Friso's perception of Nel doing anything to get a story and on the fact that Nel was the only journalist Luns ever addressed by Christian name. Lewis told me:

"Luns was very important. He was a very stubborn and rather pompous man. I would be disinclined to believe Friso's suggestion. If she did, I'm absolutely certain it would not have been for the story. She might have because he was attractive. He was a tough, tough man and an interesting man. He was foreign minister at a time of great importance when there was a big fight with France about what was going to happen with the Common Market, and later, he became Secretary-General of NATO. So he was very much part of this post-war construction of Europe. He had strong opinions and he wasn't wishy-washy, so Nel might have thought he was attractive, I wouldn't be surprised. But I'm sure she didn't go to bed with him to get a story. That is simply not Nel's style. I don't know whether she did, she would not have told me. I just know that she was such an independent-minded, strong-minded person, that she would disdain anything like that."

Nel covered a number of NATO meetings including one held at the Juliana Barracks in The Hague where she took a shortcut which resulted in a snippet titled 'Fast-moving Nel' in the AP World magazine of summer 1964.

> "Nel Slis, the AP news gal who covers the Common Market at Brussels. Fastest route from some news conferences to the tent bureau was through the men's room of the barracks. In moments of great stress, Nel Slis took this short cut. "She went through there so fast," says Tom Ochiltree (London staffer in charge of the team)," that maybe none of the men noticed her."

In a profile written for the official announcement of Luns' appointment as NATO chief on June 4, 1971, Nel gave a more extensive physical description of this man than of Mansholt. Perhaps he was more interesting to her in this way. She certainly considered he had charm, not a typically Dutch quality. Nel led off with the contrast between Luns with his predecessor Brosio:

> "Lanky, long-legged Joseph Luns (60), of the Netherlands, will bring a new touch to the North Atlantic alliance, when taking over from Italy's aging and reserved Manilo Brosio (73) who retires next fall. Luns jumps on the Nato bandwagon after Brosio has oiled its wheels for changes in the seventies, that make the emphasis shift towards greater European participation in the NATO defense effort and a detente in East-West relations. Contrary to serious and discreet Brosio, Luns is talkative and loves to quip jokes. At times he gets deliberately clownesque for the purpose of humouring his colleagues, to thaw a frozen meeting or to cajole his partners so as to get his way…

> "Six and a half feet tall, balding Luns is a great and versatile diplomat. Not an addict to sports, his long egg-shaped face, sallowed by tireless diplomatic activity, is mobile and occasionally turns into that of a sad clown. Luns is extremely courteous. He turns on his charm whenever he feels like it. 'A diplomat', he said, 'must be nice.' Chuckling, he admits that he loves to put his foot in it, when circumstances call for it."

On his new post at NATO, Nel remarked:

> "It will be a change and not always easy for the Dutch Foreign Minister Luns to serve fifteen foreign ministers in NATO, when taking over next October. For fifteen years, Joseph Marie Antoine Hubert Luns has served the Netherlands as foreign minister in eight successive cabinets, with a growing authority at home and prestige abroad."

Luns told Nel his long term in office had made him familiar with the problems of about one hundred countries, from which he had collected some hundred or more medals.

> "With disarming vanity he loves to wear as many as his chest will allow. Luns' globetrotting has endowed him with invaluable political and diplomatic experience, complementing his envied intuition for politics. His collaborators envy his political flair. He has made his foreign ministry officials breathless, when appearing seemingly unprepared at conferences, but unfailingly knowing the right answers, they say."

He was reticent about his designs for NATO - and here the stroppy French rear their heads again:

> "Asked whether he sought to bring back France into NATO's military organisation, Luns carefully said that he could give neither a positive nor negative reply. Well aware of difficulties in President Georges Pompidou's political backyard, Luns said that one should not give the impression of wanting to force France."

But earlier, Nel reported, he had been less diplomatic.

> "Angry over the Franco-German bilateral treaty, concluded outside the Common Market in 1963, he used to translate French foreign minister, Maurice Couve de Murville's name into German, calling him Couve de Murstadt. Despite Flemish-Belgian sensitivity over a Dutchman speaking French in European Common Market ministerial council sessions, when disagreeing with Couve over Britain's entry, he used to stare Couve in the face, telling him: "When I want to be understood, I speak in French.""

Still, Nel believed Luns got on with the Frenchman in his own way, with his light touch so untypical of his compatriots. This light touch was not always appreciated by Dutch MPs:

"Luns is the only minister who called Couve 'Maurice'. He is perspicacious and witty. Staid members of the Dutch parliament have blamed him for being light-hearted and flippant. 'You can never do right in parliament," Luns said. "Parliamentarians are getting too critical." He complained that the Dutch parliament had a tendency of wanting to govern, while their task was one of checking the government's action if needed. The Dutch parliament in turn often complained about his constant travelling. Foreign ministry officials used to say that Luns was visiting 127 countries each year and Holland twice."

On home and family, asked what his wife and children thought of his long absence, Luns quipped:

"When I am at home on Sunday, the children ask 'who is that pale man cutting the meat today?'"

Luns had one married daughter and a son, Hubert, studying political science at Stanford University, California. Nel was complementary about his wife:

"Pretty baroness Lia van Heemstra, a quiet, distinguished-looking lady, who is a cousin of film star Audrey Hepburn."

Born in Rotterdam on August 28, 1911, Luns graduated in law from Leiden university to enter the Dutch diplomatic service in 1938 and held posts at the Dutch embassies in Berne, Lisbon, London during World War II and New York before becoming Foreign Minister in September 1952. When we first took up the post, it was in a very modern jobshare arrangement:

"During his first four years of office, Luns shared, for politicial reasons, the portfolio of foreign affairs with former banker-minister, Willem Beyen. As Beyen took care of bilateral relations, Luns took over multilateral affairs. When leaving The Hague for his diplomatic missions abroad, he used to tell Beyen: 'behave myself'."

He was a vote-catcher, too:

"Luns has been the magnet in drawing votes for his Catholic People's Party, Holland's largest. The Dutch people have loved Luns' pre-election television shows. His tongue-in-cheek performance in reply to sharp questioning by reporters used to make people rock with laughter."

Politically, Nel described Luns as a pragmatist.

> "For many years Luns strongly opposed closer contacts with Eastern Europe. To the great surprise of Dutch socialists, when visiting these countries they found Luns had become a popular man with both Yugoslav and Rumanian statesmen."

In marked contrast to Mansholt's socialist background was Luns' conservative Catholicism.

> "A convinced Catholic, Luns is very conservative in religion and generally old-fashioned. With deeply held beliefs, he expresses his great concern over 'modernism' in the Catholic Church. In his opinion, a good Catholic must be obedient to the Church and submit to the Pope's authority in every respect. He feels strongly about extreme forms of modern literature, the arts and contesting students. He condemns radicalisation of Dutch public opinion. 'It points to a lack of tolerance, once the greatest virtue of the Dutch'. These attitudes have not always endeared him to Dutch youth."

One difficult period in his ministerial career, said Nel, was the loss of Dutch New Guinea, which he blamed partly on United States policy and partly on the Dutch socialists.

> "But it was typical of Luns' make-up that he took the loss valiantly. And like Mansholt, despite these Dutch-American tiffs, notably with Robert Kennedy over New Guinea, Luns has an unshakeable belief in Atlantic partnership. He has always stressed the need for good relations between Europe and the United States."

Luns had qualified praise for the US. He told Nel:

> "One cannot deny that some American politicians show a lack of tact. But, fundamentally, the United States is a super power, which in my experience, abuses its power less than others. More than any other big power, the United States will be reluctant to use its might as a steamroller."

From the American side, well-informed sources told Nel the Americans had had their reservations over Luns as a choice for Nato's secretary general, fearing that he might not be a 'model of discretion'. One

American diplomat said worriedly: 'He will need a very good second man'.

Like Mansholt, Luns was a true European and equally keen on UK entry into the EEC. As Nel wrote:

> "In Luns' political thinking, Europe has priority. The recent French change of heart on Britain's entry into the Common Market has been to his great satisfaction. He worked tirelessly to achieve this. His last visit in March 1971 to Pompidou, in Paris, was motivated partly by a wish to sponsor a Franco-British summit. (*Luns said*) 'I am satisfied that the European Economic Community is now a running concern. It has promoted European economic integration and enabled the six to avoid a dangerous economic slump.'"

Luns also looked forward to a European parliament with real power.

> "Luns is convinced that ultimately a United Europe needs a supranational authority responsible to a democratically elected European Parliament. Luns' method is not one of forcing feelings. He believes that imperceptibly Europe will advance in this direction to the point of no return."

He had therefore naturally fought former President de Gaulle in 1961 when the General proposed a European political union made up of sovereign nations, l'Europe des patries. Luns blocked the plan by his sole veto, which caused former German Chancellor Konrad Adenauer to accuse him of:

> "Impudence not befitting a junior minister."

Luns told Nel that Adenauer always disliked him and this was mutual. But Nel commented that Luns' respect for De Gaulle was also mutual and quoted De Gaulle as remarking:

> "Luns, you can trust. He is a man who loves his country."

On his background, Nel reported:

> "Luns holds a Latin touch from his Belgian-born mother, Henriette Louvrier from Liege. From his father, Hubert Luns, a professor in art history at Delft University, he inherited his flair and culture. He is a good historian and a Napoleon buff, who rattles off by heart all of the French Emperor's Marshalls. Despite his squabbles with the French, Luns insists, 'I like France

and the French personality.' Not to speak of the kitchen, because Luns is fond of French cuisine…"

A small undated item by Nel records the furore Luns caused in the Dutch parliament in one of his *enfant terrible* moods while head of NATO, when he compared the Dutch language to 'animal noises':

```
Nato  secretary-general  Joseph  Luns  told  US
president Richard Nixon that the Dutch language
is  to  be  compared  with  'animal  noises'  has
stirred    questions    in    the    Netherlands'
parliament.  Three  Dutch  Socialist  members  of
parliament  have  asked  Dutch  foreign  minister,
Max  van  der  Stoel,  whether  he  had  seen  reports
in  the  French  daily  'Le  Monde'  that  Luns  told
Nixon  during  the  Brussels  Nato  summit:  'Of  all
animal  noises,  Dutch  is  most  like  a  language
but  even  so,  I  don't  think  this  is  being  nice
to  animals'.  Claiming  that  Luns  had  spoken  in  a
disparaging  manner  'about  the  language  of  the
Dutch  people  and  of  many  Belgians',  the  three
MPs  asked  Van  der  Stoel  to  point  out  to  Luns
'how  objectionable  such  utterances  are'.
```

viii. Nel's eye view of EEC life

Nel wrote a detailed article for Dutch publication Vrouwen en hun belangen (Women and their interests) in June 1974 on the challenges of reporting on the EEC.. Describing how the press 'rummaged around' in the European Community in Brussels, she says:

> "The word is well-chosen inasmuch that the headquarters of the EEC - called "Berlaymont" after the exclusive convent that stood there earlier - is a modern madhouse. Only after many months does a newly arrived journalist find her way or what she wants."

At the time of writing, she says, King Boudewijn has just opened a brand-new, streamlined, six story International Press Centre opposite Berlaymont. This would become the very comfortable haven for the 270-odd journalists who represented 34 countries and reported daily on the ups and downs of the EEC. Nel goes on:

> "Hitherto, the only daily gathering point for the press was on the first floor of Berlaymont, where every day at 12 o'clock the head of the EEC press service, Beniamino Olivi, has given a briefing and provided an explanation for the journalists about new developments and

commentary on the member states who have once again infringed the regulations - for example, most recently, Italy's infringement of agricultural policy...

"A big attraction - a means used by Olivi to keep his horde together - is that immediately after this briefing, the bar in the corner of the press room opens and the journalists can fall on the tax-free drinks. Italian Anna, who every journalist knows, then displays a rare dexterity in distributing whiskeys, beer, camparis and espressos in a few seconds. She does then get a fine present from the press corps every year at Christmas. These twelve o'clocks are not only an opportunity for the journalists to exchange news among themselves but at the same time a good chance to invite experts from the EEC commission for a drink. The press benefits from having the commission's sometimes very complicated proposals explained."

She then explains the special role of the press agency to her Dutch readers:

"Among the 270 journalists, there are only about half a dozen women who hold a full-time job reporting on the EEC. As correspondent for The Associated Press, I belonged to the press agency group. These are the 'busy bees' of the press world. Their work is continuous. As well as the national press agencies, like Agence France Press, Reuters etc, new agencies have been born which are exclusively occupied with news about the EEC.

Of these, Agence Europe is the best-known and the oldest. It has the authority of a law gazette that lies on every diplomat's desk. Press agencies work 24 hours around the clock for their clients, who are spread throughout the world. This type of work means journalists must keep their ears pricked tovlisten out for breakin news in all regions , for example, the Mediterranean area, South and North America whenever trade and prices of tropical and subtropical products come into play. They have to know the difference between soft and hard (durum) wheat etc.

"Journalists normally develop as all-rounders; there are no specialists. Those who venture to (report on) the EEC have to do their homework, have a memory like an elephant, an iron constitution and strong nerves. It is rushed work and there is much competition among (reporters) to be the first and the best - especially among the agencies.

"Tribute must be paid to the press officers and experts of the EEC commission and also the specialists from the missions of the countries that are members of the EEC. They are pretty well always ready to provide texts and explanations. They know the dangers of ignorance and misinformation.

"I remember real lectures about 'special drawing rights' and 'eurodollars', as well as about the countless sorts of agricultural prices ranging from trigger prices to threshold prices and intervention prices."

The EEC of the long nights

Nel's piece gives a detailed picture of the famed long nights of EEC negotiations, and of the camaraderie and, sometimes at least, the sheer excitement of reporting on EEC affairs in those early days.

"The famous 'nights of the EEC' belong especially to agency journalists. Newspapers 'go to bed', people say in journalists' jargon. A journalist working for a morning paper simply cannot report any more after midnight. Those working for an evening paper have to have their stories ready by one o'clock. But agencies have a paper or radio station somewhere that wants news at all hours. You only have to think of the six-hour time difference with America. Many radio stations are on the air for 24 hours. That means that an agency journalist sometimes begins work at 10 o'clock on Monday morning and is not finished until 2 o'clock Tuesday afternoon when the council of ministers can find no way to reach agreement, for example, on agricultural prices or energy policy.

"The most exciting nights were during the talks on British membership. We participated in these three times, in 1962, in 1967 and, finally, the last successful talks in the 1970s. All the more so as the Six always first had to agree on what they wanted to offer the British, Danes and Irish. After that, the future members could come in and more heavy negotiations took place.

"During three out of the 12 months, the council of ministers' meetings are held in Luxembourg - in April, June and October. Not in winter, because that would cause too many accidents, during this exodus from Brussels via the misty and often icy roads in the Ardennes. This is tiring, because it is after all still a 2 to 3 hour drive and not always good weather. But it also has its charm. The European journalists know all the beautiful spots in the Grand Duchy and all the good game restaurants that lie hidden away in the Ardennes.

"The work has been inspiring, particularly in the time when there was still momentum in the community. It was initially a group of fifty journalists, which has now grown to 270. It is a colourful mix of nationalities, with Russians, Chinese, Japanese, Egyptians, Israelis and Nigerians who have added themselves to the ranks of the Europeans, Americans and Canadians.

"You normally begin fresh on the Monday morning with a council of ministers. On this kind of first day, it goes well, as you eat more or less on time, because the ministers also do that. After midnight, the company of journalists thins out. The agencies and one or two others are left. But still generally a good fifty people. These take it in turn to get a breath of fresh air. Because the press corps in Brussels is exceptionally fraternal - nobody sees any possibility of gathering the opinions of nine delegations on their own - you help each other out. If, out of boredom, you go to eat in one of the restaurants which stay open at night, you always leave your telephone number. Then sometimes you might get a quick alert from your fellow-journalists. They cannot avoid doing that either, because there only has to be a rumour running like wildfire through the press room and the journalists' work rooms and everyone flies to a corner where an expert is making some statement.

"Up to now, the ministers had met on the 14th floor of the Charlemagne building, next to Berlaymont. Often experts are so worn out there that they set forth downstairs to chat with the press. Often there's nothing in it but sometimes it means 'news' and an interim report. Assiduous colleagues that don't want you to miss it alert you.

"But often these are long nights with lots of sandwiches, beer, coffee and whiskey according to the preferences of the northern latitude. German colleagues swear by beer and white wine, the French drink red wine and the Scandinavians and Anglo-Saxons throw in their lot with the whiskey. There is also a lot of gambling. The Italians play poker; the Dutch play dice; the Germans play chess. Others read, sleep or work on something else. Heated political discussions are also held.

"In view of the endless controversies among the Nine, one must above all not build anything on the remarks of a single delegation. Every country at some stage has its weaknesses. I remember the creation of the community sugar policy based on the production quota, which cannot be exceeded. The Belgian sugar lobby, a powerful group, just wanted to produce at random (*as much as they liked*). In that case, you must not believe everything that a Belgian tells you. And whatever they may say, all Nine are afraid of losing some of their sovereignty - and it is often easy to hide behind France.

"Little remains secret for the journalists, who often have the chance to play off the weaknesses of one against the other. As well, there are the many bodes (spokespeople), often Belgian or Italian, that have been around so long already. If, for example, you want to know who the permanent representatives preparing for a council of ministers are, then you go along to the bodes (*spokespeople*), who have to carry endless mountains of documents. Or you catch snippets of the talks from them. 'Oh', the spokesman may say then, 'they're arguing about tobacco'.

"There is no question of discrimination against female journalists. But one thing is for sure: a female journalist must come very well prepared, because an expert begins by thinking that a woman after all does not know much about it. If he sees in an interview that you are well-informed, then you have no problems any more. But woe betide a woman journalist if she makes a mistake! This is much worse than if her male colleague makes the same mistake. Sometimes being a journalist at the EEC is a thankless job. For many, it is difficult to get the fruits of their hard work into the papers. What seems very important in Brussels is often overshadowed in their own country by national events. And this will not change either, so long as the Nine do not have any real communal interests."

As well as photos with key political figures in Brussels, I found one of Nel tête-à-tête with world renowned composer Igor Stravinsky and US Ambassador Celdon Chapen at a Brussels cocktail party in the mid-1960s.

UK Foreign Minister Ted Heath, Brussels, c.1963

by newsmen on arrival at Brussels military airport. Clark Clifford
in Belgium for the NATO defense ministers meeting held in Brussels.
CIATED PRESS WIREPHOTO) (str.Gr.10-5-68pt)

US Defence Secretary Clark Clifford

With German Minister Schiller, Luxembourg, 26 October 1971

With EEC President Gaston Thorn, Brussels, 28 June 1972

In conversation with Igor Stravinsky, US Ambassador Celdon Chapen,
Brussels cocktail party, mid-1960s

ix. A Car Crash in Holland: Nel's Hartman nemesis

In November 1969, Nel had a serious car accident on her way to the first key press conference at a Common Market summit in The Hague - not surprising considering her appalling driving. Yolanda Frenkel-Frank remembered this from her visits to see Nel from time to time in Brussels.

> "She had a terrible car accident and had to stay in hospital with whiplash, cursing like mad - the whole time cursing bloody Dutch drivers but *she* was a completely awful driver."

Near her old apartment in Javastraat, the one-way system around the corner in Frederikstraat had been changed since she left and Nel followed her old route and drove down it the wrong way. She crashed into a taxi and was badly injured and was forced to spend a lengthy period in hospital.

Gradually she recovered. In January, she wrote to Gallagher to thank him for his friendly note urging her to take time to get well and for a gold AP decoration she had received the previous October. Nel was perhaps less impressed by that than she would have been by a pay rise. But in any case, she assured Gallagher she would soon be back on the beat.

> "Presently I am training to walk properly - a little better and longer every day. My doctor assures me that by the end of January, I will be able to resume sprints for the telephone."

While recuperating, she stayed with her great friend near Brussels, Viscountess Laure de Jonghe d'Ardois. The accident had forced her to miss the November Common Market summit, as the AP's November 23-29 World Service reported. The summit was a landmark in that it introduced the English language for the first time, in anticipation of UK accession:

> "There were 450 journalists at the Common Market's summit conference, and they found the Dutch admirable hosts Foreign Minister Joseph Luns personally escorted an overflow of more than 100 journalists to the floor of the meeting hall with one mild request: 'Just don't sit on the tables'.

> "But there was one absentee - the AP's Nel Slis, who knows the way through the mysteries of this organization like few others. Nel was injured in an automobile

accident on the way to the first important news conference and probably will be out of action for the rest of the month.

"The Dutch, with a bow to the great British interest in the meeting, opened up the Common Market's press relations to a new language - English. It had never been considered necessary before. The AP staff - Carl Hartman, Eric Esih of the Bonn office and Bernard Veillet-Lavellee and Stephens Droening of the Paris bureau - welcomed the innovation although between them the AP correspondents could handle half a dozen languages.

"Hartman got the first tip on how it would all come out. He saw a Luxembourg official standing alone in the Senate lobby. Hartman asked him how the negotiations with Britain had been worked out and the man told him. Six hours later, the final result was announced just as he said."

Nel must have been chafing to get back, furious about missing the summit. She was probably also extremely miffed by the reference to Hartman's tip, as there was fierce rivalry between them and they did not get on well. Hartman was to become a major source of problems. The AP appreciated Nel's qualities as a reporter but was inclined to carp at her occasionally strange use of English. It is possible the AP's reservations about a woman reporter had not completely disappeared, especially such a 'difficult' one. Also, news agencies generally have a weakness for 'hot young reporters' as against age and experience. Nel was well into her fifties by this time.

Her efforts did however receive some recognition. From 1 October 1966, she was given a salary rise to 1,950 guilders (885 euros) a month 'upon merit considerations'. Brussels bureau chief Fred Cheval, who was clearly impressed by her energy and persistence, said in his letter to her:

"No doubt, you have fully deserved it, if one considers your tireless, day and night aggressive gathering of European Affairs information. I do not believe anyone could have maintained your pace in that facet of your duties and remained alive. You have survived and deserved the increase granted. You are an almost unequalled master in collecting information."

Nonetheless, the AP still felt her style and use of language left some room for improvement.

To Nel's fury, she discovered less than a year later that her bête noir Hartman was to be sent from Bonn to Brussels because of the increasing importance of the EEC and the UK's impending accession. Kersting had to work hard to prevent her from writing an angry letter to AP General Manager Wes Gallagher in New York. Hartman himself was clearly aware of how sensitive Nel was about his imminent arrival, saying in a letter to her from Bonn on 4 September 1967:

> "If this seems hard on you, perhaps you can believe that I would like to do everything I can - in my own interests - to make it easier... What can we do to make it as painless as possible for one another? It would be nice to have a word from you."

It would be nice to know whether Nel ever replied to him.

Nel also continued to fret about her salary and pension as her salary did not leave much room for salting anything away for retirement. She always told younger journalists she would have to work until she dropped after retirement because she had such a meagre AP pension, and that only extracted after a huge battle. At the end of 1967, aged 54, she wrote to Stan Swinton, who she knew best among the AP chiefs in New York. But she got nowhere, and even Kersting got fed up with her harping on the subject:

> "I ask you emphatically not to phone me any more about this personal salary question and not to phone the bureau either. First you phoned up Anneke and me (both working people) in the depths of the night and then you phoned again to Mr Van Mierlo at the bureau. Everything would have been easier with a little letter. We are not a grocery store."

However, on Kersting and Cheval's recommendation, Nel's persistence was eventually rewarded by another salary rise of 50 dollars a month from 1 March 1969.

The Nel/Hartman rivalry meanwhile got worse rather than better and the AP was unhappy with their disparate and uncoordinated Common Market coverage. Critical letters from London Bureau Chief Dick O'Regan in 1970 described Hartman's stories as too superficial and written too much from an American perspective while Nel's were too detailed and too regionally oriented - giving some inkling of their essential incompatibility.

> "There is a job for both of you to do in improving our Common Market coverage,"

O'Regan still insisted.

A year later, O'Regan said in a letter to Cheval, Hartman and Nel dated 26 May, 1971 that there were still complaints from some AP bureaus that

> "Hartman's copy can be too elementary and Nel's copy
> is too confused."

Because of the lack of communication between Nel and Hartman, the AP was also irritated by double coverage and ordered Nel and Hartman to confer every morning on what they planned to write that day and what press conferences they would attend. They were also told to read each other's stories and keep each other informed about long-term projects they were working on. Despite the AP's pleas that

> "there should not be any competition, but organized
> teamwork to produce the report wanted,"

these directives must surely have added fuel to the fire.

The message was repeated from New York, adding insult to injury from Nel's point of view by stating that 'Miss Slis' came administratively under Cheval, but the AP production relating to the EEC was 'the responsibility of Mr Hartman': all Nel's copy should be read by him for 'editorial control'. That must have been the final indignity for Nel, with her vast experience, to have to submit to this younger, probably better paid and even in the AP's own view, 'superficial' reporter. No doubt her copy did need editing, but this was no way to solve what was clearly by then a serious personality conflict between the two.

Notes from Hartman demonstrate this, and must have rubbed salt into Nel's wounds.

> "Please check with me BEFORE requesting interviews
> with members of the EEC Commission... When you
> give me information on the telephone, please do NOT
> send the story to London yourself unless I ask you to do
> so."

This would have been impossible for Nel to swallow and no doubt she gave Hartman hell in return. It must have been an intolerable situation for both of them.

In due course, a diplomatically couched letter dated 6 April 1973 came from New York, 'neither punitive nor in any way connected to your relationships in Belgium' informing her that she was being transferred back to The Hague with effect from 1 June.

x. Leaving Brussels: Slis on Belgium, Slis on Europe

Nel left Brussels with mixed feelings. The Hartman affair soured her last years there, but it had still been a wonderful period for her and she had many good old and new friends there. Among the Dutch were Han Boon, who had become Dutch ambassador to NATO and Rudolf 'Peek' Pekelharing, formerly foreign ministry spokesman in The Hague, who became head of the NATO press service. Other friends who had visited her in Brussels included Isaac Stern and his wife, when on a European tour. Best of all, her very close friend Laura, Vicomtesse de Jonge d'Ardois, lived in Ukkel near Brussels and she had spent many happy weekends there.

Tyna Wynaendts often went to stay with Nel in Brussels for long weekends and holidays and had cause to be grateful to her for her continued admonitions to study languages.

> "Her own career was built on languages, and she always told me to be careful of your languages - it's so important, in the modern world you have to be international. She also influenced my parents to send me to France. Maybe they would have done this anyway, but she was very insistent. And it is true that I got my job at the OECD library because of languages; I wasn't really qualified to be a librarian, but they needed somebody who was at least bilingual or trilingual. So it helped me. As she told me, when you have your languages, you can always find a job."

Comparing Belgium and the Netherlands while she was working in Brussels, Nel said she found Brussels pleasant to live in and liked the Belgians, but added:

> "It isn't always easy for the Dutch here, partly because of the linguistic problem. People don't realise that we don't take sides on the matter."

In an interview with Brussels Bulletin magazine while she was living there, Nel spoke of a perennial misunderstanding between the Dutch and the Belgians:

> "They are so different. I think it's partly because the Dutch, whether they're Catholic, Protestant or Jewish, think like Calvinists, while the Belgians have a more flexible Catholic way of life. It's also a question of history. Belgium has been the victim of war and the

balance of power; the country has been an eternal battlefield. It's very different from Holland, which has never had any wars except the Spanish and the German occupation."

Nel also had praise for Belgian women:

"In Holland, women put great emphasis on getting university degrees, then they get married and give up work and just settle down to giving coffee parties. In Belgium, the number of women who work is much higher. And whereas the Dutch woman spends very little time on her looks, her Belgian sister takes great pains and looks much prettier."

Enlarging on this theme in another interview from around the same period, she said:

"There are certainly just as many capable women in the Netherlands as in other countries, but I find they are way behind the women in other countries. It is a question of mentality. This is the only country where emancipation is subsidised."

She tossed her head back and bellowed indignantly:

"It's a hopeless business, a joke!"

Lowering her voice again, she added:

"In Belgium, where they still have Napoleonic laws, where women in any case until recently still needed written agreement from their husbands if they wanted to take a trip to England, there they are much more independent. They work harder and take care that they still look good."

Nel also remarked in the Brussels Bulletin that at the height of Holland's socialist era in the 1960s and early 1970s, there was a strong element of protest among the young, with movements like the Kabouters (hopgoblins) and Dolle Mina. But there was nothing comparable in Belgium.

"I think partly because of history: under stress, the Dutch protest, the Belgians are saboteurs; partly because of the preoccupation with the linguistic problem, partly because the social structure here is more rigid than in Holland."

What Nel most admired about the Belgians was their ability to cope, she went on:

> "I admire the way they've absorbed the big international organisations like the Common Market and Nato."

What surprised her most was the way drivers did not move when the traffic light went green, a strange comment for a Dutchwoman since much the same happens in the Netherlands. Perhaps she was contrasting Belgium with countries like Italy and France.

Asked whether journalism was a suitable profession for a woman, Nel said:

> "Certainly. Women are discriminating and perspicacious, which makes them good journalists. But it's not true, as some people claim, that their sex gives them an advantage over men or it may give them a short-term advantage but this is offset by the fact that men find it hard to take a woman seriously on a serious subject."

In many ways, the Brussels period seems to have been the high point of Nel's career, not least because she was so interested in Europe. After the initial struggles to master the EEC's complexities, she surely hit her mature journalistic prime, becoming a dominant figure on the Brussels scene. Later, even after her memory had begun to fade, she was to enjoy a final revival at the Maastricht Summit in 1991.

Mulling European developments in 1981, seven years after leaving Brussels for The Hague and not long after she had retired from the AP, Nel told me:

> "I still believe in Europe, very much. We mean nothing any more as individual countries, in world politics and I think Europe is still the best place to live, personally - I love other parts of the world but I wouldn't live anywhere other than Europe.

> "Economically, we would benefit enormously by a united Europe. Also, culturally. That's not even in the Treaty of Rome. It's done a little bit, but not enough, by the Council of Europe. I very firmly believe in the great advantages of a united Europe politically, economically and culturally, while maintaining our differences."

(What sort of Europe?)

> "Freedom in goods, services and people; a journalist should be able to work in Sicily, and doctors and nurses should be able to work anywhere. Freedom of capital of

course - that's very difficult because of the different tax systems everywhere. Social systems: the Dutch is a lot better than the Italian, Spanish or Greek. The farmers here are better off than elsewhere. People forget - it's so easy to say, ah, that's the fault of the Common Market. That's not true. Politically, a lot has happened."

(How big should it be?)

"Well, I think personally we should start with what we have - and of course, we now have Spain, Greece, Portugal coming in. *De Gaulle's idea of Europe from the Atlantic to the Urals?* Mmm Why not the whole Slav world - I often wonder if the Russians would ever go in for that but the satellites, yes. Then there's Scandinavia - that's a world apart, Europe stops at Denmark in a way. Sweden wouldn't mind. Finland would be in a difficult position, though I think the four would eventually, if they had their heart in it, be an asset for democracy, stability - definitely.

Here her answer seems quite prophetic by the new millennium, in the wake of the collapse of the Soviet Union and with former Soviet bloc countries queuing up to join the EU. From the Scandinavian side, Denmark and Finland have since joined, but Norway is still absent.

(Holland's contribution?)

"Well, it's a belief in Europe. Mostly selfish - its bread is buttered by Europe, certainly in the agricultural field but also in many other respects. Also Belgium and Holland are so central, we *are* Europe in a way.

"The achievements of Europe are I think enormous - very fast. In the beginning, it was a starry-eyed period, it has slowed down enormously, but imperceptibly it makes constant strides. A great breakthrough was Britain joining.

"The first thing is getting people across borders. The agricultural market, however you want to say it, it's still a major feat because had it not been achieved, southern Italy and Germany would be empty with all the poor farming people going to the cities and there boosting communism. It prevented extreme leftism.

"Secondly, the free market - you can move goods across very easily - camembert and French wine here; that was impossible before the war - now you can get anything anywhere. Perfume costs the same here as in Paris. Thirdly, the exchange of capital. The European Monetary System has greatly helped the movement of capital and money matters; it helped to stabilize the system.

"People always forget what has been done since 1952 when we emerged from war, when people were at each other's throats. Now, in less than 30 years, it's made a lot of progress. Europe can play a very important role in the future, if it plays things well; the French can have great influence in Africa. Britain is fairly well off compared with Greece, the poorest, but we can have the whole Mediterranean as one big family. Look, from Italy to, I don't know where, nationalities are so interwoven. I think it's a very close world and we can have tremendous influence because the Spanish are after all half Arab and the French have always said that we should be an influence in Africa. Like North America can have great influence on Latin America."

(Could the EEC foreshadow a world federation?)

"No. Europe is totally exhausted in raw materials, very little iron, a bit of coal here and there. America still has some, but it's also fast being exhausted. We'll always be interdependent, more and more so. We in Europe have become, not so much tired but wise, it no longer makes for great civilisation - it's an old civilisation."

xi. Dale on La Slis

For a personal portrait of Nel in Brussels at the height of her powers from one of her fellow-journalists, Paris-based journalist Alan Tillier came up with the name of Reginald Dale. Dale was in Brussels to report on the EEC for the Financial Times from 1968, when Nel had already been there for six years. In fact, Alan himself had also met Nel in Brussels and later visited her at her apartment in The Hague with Reggie Dale. He was complimentary about her:

> "Nel always made the EU understandable to a visiting fireman like me, cutting through the gobbledegook."

Dale spoke enthusiastically on the phone from Washington about Nel in her Brussels heyday:

"I can still see her clearly, a wonderful person. She could be very aggressive - that's not the right word; feisty, that's the right word - when dealing with people who weren't very co-operative. She was incredibly friendly to new journalists arriving in Brussels and often took them under her wing.

"She knew a lot of people, all the main players. She was close to the Dutch, of course, and also to the French as she spoke French. Also to the Luxemburgers including Boschette, the Luxembourg commissioner and Jen Dondlinger, his successor. She knew everyone and everyone knew her. Another friend was a Dutchman in the Commission, Edmund Wellenstein, a very senior official with a very good brain... A great friend of Nel's in the Commission was Clara Meyers, spokesperson for agriculture; they'd go off places together. Another good friend was Emanuel de la Taille, well-known on television. Later, when he stopped doing television, he ran a club for journalists in Paris...

"I can see Nel now, driving her little car, peering ahead with a determined expression. She was an erratic driver... But when she got stuck into something, she stuck to it. She had huge concentration in everything; whether it was driving or complicated European questions like agricultural prices, it was the same spirit. She would go on and keep pestering until she got enough to explain it, enough for a story.

"Everyone knew her, she was a charismatic figure. You always knew when she was around, she was a huge presence. You'd see her frown of concentration then she'd suddenly burst into a radiant smile.

"The main subject while I was in Brussels was enlargement, Britain, Ireland, Denmark, Norway. And the whole question of how the EEC should adapt to take in more members. The Hague triptych (the three pillars of policy) for enlargement and deepening came from a summit in The Hague in 1969. We also covered NATO, and I went on covering it afterwards.

"But I remember Nel much more in the EU context. We would wait for hours and hours outside, often all through the night; the press corps all knew each other well. Commission meetings were then in the Berlaymont building; you walked across the road to the Charlemaigne building, where the Council of Ministers met. The press were on the ground floor and the ministers met on the 14th floor, so they had to get by us.

"When I first went to Brussels, it was a cosy little club with just the Six (Common Market members). There was only a handful of journalists (compared to later) and we'd swap information on the six countries.

"Because Britain was not a member but the Dutch thought they should have been, they would brief journalists as an unofficial favour, first their own in Dutch and then the others in English. Though in England there wasn't much interest in the EEC. There were only three British staff reporters at first, Charles Stevens at Reuters, P. Taft of The Times and me.

"Then De Gaulle died in 1969 and the negotiations started in 1970, it was the beginning of a huge influx of journalists. Later, oil prices in 1973 was a big story: Saudi oil minister Sheik Yameni came to Brussels, but the EEC had no common energy policy.

"I didn't see Nel outside work because work took up so much time - occasionally we would go riding if there was a meeting in The Hague. When I moved to Paris later, Nel came for a short stay. I was in Nel's apartment in The Hague a couple of times. I was with her on the night they announced the new pope (Pope John Paul II). Neither of us liked the cut of his jib.

"I loved seeing her there, but she was much more in her element in the huge press area in the EU, her laughter. So much of life there was in public. Nel liked a drink but I never saw her the worse for wear for drink. At the time of the British entry negotiations, we'd be up three nights running to three or four in the morning.

"I can just picture her now very vividly, laughing. She had a great sense of humour and a lot of funny stories, strange things in Dutch, which she'd translate, quite obscene, some of them. Part of her good heart. A very generous person with a big heart.

"As you go through life, you meet a handful of people who are clearly larger than life. It's a privilege to have known them, and Nel is one of those."

Leaving card from Brussels colleagues, Nel

HELLCAT
OF
THE HAGUE

9.
Return to Holland

Slis on the Dutch

When she left Brussels, Nel still had yearnings for her first love, Paris. But at the age of 60, she was not at all averse to establishing herself in Holland. With only five years to run to retirement, the tiny AP pension she complained about must have made the relatively generous Dutch state pension attractive and it was necessary to be living there for five years to secure it. In any case, the AP wasn't offering Paris but The Hague. As she explained:

> "If they had asked me, I would have gone to Paris immediately but press agencies are *frugal*. There was a staff shortage in The Hague, so I went back. There was also a question of an inheritance. It was time to think about the future. My pension from AP is *poor*. Americans do not understand what a pension is and Europeans are in their eyes *second hand*, they come completely at the bottom of the ladder."

American news agencies generally treated 'local hires' very poorly financially compared with correspondents parachuted in from the US, in my own experience as wel, working for AP-Dow Jones. Some non-Americans managed to beat the system and claw their way higher up the salary-and-status ladder but only very few. Luckily, Nel had an ace up her sleeve, in the form of that piece of fertile land she had inherited in Goeree-Overflakkee.

As soon as she heard about her transfer, Nel wrote to her new bureau chief John Gale about her plans for her return. True to form, this was to be after a holiday, this time in Portugal. Her letter shows her mixed feelings about leaving Brussels.

> "Naturally I am sorry to leave so many friends in Brussels. The work on the Common Market has been most inspiring... Your kind letters have contributed to soothing my traumas due to a lack of courteousness at the Brussels office."

The last sentence is a veiled reference to that thorn in her flesh, Hartman.

i. Cashing in those fat Goeree hectares

Almost the first thing Nel did back in Holland was to return to the island where she was born to sell her land there. She was immensely pleased that she went in person instead of leaving it to intermediaries and she found the people there also appreciated the personal contact. With the money, she bought an apartment in The Hague that Yolanda's mother had found for her.

It was a pleasant first floor apartment in a group of modern apartment blocks near the sea, about 20 minutes by tram from the centre of The Hague. The rooms were arranged off a small hallway. In Nel's study, I saw the faithful filing cabinet, telex, telephone and fax. And of course there were the piles of newspapers no journalist can do without. She had a comfortable, relatively large sitting room on the same side as the study. On the other side was Nel's bedroom and a guest bedroom, as well as the bathroom and small kitchen. Good furniture inherited or picked up by Nel along the way, bookcases, pictures and photos of friends and places lined the walls. The surrounding balconies gave a glimpse of the nearby dunes.

Nel's finances were something of a mystery to me. She often complained about her meagre AP salary and pension, and the extra expenses that a woman correspondent incurred in order to be well turned out. But she still managed to buy expensive clothes and she always looked extremely smart. She also travelled extensively, well into her later years. How, I wondered, did she manage all of these expenses. Part of the answer was that, like other journalists, she supplemented her AP income by those schnabbeltjes, writing for magazines and other publications. She also inherited a house in Biarritz from her friend Jacqueline and presumably salted something away when she sold it. Probably the biggest help came from those 'fat hectares' of Goeree, enabling her to buy the apartment in The Hague outright and thus live rent and mortgage-free. This was the first time in her adult life that she had ever had a home of her own.

Nel was to live in Holland for the rest of her life. In 1981, she told me a little wistfully:

"I feel, frankly, at home in most countries in Europe. I'm even getting used to post-war Germany, a beautiful place. Yes, I found it very difficult to get back. Personally, I find other countries more attractive and if I had money and time, I would have a second house in France or Italy - still the cradle of European civilisation."

This wish was not realised. Tyna also told me she wanted to move to Portugal at one time when she had a group of older friends there but they all died off before she got around to it.

Still, with her endless restlessness and curiosity, Nel always considered herself European more than Dutch. She relished wider Europe and indeed the world stage. Nonetheless, at the point where she was embarking on her 'last fling at covering the Dutch' as her bureau chief Gale called it, I naturally found myself hunting for some pieces she had written that would show what she thought about her own country, its culture and its people.

ii. Nel's-eye view of the Netherlands: Climate, Calvanism, Curiosity

A thoughtful undated draft article on the Netherlands written shortly before the Brussels period gives us a Nel's view of a number of elements of the country and its people. It also shows the international dimension of the Dutch persona. Some warmth about the Dutch nation and its peculiar history emerges in the piece, along with evocative images of the countryside. It ends abruptly, but its circa 1960 snapshot encapsulates many enduring characteristics of the country and its people. Nel wrote:

> "The Netherlands is conditioned by three C's - the climate, Calvinism and curiosity about peopleand things abroad...The Dutch are apt to apologise for their climate, as though they themselves had invented it. Most Dutchmen take a wry pride in the fact that the climate of the Netherlands is damp, that the skies are always a luminous grey and that the sun only makes its appearances on the birthdays of the members of the House of Orange. Making depreciatory remarks about the Dutch climate is one criticism that the Dutch themselves still enthusiastically agree with. And yet, the Dutch evidently thrive in this climate, for they are an active, bustling lot, almost bursting out of the dykes which protect them from the ever-covetous waves.

"In fact, Holland's birth rate is the highest and its mortality rate the lowest in the world.

For a long time Holland's statesmen have been considering making marriage a little less attractive, by cutting the exorbitant taxes on bachelor workers. But their alibi is still that the taxes can't be cut because of ever-threatening inflation. In Holland, there are still high premiums paid for babies. The only thing that might deter young couples from getting married is the shortage of housing.

"Despite an upward trend in the number of emigrants, the Dutch, like Don Quixote, are fighting windmills in their attempts to reduce their numbers. Don't have illusions about all the windmills left in Holland. Out of the 7,000 that existed in the 17th century, there are only about 1,200 left, of which some 1,000 are still in working order. These few left over from the pre-technological era are reverently guarded by the Dutch society as "monuments" and are likely to remain a characteristic feature of the flat Dutch landscape."

This was written before the successor of the traditional windmill, the lanky 'sustainable energy' wind turbine began to dot the land and seascape around the Netherlands. From a distance, they look rather attractive, but some say they are noisy neighbours. Nel goes on:

"This landscape, dead and dreary in winter and blossoming in the summer with green foliage and the white sails of boats floating along the canals, is always dominated by the huge expanse of luminous and ever-changing sky. This wonderful light helped to create the golden age of painting in 17th century Holland, when wealthy Dutch merchants were immortalised in canvas by such masters as Rembrandt and Frans Hals. Holland's museums are bulging with masterpieces of this era, although newer trends can be seen at the municipal museums in Rotterdam, Amsterdam and The Hague and at the Kroeller-Mueller museum on the edge of the Veluwe National Park.

"This park is the only spot in the Netherlands where a Dutchman at times can claim to be 'alone'; it is strictly guarded as a 'reservation' from which homes and factories are barred from being built, in order to provide a breathing space in this overcrowded country. In fact the shortage of open spaces is getting so acute that the government had to ask neighbouring West Germany for space to exercise Dutch NATO forces.

"The disparity between Holland's growing population and the country's microscopic size has kept the nation's leaders worried for generations. Some 10 million Dutch people are living within an area of 12,530 square miles, and more than half of them prosper well below sea level. Those of you who have traveled through Schiphol airport landed some fourteen feet below sea level. Ever since the 13th century, the Dutch have been building dykes to keep their feet dry. Four of Holland's largest towns are below sea level: Amsterdam, Rotterdam, The Hague and Haarlem. At the rate the population is growing these cities, in another half century, may well become one sprawling entity."

By the end of the 20th century, the population had expanded by 50 percent to 15 million. In 2000, a young Japanese architect described his impression of a train trip through the 'sprawling entity' of the Randstad, the western urban agglomeration. Pondering its alternating urban and apparently rural patches, he found this an ingenious managed Dutch solution for the problem of an overpopulated country.

"Leaving the streets of Rotterdam, I came across windmills and an endless pasture that precisely reminded me of the very image of the Netherlands' sight-seeing spots.

"The moment I thought I had a moment to enjoy the pastoral landscape with scattered sheep and cows on the green carpets of grass, the city area would start again and I would arrive at the next station...

"Through this repetition, I arrived in Amsterdam with a strange feeling of the good and rhythmical combination of nature and city.

"In Holland, nature and cities are linked in an integrated network rather than in confrontation. 'Green Heart' slides its greenery in between the cities.

"Yet as drainpipes control the level of underground water using electric power 24 hours a day in the soil of the meadows where cows and sheep are dozing calmly, we realise that the relaxing meadows exist as completely artificial and high-tech areas.

"Protecting the environment is not protecting the existing nature, but controlling it."

Controlling nature is an integral part of Dutch history, as Nel goes on to point out in her circa 1960 piece:

"In the last two thousand years the Dutch have gained 1,453,000 acres from the sea and lost 1,400,000. They are now concerned with creating their twelfth province, by turning the eel-rich Zuyderzee into the province of Flevoland, thereby wresting 550,000 acres from the sea. Meanwhile don't miss Holland's eel, as it is freshly smoked on the doomed Zuyderzee coast."

Also threatened by the push for land are Holland's world-famous oysters. These vitamin-rich plump morsels, responsible for substantial export income, may well be on the way out. At present a war is being waged between the wealthy oyster farmers of the southern province of Zeeland, and the hydraulic engineers in charge of the Delta plan.

"This pre-war project received added impetus after the 1953 disaster, when one-sixth of the Netherlands was submerged by salty sea water, which drowned some 2,000 of the Dutch. This project is being implemented only this year. Its purpose is to join the Zeeland and the southern islands with the mainland by connecting dykes. The plan will interfere with the oyster beds, but it opens new vistas for the hitherto agricultural province of Zeeland."

Thankfully, the delicious eels survived and flourished, as did the oysters. Although Yolanda told me the eels and oysters were on the verge of extinction and are farmed today. The oysters at least travelled far and wide, to my delight turning up in Prague when I moved there at the start of the 21st century. Oysters are either loved or hated. For those who love them, it is like eating the sea, which had extra piquancy in the land-locked Czech Republic. Nel's piece continues:

"The plan opens new vistas also for an evolution from Calvinism, for Zeeland is the bulwark of Calvinism. One of the main concerns of the Zeeland farmers' wives when they were saved from the disastrous 1953 floods was to have their sea-soaked white lace caps stiffened in time to go to church in them the following Sunday. The Calvinist women also had pangs of conscience when the Red Cross provided sophisticated clothes from other areas of the country, and even from as far away as Paris where sympathetic Parisians doffed their chic clothes upon hearing about the water-stricken Dutch. The Red Cross had a hard time convincing the Zeeland women that wearing stockings - other than the familiar black ones - was no sin.

"Calvinistic sentiments can be detected throughout the country. One elegant lady discussing the floods with friends in a bar in The Hague was heard to say that her first action when she heard of the disaster was to take off her red nail polish. Dutch women in general, naturally wholesome but tending to be plump, are apt to cut down on grooming for fear they should lose that God-given look…

The Netherlands' denominationalism which Nel describes next did largely get eroded later on,but has played a significant role in its history.

"One result of the Calvinist influence is that everything in Holland is run along denominational lines, including education, radio and television, trade unions and even political parties. There are some fifty different shades of protestant Christians, and arguments about such things as the role of the snake in the Garden of Eden take place even among Dutch rightwing political parties. Parliament spent twenty-four hours debating whether to sign the now defunct European Defence Community agreement, but argued for three weeks on whether or not cremation was legal in a Christian country.

Of the eight parties in parliament only three are non-denominational: the Labour party (PvdA), the Liberal party for Freedom and Democracy (VVD), and the Communist party, which is shrinking rapidly. The Anti-Revolutionary party is still protesting against the French Revolution, but its influence, too, is on the decrease. During the war, denominational differences seemed forgotten in the fight against a common enemy, but they have sprung up again in full vigour, not diminished in the slightest by the more fundamental rivalry between the Protestants and he Roman Catholics.

Denominational thinking has also influenced Dutch literature, little known in the outside world because of the language barrier. Only about 15 million people in Holland and Belgium, plus the descendants of the Boers in South Africa, speak the language. Three of the great figures of Dutch literature are internationally known because they wrote in Latin: the fifteenth-century humanist and theologian Erasmus, the seventeenth-century jurist and theologian Grotius, and his contemporary Spinoza, the theologian and philosopher. Spinoza's Jewish-Portuguese parentage is also evidence of the open-armed welcome that Holland has given to refugees. This attitude, a blend of charity and of stern justice, is a natural result of the country's strong religious tradition.

The average Dutch citizen is however far less reserved, serious, non-effusive and plodding than he looks. Climate and Calvinism may stiffen his spine, but his curiosity, imagination, individualism and sense of humour make him far from stodgy.

It was the Dutch who discovered Australia and New Zealand; they established colonies in the two Americas, in Asia and in South Africa; they sailed up the Hudson and they founded New Amsterdam, now New York.

In the Dutchman, brought to a halt by the sea, there is that deep-lying urge to pioneer and explore, to innovate and invent in all spheres of human activity.

World travellers will run into Dutchmen all over the globe, from the Far East to Africa, from New York city to exclusive French nudist camps. A reporter, visiting one of these camps, asked a Dutch inmate how he liked it there and was told: "Well, it's all right, but a bit hard on the feet".

Throughout the centuries the Dutch have sailed the seven seas. They are a nation of traders, transporters and brokers. Invisible exports play a great part in the national economy.

Two of Europe's main arteries, the rivers Rhine and Meuse, reach the North Sea through Europe's largest harbour, Rotterdam, the city that sprawls across the Rhine estuary as a gateway to the continent. Rotterdam breathes activity, and is the only Dutch city endowed by wealthy citizens with works of art.

Amsterdam, the Netherlands' capital, at the same time is Holland's pride, because it is Holland's most beautiful city".

The Netherlands' Calvanistic flavouring which Nel describes did largely erode later on but has played a significant role in the country's history.

Nel frequently drove to Amsterdam for press conferences, parties and Foreign Press Association meetings. This went on until well into her seventies, with her driving becoming increasingly terrifying for any unwitting passengers.

A few remarks Nel made to me about her country in 1981 add another facet of the Dutch:

> "Another feature of Holland is its lack of moderation - they either go overboard one way or the other. In the 60s with sex on the radio, they had it up to the point of impudence, on TV and radio. I mean, I'm all for freedom of sex and such things, but there were such unsavoury programmes on these things, it was totally unnecessary. The same is true when they go the other way, being too priggish. There is a lack of moderation sometimes".

But she conceded that the Netherlands had its own particular strengths as well.

> "A country of tremendous freedom and charity. I think it comes from Calvinism - there's a good and a bad side, the Dutch get nice when you're really in the soup. Of course, I feel why not profit from it earlier but, here, you have to be really *dans la merdre*... But they stand by you then; it's a good quality. They immediately collect for the Chinese or whatever - partly Calvinism, you know, the bible, feelings of guilt. They're helpful, they don't like to see people in trouble".

Nel had a couple of other approving comments, though she couldn't resist a sting in the tail:

> "And I do think on the whole culturally they make a great effort. We have wonderful music, better than Belgium, and there's still a lot of art, painting; the bookshops are thriving, much better than we had in Belgium. I mean, there are advantages to Holland - art, culture. Even though the Dutch always know everything better, they sit there judging, they're very, very smug".

iii. A changing country... but what about women?

A partly illegible draft of an AP feature on changes in the Netherlands, written around 1972-3, focuses on increased prosperity and revolt. Nel found the Netherlands had changed from a 'staid and stable country' into an 'avant-garde land with a radical youth and aggressive media' and action groups on everything under the sun. She noted a new openness on television, demonstrated by the filming of an abortion and by TV discussions of death and other previously held taboos. No doubt she was pleased to find the formerly meek press corps at last getting tough with taboos and authorities.

From her regular coverage of religious affairs, Nel had an acute grasp of the role these played in society. Her piece reports on the theory of a socialist professor and former politician that the Roman Catholic Church's collapse had made aid to poor countries and anti-pollution the new religion. This is contrasted with the views of a Roman Catholic former woman minister. She believed that people felt under threat and that national authorities could no longer cope with global problems like the atom bomb and pollution.

Despite the shift to free thinking, the 45% Roman Catholics versus 25% Protestants and 30% humanists breakdown of the day seems to show a surprisingly high proportion of the first group. But as Nel points out elsewhere, even the Catholics and no doubt also the humanists in Holland seem in a certain way Calvinistic. However, it seems that the Roman Catholic Church had come a long way from 1955 when the Dutch bishops had actually prohibited "their" politicians from joining the socialist party. Almost half the 150-seat parliament was by then leftist and this group included many Roman Catholics, Nel reported.

She also found that older people were aware of increased prosperity. Nel's own faithful Aagje was roped in here as a 78-year old charwoman who said she has 'never had it so good'. Among the young, Nel found a growing tendency to revolt. She attributes this partly to overpopulation and partly to the loss of the old 'outlet' of the Dutch East Indies (Holland's former Indonesian colony). In the early 1960s, there was a wave of rebellion against the establishment and obsolete traditions by campaign groups calling themselves the 'provos' and 'kabouters' (gnomes). Nel notes that these groups also took up the fight against pollution as 'the most acute symptom of a sick society'. The piece finishes with Nel's faintly hopeful consideration of a prediction that the next wave of revolt would come from women.

Nel was often quite scathing about her compatriots and their culture but never more so than on the subject of women and emancipation. In 1981, she told me:

> "I think Dutch women are a case apart - they're so smug and self-satisfied on the whole. One, they're the most backward, even compared with Ireland, Italy, Austria. The younger women are a little different but I find even among Dutch women journalists very little solidarity, very little interest one for the other. The best crowd of

women in Holland are the platteland (country) women, farmers, because they have started courses on politics and so on. There is also a great deal of class business too - though less among the younger women. But in all the places where I've worked, London, Belgium, France and all over, I've found there's greater friendliness and solidarity among women journalists than in Holland. Here, they're still, as they say, catching flies off each other (*denigrating each other*)"

Warming to her theme, she burst out:

"I think it is *grotesque* the way they go about subsidising so-called emancipation. The Rode Vrouwen and the countrywomen are the only two organisations that have some goodness in them. *why* subsidise emancipation - why not have it come from the various organisations to help each other push for women's rights. They should subsidise creches - what women need - so that women who want to work have the facilities. If they don't know what they need, then they should not be subsidised. Now they use the subsidies for sitting and meeting and commissions and all sorts of useless things. It is a scandal. Here, women are all divided - the academic pooh-poohs the businesswoman; they pooh-pooh the soroptomists, the soroptomists pooh-pooh someone else. They're all divided in little clubs and they're an unbearable lot anyway."

Many foreign career women settling in the Netherlands would be inclined to agree. In 1979, when I came to live in Holland, I was shocked to discover the meagre extent of women's participation in the working life of the nation compared with other European countries. Single men as well as working women suffered from the fact that society was arranged on the assumption that anybody working would have a wife at home to take care of things and do the shopping, let the plumber in and so on. And virtually all the shops closed at 5 p.m. After debating later shop opening hours for more than two decades, these did eventually arrive at the end of the 20th century. Sunday openings followed. Unfortunately, progress in women's participation continued at a snail's pace. Combining family and career still seemed to be a choice reserved for men, naturally equipped with wives to take care of the family.

This aspect of the Netherlands, with its liberal reputation, is a puzzle. Good educational opportunities were available for some if not most Dutch women even when Nel was growing up. But she found that those with degrees did nothing with them and then apparently felt jealous when they saw what Nel had achieved. It is true that by the 1970s, quality day-care for children was widely available in Belgium, where many women went out to work, but scarcely at all in Holland. And it was typically practical of Nel to call for more crèches. But the fact is that if women are sufficiently keen to work outside the home, they create a market for day-care facilities. This did happen in Holland from the 1970s onwards, but the preference for part-time work rather than a serious career has persisted among those women who do work outside the home. Few women had broken through the 'glass ceiling' in management by the start of the 21st century. It seems to me there is still room for a change in women's attitudes in Holland.

Nel herself was an almost unique role model for Dutch career women. A fellow-journalist once remarked that if more Dutchwomen were like her, there would be no need for an emancipation movement. Gradually, though, Nel's pioneering lead was followed at least in the international news agencies and to some extent, in the newspaper world in the Netherlands. In politics, there was something of a breakthrough after the exceptionally turbulent year of 2002. This was the time of the meteoric rise and subsequent murder of flamboyant, outspoken gay populist politician Pim Fortuyn. Two successive governments collapsed, the second mainly due to the chaotic nature of the party Fortuyn left behind him. After the general elections in early 2003, more women held government posts than ever before. There were five full ministers, compared with just one in the previous administration, and four state secretaries. And the conservative VVD parliamentary party was led by a woman. As I write in 2013, the figures are holding up quite well with six ministers and two state secretaries. So there is some progress within politics.

If Nel had married Dan Schorr and had children, though, I fear that she would have found it virtually impossible to combine this with a career in journalism. The ambitious Schorr was hardly house-husband material. Also, even right up into the 1970s, combining motherhood and work was extremely difficult for news journalists in most parts of the world. As Isabel Conway, an Irish journalist who moved to Holland, remarked:

> "You see all those photographs of Nel in the old days. Oh, she was so stylish, she was the real thing, she was tough because you had to be as a woman journalist then, and there was no compromise, you just had to, you were married to your job, that's how it was then. To be honest, when I started in the 1970s, it was very similar in Ireland, you couldn't combine it with other things. You

were either in for it, the whole thing, or you didn't do it, you retired, got married."

It was Tyna Wynaendts who explained just how important Nel felt independence and access to wider horizons were for women. This was the core of her own emancipation credo, and was also what she encouraged in other women. Growing up in Goeree-Overflakkee, she must have seen how the wives lived, as 'a slave to their husbands', Tyna said. She added that Nel also detested the small-mindedness and cramped, watchful attitudes, 'where everybody knows everybody else and comments on them'. This was certainly not confined to her island. One can think, for example, of the small mirrors still to be seen outside the windows in Dutch houses everywhere, used to watch everything going on outside.

Therefore, Tyna said,

> "Knowing how difficult it was for women to get on professionally, Nel would privilege women and help them a lot,"

Occasionally, Nel's determined support for women had bizarre results. When Tyna became engaged to Jean Jacques, the ambassador in Brussels remarked that she was very lucky.

> "Nel said no, *he* was very lucky and that became a real fight, they were both competing on who in this new couple, Jean Jacques and myself, was the luckiest one to have found the other one. And it was a real fight; they never spoke to one another again."

All the same, said Tyna,

> "Nel didn't want anything to do with the feminists, the Dolle Mina and some women who would aggressively and in a vulgar way fight for their rights. She wasn't with them at all, but she wanted to help people in their professional life and would go out of her way *because* they were women. For instance, when she was younger, she left all her money and land to an association in Holland to promote birth control (in her Will) because she said that was what women needed to get their freedom and to be able to build up their career. She thought women should be able to chose whether to have children or not and she wanted to help this."

Later, with contraceptives widely available, it became unnecessary for Nel to leave her money for their promotion and Tyna became Nel's heir.

Though Nel was doubtless delighted about the arrival of contraceptives in the 1960s, she was out of tune with the provocative sexual liberation movement of the day and would never associate herself with aggressive feminism. Speaking of such women, Tyna said:

> "They had a very revolutionary way of looking at it. These people often are provocative, and she   would have nothing to do with that, she was very much a lady,"

This seems paradoxical, in view of Nel's own often unladylike behaviour. Mulling this aspect of Nel's character, Tyna mused:

> "She was too neutral to be engaged politically but she had very strong opinions - without being like others who had similar opinions: she would never mix with the Dolle Mina."

Perhaps, I suggested, she disliked their sometimes extreme, aggressive and shrill behaviour.

Tyna replied:

> "But sometimes you need those kinds of people too. But I think Nel was very much a *lady*, with all that that means. She had a very high sense of quality for all things - in her personal life, but also in literature, in the friends that she chose. She was not influenced by the idea of being a part of a social section of society. She made up her own mind on everything".

Something invaluable that Nel showed her, said Tyna, was the perception of the world from a broader perspective beyond the confines of Dutch opinion.

> "She always said, don't just stay here in Holland, there's much more. And when we were travelling, she always gave me another perspective on things - really that it's not just the opinion of high society in The Hague that's important; the world is a lot larger and there are other opinions. And that was very valuable."

Independence was also the pleasure of simply being able to buy things.

> "She liked buying a lot and that's one of the things she said, it's wonderful being independent, you don't have to ask anybody whether you can or not and, if you spend it foolishly, it's your own responsibility and nobody can tell you maybe you're spending too much on shoes or whatever. She said make sure you're in that position, so that you can do exactly what you like."

For Tyna, Nel was an influence complementing that of her mother, Nel's best friend.

> "I'm grateful that the adult woman I could identify with was my mother, for many, many very good things, but Nel was sort of additional, a role model of a woman who could look after herself and earn her own living and who was intellectually creative and I'm very grateful for that."

Nel's often derogatory views of Dutch women and their movements in the 1970s did not deter her from taking a professional interest in matters relating to women and feminism, and she was always willing to write for women's publications. She wrote about feminist magazine Opzij when it was launched in the early 1970s and later she herself wrote for Opzij. Another report I found was on a woman that made it into an important political post, that of Labour leader. In an odd slip-up in the lead, Nel likened her to Peggy, presumably meaning Maggie, Thatcher, an odd comparison considering Thatcher was a Conservative with a very large C. There are no obvious clues here to Nel's private reactions to the Dutch Labour leader, but she probably approved of her undogmatic, democratic views and her contacts with other women socialists around Europe (Appendix D).

iv. Primeurs, Politics and Premiers

With her indefatigable nose for news, Nel continued to have her share of 'primeurs' or scoops. Among the stories she covered were the French embassy hostage-taking by Japanese Red Army terrorists in The Hague; the armed hijacking of a train by South Moluccan independence fighters, for which Nel spent a few days in Beilan where a crisis centre was set up in Hotel Prakken; the assassination of a British Ambassador; KLM hijackings; and the granting of independence to Holland's Latin American colony, Surinam.

In general, she found the AP was looking for more financial news from Holland than in the earlier period, though the Royal Family remained a topic of great interest for the American market. Financial news was evidently more of a necessary string to her bow than something that passionately interested Nel, judging by the paucity of such items in her archives. But a small item on natural gas from 1976 is historically interesting as it features both Ruud Lubbers and Wim Duisenberg, as economy and finance ministers respectively. Lubbers was to be prime minister from 1982 to 1994 and later the UN High Commissioner for Refugees. Duisenberg later became president of the Dutch central bank and subsequently, the first European Central Bank president.:

"The Dutch government said Tuesday it plans to renegotiate export prices for natural gas supplies before the end of this year.

"Economics Minister Rudolf Lubbers and Finance Minister Willem Duisenberg said in parliament that export prices had not kept pace with steeply rising domestic prices.

"The ministers said contracts with most countries contained a re-negotiation clause.

"Countries to which Holland supplies natural gas -- its biggest export commodity -- include Belgium, West Germany, France and Italy.

"Lubbers and Duisenberg made their remarks in reply to questions from labor legislators who wanted to know why domestic prices were considerably higher than those for export."

An item on 6 September on a 1976 KLM hijacking reports:

"KLM said all 79 passengers and five crew of the hijacked KLM Dutch Airlines DC-9 released by three Palestinian terrorists Sunday arrived safely in Amsterdam on Monday. The plane was hijacked late Saturday when it left Nice, France after stopping there on a scheduled flight from Malaga in Spain to Amsterdam. The hostages were released after the three terrorists were given safe conduct by the Cyprus authorities. Earlier the Palestinians threatened to blow up the plane in mid-air unless Israel released eight jailed guerrillas. The Tel Aviv government refused."

In a followup the next day, the captain, Piet Janssen, told reporters that one of the hijackers came into the cockpit and said, 'you remember me, three years ago?' But he did not remember this repeat hijacker because Janssen was not on the plane hijacked in 1973. That hijacking ended when three Palestinians released 264 hostages in Abu Dhabi in the Persian Gulf after 68 hours of captivity. The three Palestinians in the later episode were also promised safe conduct out of the country. Captain Janssen told a news conference they had enough explosives to blow a big ship clean out of the ocean. The Palestinians joined the DC-9 Saturday evening at Malaga, in southern Spain, and carried the explosives on board. There was apparently no security check at Malaga. They seized the aircraft shortly after it had stopped at Nice, France, on its way to

Amsterdam. Dramatically, it then landed in Tunis with enough fuel for only another 14 minutes flying. The airport horrified the pilot by refusing landing permission, turning off its approach lights and placing obstacles along the runway to prevent the aircraft landing. Captain Janssen was furious:

> "I think it's a disgusting scandal that the authorities there bluntly refused to allow us to land. We were an aircraft in an emergency situation. We didn't have enough fuel to go anywhere else."

Fortunately, they were able to touch down safely because the airport had forgotten to switch its automatic landing system off. The landing gear was slightly damaged when it hit some oil drums on the runway.

The Japanese hijacking of the French Embassy is well documented, and provided another scoop for Nel. According to the AP's obituary on Nel written by Anthony Deutsch in December 2001,

> "Slis actually witnessed the takeover by Japanese Red Army terrorists of the embassy. After scrambling to the rooftop of a nearby bookstore, she lay crouched in the shadows as they emerged with heavy weapons. She later told the story in an eyewitness report."

Nel's dramatic reporting received wide international coverage.

v. Joop den Uyl: A Knighthood for Nel

Returning to Nel's abiding interest in politics and premiers, she wrote solid pieces on the socialist government which took office in May 1973 and its premier, Joop den Uyl, as well as on the granting of independence to Surinam under Den Uyl's premiership, marking the end of the Dutch colonial period.

The first piece on Den Uyl looks at the incoming government's income-levelling plans for taxation and what people thought of them at the time. For this piece Nel hijacked her friend and advisor Piet Wackie Eysten to give a coolly negative assessment of the plans, arguing that low-wage earners already had numerous advantages over higher earners. After this, Nel's piece weaves its way neatly back and forth between pro and contra income-levelling arguments

This is followed by a short undated interview with Den Uyl, in which he talks about Europe, a subject close to Nel's heart. She also takes a broader look at Den Uyl's foreign policy stance in a May 1975 piece. Den Uyl, one feels, enjoyed being interviewed by Nel, and the pieces are historically significant. Den Uyl was a backer of European integration, but wanted democratisation via a strong European parliamentary system; he also wanted to bring the Scandinavian countries into the EU.

In the same interview, Den Uyl, who was about to be the first West European leader to visit US President Ford after the fall of Saigon and the ending of the Vietnam war, took a fairly hard line vis-a-vis the US, expressing his preference for a strong Europe, independent of the US Privately, Nel probably found some, if not all, of his views attractive.

On decolonisation, Den Uyl could be said to have 'put his money where his mouth was', with Surinam becoming independent at the end of 1975 under his premiership. The last piece I found from Den Uyl's period as premier was written by Nel about Surinam just ahead of its independence. Considering that most of its miniscule population wound up in the Netherlands, it is startling to read that Surinam is four times the size of Holland, and that 80 percent of it was then unexplored jungle.

While he was prime minister, Den Uyl personally recommended Nel to receive the insignia of the Orange Order, symbol of knighthood. To be nominated by the Prime Minister was an honour in itself, as most journalists who were nominated were chosen by the ministry of culture. As a result, Nel's name appeared at the top of the list of decorations in the official Gazette. Piet Wackie Eysten recorded that Nel received letters, telegrams and telexes of congratulations literally from the entire world. Fred Cheval in Brussels found the honour all the greater, coming from 'those you have been *after* all these years' and Wes Gallagher told her it was 'a great recognition of your many talents'. A former ambassador, Van Royen, referred to the time of the Indonesian Round Table conference and the fact that he had never had to hesitate in trusting Nel.

Den Uyl also presented the decoration to Nel himself. A later 80th birthday interview with Nel recorded that Den Uyl stuck at least three safety-pins in her chest trying to put it on. Former government information service Gijs van der Wiel told Nel's interviewer:

> "In my entire career, she is the only journalist who was awarded the decoration by the prime minister himself."

The AP obituary of Nel quoted Den Uyl as remarking:

> "She is certainly difficult but I still love her a little."

vi. Dries van Agt: Enemy and bête noir

On March 22, 1977, Den Uyl's government resigned in a dispute over land reform. Following the May 25 general election, it took 205 days to form a new government, a record even by Dutch standards. As a result of

Den Uyl's failure to form a new administration, a centre-right coalition took over with Christian Democrat Dries van Agt as premier even though the socialists emerged as the largest party. Nel's report appeared in the International Herald Tribune of December 19, 1977. The change of administration heralded a watershed moment in Dutch political history. Noting that "Dutch Liberals are really conservatives and politically right-wing," Nel's piece continued:

> "Together with the small leftist Democrats '66 (D66) party, the Socialists and Christian Democrats bargained for months before agreeing on government policy and then talks broke down on the allocation of posts. The Dutch were surprised by Den Uyl's failure to put together a new administration. The 58-year-old socialist leader is regarded as a shrewd politician but many Dutchmen believe he may have overplayed his hand on the ministerial issue... He wanted to lead what he called a 'progressive' administration."

Nel also noted that a coalition between those three parties would have held 110 of the 150 seats in parliament compared with the bare majority of 77 for Van Agt's coalition. Her piece warned that Van Agt might run into problems as a result, which was to be confirmed by events.

For a newcomer to the Netherlands arriving as I did in late 1979 in the middle of Van Agt's first term of office, politics over the next few years appeared to be entirely dominated by the question of stationing American Cruise missiles in the Netherlands, vehemently opposed by the Socialists.

The Socialists did indeed provide a tough opposition, and though the Cruise missiles did eventually arrive and Van Agt and his precarious coalition served one full term, his second administration did not go to term. Nor, incidentally, did Van Agt's administration succeed in its aim of curbing government expenditure. Finally, there are a couple more details in Nel's piece on the views of Van Agt, a law professor:

> "A Roman Catholic, Van Agt firmly opposed moves by the Socialists to liberalize abortion which is in conflict with his personal beliefs. Abortion was also one of the major stumbling blocks during talks with the Socialists on a new administration."

Nel heartily disliked Van Agt and the feeling was entirely mutual; he was certainly one of the enemies she made. Van Agt once said tartly to her at a press conference: "Ach, Miss Slis, you always know better." "Yes," was Nel's curt reply.

Tyna Wynaerdts remarked that there were quite a few people who were scared of Nel.

> "Because she had a way of getting news of out of them that they didn't really want to give. She was so insistent. But there were quite a few politicians who really loved her and she could phone them in the middle of the night and they would answer her. Like Lubbers. And she could be discreet if she was asked to be. They knew that if they said something off the record, she wouldn't use it. They trusted her completely".

I also found a prescient 1978 draft interview with Wim Kok while he was president of the Dutch FNV trade union federation. Kok later became leader of the Labour Party (PvdA) and succeeded Lubbers as premier. Nel was clearly impressed by the handsome young rising star:

> Wim Kok as FNV chief

> "President of the Dutch trade unions, Wim Kok (39), has been invited to make his first trip to the United States April 11 to May 4 and is anxious to persuade American labour leaders to return to the International Confederation of Free Trade Unions (ICFTU) and to carry their weight to bring the United States back into the International Labor Organisation (ILO).

> "Kok, who is young, smart and intelligent, feels that all conditions for America's return to the ILO can be fulfilled.

> "America's conditions are that the ILO should do more for the underdeveloped countries, should be more critical of Eastern European labour leaders and does not accept the Italian Socialist-Communist labour union 'Confederazio ne Generale Italiana di Lavoro' (CGIL) into the ICFTU.

> "A few weeks ago, the CGIL severed relations with the communist World Federation of Trade Unions (WFTU), giving up its observers status with the organisation, " Kok said in an interview.

> "'George Meany, president of the AFL-CIO, claims inclusion of the CGIL into the ICFTU dangerous', Kok said, 'but the fact that they broke off relations with the communist organisation is a positive step towards democratising unions in Europe.'

"Kok, described as 'a very reasonable man' by both employers and most workers, said following recent contacts with Hungarian, Romanian and Yugoslav labour leaders he feels that European unions can learn from them and their mistakes as well as vice-versa.

"Dutch government officials hold Kok in considerable esteem 'because his merits are mainly that he can rally together the radical as well as moderate elements of the unions and has constantly stressed the importance of wage moderation,' a social affairs ministry spokesman said.

"Kok, tall and handsome with dark wavy hair, looking more like a young diplomat than a workers leader, is the son of a carpenter. He graduated in economics and is the youngest trade union leader ever in this country.

"It was also Kok who gave the last push to fusing the protestant, Roman Catholic and Socialist unions into the largest federation of Netherlands trade unions (FNV)"

In 1982, new Christian Democratic (CDA) leader Ruud Lubbers took over as premier. Although Nel was a huge fan of Ruud Lubbers, her archives did not produce any stories about him while she was still at the AP but he does feature in one reproduced in Chapter 12

Lubbers enjoyed great personal popularity as premier but with his departure in 1994, his Christian Democratic (CDA) party was to stumble badly and find itself out of office for the first time since the war. The CDA remained out of office until the end of Kok's second administration just before the general election in 2002. Kok's personal popularity as premier if anything exceeded Lubbers', even as his Labour party continued to lose ground during the 1990s. But his term ended badly in 2002 as a damning report on the role of Dutch UN troops in the massacre of Muslims in Srebrenica five years earlier caused him and his cabinet to resign just ahead of the scheduled general election. This was followed by the murder of outspoken populist politician Pim Fortuyn by an animal rights activists. In turn, this became another factor leading to a crushing defeat for the PvdA and the revival of the fortunes of the CDA as many accused Labour party leader Ad Melkert of inciting hatred towards the controversial Fortuyn.

Nel would have relished covering 2002, an eventful year in Dutch politics. It was also the year of Crown Prince Willem-Alexander's marriage and of the death of his father, her old friend Prince Claus.

10.
The Lockheed Affair (1976)

The Prince and the Aircraft-maker - The Big Fudge

The big story during Nel's final stint with the AP was also among the biggest in her entire career. The Lockheed scandal involved Queen Juliana's husband Prince Bernhard and occurred during Den Uyl's premiership. In February 1976, a US Senate subcommittee on multinational corporations revealed that bribes to promote Lockheed aircraft sales in the Netherlands were said to have been paid to an unidentified high-ranking Dutch official. The official was subsequently inferred to be Prince Bernhard. A Commission of three distinguished Dutchmen was set up to investigate the allegations that one million dollars was paid to the 'official' in 1960-62 and a further 100,000 dollars in 1972.

Voluminous quantities of AP copy in Nel's archives take up the story from the completion of the commission's report in August. Although the huge output was a team effort, it is easy to imagine Nel herself engaged with the story virtually round the clock for weeks on end. She was by then approaching her 63rd birthday.

i .Curtain-Raiser

Nel's bulky AP archive started on 17 August when the news emerged that the independent Commission had delivered its report and it was being studied by the cabinet. Den Uyl planned to report to parliament about two weeks later. Ahead of this, Dutch press reports claimed variously that Bernard had not been cleared or that there was no evidence that he took the money but he must have known some of his associates accepted Lockheed payouts.

A Slis report for the AP six days later said:

> "Queen Juliana arrived home Monday to take a hand in the political situation produced by the involvement of her husband Prince Bernhard in the Lockheed payments row.
>
> It was the second time in less than a week that the queen had interrupted her vacation on the Italian Riviera for talks with the Dutch government. She was expected to consult with Premier Joop den Uyl on Tuesday.
>
> Prince Bernhard accompanied the queen to the Netherlands.
>
> Since the queen's earlier visit, the entire Dutch cabinet has received copies of the report of an independent commission (the Donner Report), which for six months probed Bernhard's connection with the Lockheed affair. However, the commission's findings are still unpublished and the government has been careful to avoid any statement imputing blame to the 65-year-old prince.
>
> One highly placed source said it now seems clear that there will be no proof that Bernhard accepted Lockheed funds but there are indications his business dealings have created a delicate political situation for the monarchy.
>
> The same source indicated however any indirect embarrassment to the queen was unlikely to lead to an enforced abdication, as no Dutch cabinet minister would support so drastic a step.
>
> Another government source said nothing in the Dutch constitution says the queen would have to go even if the commission's 70-page report fails to absolve the prince.
>
> Bernhard is Inspector General of the Dutch armed forces and a member of two government

> advisory bodies - the defense council and a
> cabinet committee which helps prepare the Dutch
> budget.
>
> His affairs have been under investigation since
> testimony before a U.S. Senate sub-committee
> last February revealed that bribes totaling 1.1
> million dollars were paid out by Lockheed to an
> unidentified Dutch official to influence
> aircraft sales. The prince has denied receiving
> such funds.
>
> In political circles here, there was growing
> belief that the prince may decide to give up
> some of his official functions in the near
> future. However, an official said this could
> result from his having reached the normal
> retirement age of 65 rather than as a result of
> the commission inquiry.

The queen went back to Italy the next day after talks with Den Uyl. As head of state, the queen had an important voice in the final formulation of the government's conclusions about the report findings, Slis noted. On Wednesday 25 August, the government said it would report to parliament the next day. The royal couple were to fly home yet again on that same day. They did a lot of commuting to and from Holland during this period.

ii. Den Uyl Reports, Bernhard Resigns

The next morning, an unattributed report in the Dutch daily De Telegraaf said Prince Bernhard would resign as Inspector General of the Dutch armed forces. When Den Uyl reported to parliament later in the day, this turned out to be true. From 19.25 to 05.30, a vast flood of AP news reports and text excerpts from the inquiry report flowed out, scarcely pausing for breath next morning before launching into commentary. The AP continued to pour out reports well into September. The lead paragraph in the first Slis report on August 26 trumpeted:

> "Prince Bernhard was accused Thursday of damaging the
> Dutch national interest in the Lockheed affair and was
> swept out of his various defence posts including his job
> as Inspector General of the Dutch armed forces."

Among wide coverage of the story in international newspapers the next day, here is the front-page lead in the Salt Lake Tribune:

Dutch Prince Resigns Posts Over Lockheed Affair

By Nel Slis

Associated Press Writer

THE HAGUE, Netherlands - An inquiry commission accused Prince Bernhard on Thursday of damaging Dutch national interest by improper dealings with the Lockheed Aircraft Corp., and he resigned his public functions.

Premier Joop den Uyl told a tense and sombre parliament the government has asked queen Juliana's 65-year-old husband to resign all posts where a conflict of interest might arise, including his duties as inspector general of the Dutch armed forces.

The Socialist premier said a three-member independent commission reported there was no conclusive evidence to prove the allegation that the prince received $1.1 million from Lockheed to promote the sales of its aircraft in the Netherlands and there was no evidence the prince had influenced official procurement policy.

But the inquiry had concluded he "entered much too frivolously into transactions which were bound to create the impression he was susceptible to favours," den Uyl said.

"Later, he showed himself open to dishonourable requests and offers.

"Finally, he allowed himself to be tempted to take initiatives which were completely unacceptable and which were bound to place himself and the Netherlands procurement policy in the eyes of Lockheed - and it must now be added also in the eyes of others - in a dubious light."

Den Uyl's statement, broadcast to a nation that holds the royal family in high esteem, said the prince would also get out of business life.

Official spokesmen said there was no constitutional crisis affecting the queen's position. They said none of the five parties in den Uyl's left-center government want the queen to step down as a result of the Commission's finding and the government's decision to force Bernhard to resign his public posts.

There had been speculation in the Dutch press that the 67-year-old queen, an immensely wealthy woman who has an unpretentious style, might abdicate...

Considerable background on the prince was given in AP wire reports:

> The prince has been a key figure in the Dutch armed services since World War II. He returned to the Netherlands from exile in London with the liberating allied forces and subsequently occupied advisory posts with the navy and from 1953 with the air force before becoming inspector general for the combined services in 1970. The post entails informing and advising the defence minister.
>
> In a personal statement read to parliament by the premier, the prince announced his resignation from his various defence assignments and said contacts of many years standing with old Lockheed friends had developed along "the wrong lines."
>
> "In particular, I have not observed the caution in these that is required by reason of my vulnerable position as consort of the queen and as prince of the Netherlands," he declared...
>
> The premier told parliament that the country's readiness to act "in a sense of solidarity" would strengthen the queen in continuing the performance of her state duties.
>
> The (commission) report did not provide conclusive evidence that the prince ever took possession of the 1.1 million dollars in Lockheed funds.
>
> The commission said however it could not be excluded that money reached the prince or his nominees without being recorded in the royal bookkeeping.
>
> The report said there had been increasingly friendly contacts between the prince and Lockheed's former head Robert Gross in the 1950s.
>
> In 1959-60, Lockheed officials considered making a gift of a Jetstar to the prince for his personal use. However, because of difficulties in registering the title, Fred Meuser, the company's Dutch-born former Swiss representative, suggested a one million dollar gift instead.
>
> (Meuser turned out later to be an old friend of the prince).
>
> The report recorded testimony by former Lockheed vice-chairman A.F.C. Kotchian to the

U.S. Securities and Exchange Commission and the US Senate subcommittee on multilateral corporations. It quoted Kotchian as saying the payments were made abroad using Swiss lawyer Hubert Weisbrod as an intermediary. Weisbrod had been appointed for the purpose by Meuser.

Kotchian was further quoted as saying the payments took place as follows: 300,000 dollars in 1960, a further 300,000 dollars in 1961 and 400,000 dollars in 1962. They were authorised successively by Robert Gross in 1960 and other officials in the later years.

In a letter to the Dutch commission, Prince Bernhard told the investigators he neither received the money nor had it directly or indirectly at his disposal.

The prince said however that about 100,000 dollars went to "a few mutual acquaintances" who need financial support for social reasons, the report declared.

In tracing the transfer procedure from Lockheed to bank accounts in Europe, the commission encountered the name of a former Polish army officer, Col. Pantchoulidzew, who was a personal friend of Bernhard's late mother Princess Armgard. The commission said it concluded Pantchoulidzew was to tell Weisbrod to which accounts the money should be transferred.

Under the circumstances, the report said, Lockheed had a valid reason to assume the money intended for the prince had in fact reached him.

The AP records later:

"In 20 crowded minutes, Den Uyl signalled the end of Bernhard's long career as one of Holland's leading men of affairs," leaving the Dutch to take stock of the shattered image of their merchant prince."

Den Uyl's speech was broadcast live on television and radio. MPs 'listened somberly' and then went off to read the 240-page commission report. The numerous business activities from which the prince was also to withdraw included seats on the boards of the national airline KLM, the Dutch-German VFW-Fokker Aircraft and Hoogovens steel group. The AP also noted he lent his patronage to more than 300 organisations.

iii. More Dirt from Donner

The Commission said it could not state with certainty the destination of nine-tenths of this famous one million dollar sum. It did establish that in 1967-68, Lockheed management had approached the prince on several occasions for information and intervention in the possible procurement by the Dutch of the P-3 Orion naval aircraft. The prince was offered 500,000 dollars if he used his influence on their behalf. Although he refused, this was only based on the impracticality of the request and not on principle. His friendly relationship with Lockheed continued.

In or around 1968, Lockheed established an off-the-books account for a sum of 400,000 dollars, administered by the Paris law firm Coudert-Freres. From this sum, a 100,000 dollar payment was made to a Swiss bank in the name of Victor Baarn. Baarn is the name of a Dutch village close to the Royal palace at Soest, The commission said Bernhard explicitly denied receiving the money and it found no evidence to the contrary. Nor was the commission able to identify the person using the 'apparently fictional name' of Victor Baarn.

Another damning revelation by the Commission was a hand-written letter in September 1974, in which Bernhard returned to the subject of the P-3 Orion and asked for a commission on the sales if the Dutch decided to buy the aircraft. This would have been worth about one million dollars. The prince told the commission he wanted the money for the World Wildlife Fund, of which he was the long-time head. But the commission commented sourly that, 'the end did not justify the means'. The report continued with a further genteel rapping of Bernhard's knuckles:

> "The concealed threat contained in the second letter written by HRH and the reference to the many efforts he had made to get the right decisions based on political considerations, form a whole which must be described as extremely questionable."

The commission also pointed out that with a company like Lockheed, which is permanently in the market for the sale of its aircraft, it was absolutely essential to avoid even the appearance of being open to influence.

> "Through his conduct, the prince achieved exactly the opposite and this must be regarded as extremely imprudent and unwise,"

the commission remarked, rather mildly in the circumstances.

Giving more background, it said that over the 10 years or so prior to 1960, there had been regular and increasingly friendly contacts between HRH and Lockheed Chief Executive Robert Gross. In the same period, Lockheed had done good business in both civil and military aircraft in the Netherlands, including the sale of the F-104 Starfighter. This explained why the idea of giving Bernhard an expensive jet was attractive to Lockheed as a gesture of thanks from Gross to a 'good friend'. It would also be a means of cementing its close relationship with the Netherlands for the future, plus it would be good propaganda for its products. When this proved impractical, the report concludes, the idea of a gift of one million dollars instead of an aircraft,

> "carries conviction only in the context of Lockheed's relationship to the prince and the importance which the company attached to it."

Although the Commission found no evidence that the offer of gifts had influenced the prince's judgement, nonetheless it stressed the fact that Lockheed felt able to make these 'improper requests' and offers, which were not unequivocally refused. In any case, the prince himself had approached Lockheed with equally improper requests for commission.

In the event, the Orion project fell through. The proposal to purchase new naval aircraft was scrapped from the Dutch defence budget on economic grounds.

Perhaps most mind-boggling was the Commission's statement that although it found no conclusive evidence that the prince ever took possession of the 1.1 million dollars, it could not exclude the possibility that the money reached Bernhard or his nominees without being recorded in the prince's books. In effect, it appeared to be saying that we can't prove you have the money but we can't prove you don't. Today, the whole thing looks like an almighty fudge.

iv. Reactions and repercussions

When the Donner report went on sale to the public the next day at 15 guilders (5.60 dollars), the state publishing house told the AP that the first two impressions of 5,000 and 10,000 copies were sold out within hours and it was printing a third impression of at least 10,000.

Dutch newspapers were quick to condemn Prince Bernhard for his dealings with Lockheed. The leftist Volkskrant, for example, found the Donner Commission's report

> "extremely painful reading and Prince Bernhard's statement in which he admits making 'mistakes' no less

so. The display and admission of actions which are contrary to the views and values of the Netherlands is in itself depressing. And when it concerns the husband of the head of state, it is a traumatic experience for a large part of the population."

Agreeing that the prince had damaged the interests of the state, it goes on:

"But there is more. The prince has moved in a corrupt atmosphere that is to be abhorred and which has injured the feelings of very many people towards the royal family."

Premier Den Uyl commented that the government had allowed the prince a great deal of freedom of movement in the exercise of his functions, based on the confidence that members of the royal house were aware how interwoven their private lives were with the national interest. If the national interest could be damaged by contacts or activities, there was a duty to consult with responsible ministers. It was unacceptable that the prince should have failed to report on his relations with Lockheed.

Den Uyl said the government recognised the exceptional services the prince had rendered to the country and endorsed the inquiry's view that his performance had been 'fruitful and admirable' in many fields. But, he added, the government

"deplores all the more that Prince Bernhard has become involved in relationships and situations which are unacceptable."

An opinion poll showed a surprising 71 percent saying that their feelings about Prince Bernhard were unchanged and 28 percent, that their feelings were changed by the scandal, while 61 percent agreed that the prince should no longer carry out official functions. Ninety percent said the monarchy should stay.

From the other side of the pond, Lockheed director Robert Haack said in an interview screened by Dutch television on Monday 30 August that the Dutch commission of inquiry had carried out a painful assignment with integrity. He added:

"I'm sure the whole aftermath of the report is as unhappy for them as it is for us. I hope both the people of the Netherlands and Lockheed can put this phase of history behind them."

That Monday was another hectic reporting day as the parliamentary debate took place. Nel's wrap was running on the wire in the small hours of the next morning.

Bernhard

By Nel Slis

Associated Press Writer

The Hague (AP) -- The Dutch government is now committed to a searching review of its future relationship with the royal house and the freedom of royal figures to fulfil their public roles as they please.

Premier Joop den Uyl told parliament Monday his cabinet will submit a bill which will define who in the royal household will fall under the doctrine of ministerial responsibility. In Dutch terms, ministerial responsibility for royal actions implies supervision, on grounds that responsibility cannot otherwise be exercised.

Den Uyl spoke as parliament overwhelmingly approved his government's handling of the Dutch connection in the Lockheed bribery scandal, which led last week to Prince Bernhard's resignation from all his defence and business posts.

The Socialist premier said his government intends to establish which royal figures will in future "particularly have to take into account the interests of the state."

Bernhard operated throughout his long career with very little reference to the government. This was possible since the constitution fails to spell out ministerial responsibility in precise terms for any other royal figure except Queen Juliana. The government now feels the activities of the freewheeling prince have produced a situation in which the supervision of royalty's public role must be closely reviewed...

In spite of the gravity (of the charges against Bernhard), the government is not expected to seek ministerial responsibility for the whole royal household. The queen and Bernhard have four daughters and eleven grandchildren. According to informed sources, the acceptance of ministerial responsibility for all of them would be a costly affair. These sources said inclusion under the doctrine -- as proposed by the last government of Barend Biesheuvel -- gave the right to live in state-owned and state-financed palaces and provided tax exemptions as well as government funding of most staff costs. The proposals never became law.

Parliament Monday also endorsed the government's decision not to proceed with any criminal investigation into Bernhard's activities.

The prince is still the consort of the queen and the government has said that a prosecution would have 'serious consequences' for the position of the head of state.

Den Uyl also said the government would not object to the prince sitting in the Council of State -- an honorary right that Bernhard has exercised only rarely. The Council of State advises the queen but has no executive powers. Members of the royal household may attend sessions but are not permitted to vote.

The government still has to decide, qualified informants said, on numerous other matters in the protocol area where the prince would normally accompany the queen in the performance of her state duties.

Primarily, the Dutch appeared concerned to keep the monarchy in one piece, while reviewing the safeguards open to the government.

"The prince has brought the royal house into a delicate position," Frans Andriessen, spokesman of the influential Catholic People's Party, told parliament. "A repetition might be fatal. The knowledge of this must weigh very heavily on the prince."

v. 'We just had a cup of coffee...'

There was also a fuss about two Dutch MPs being approached by Lockheed in 1974 to win support for the Orion. This rumbled on for a while, but eventually fizzled out as there was no sign of improper activity. The two, Joop van Elsen of the Catholic People's Party and Adrianus Ploeg of the Conservative (VVD) party, visited the Lockheed and Fairchild plants when they were in the US in 1974 for a NATO meeting.

Ploeg told De Telegraaf rather plaintively: "We just had a cup of coffee or orange juice with them."

Yet another revelation followed on 2 September, when it emerged from letters that Prince Bernhard discussed the purchase of planes produced by Northrop Aircraft Corp with West German Chancellor and former defence minister Helmut Schmidt. The letters were released by the Ministry of Information at the request of two socialist members of parliament. They involved an exchange between Schmidt and a former Dutch defence minister, Willem den Toom, about efforts by Northrop to promote its F-17 Cobra combat aircraft as a replacement for the Lockheed F-1046 Starfighter. An article in the New York Times said it was widely assumed in The Hague that Prince Bernhard's links to Northrop, which was Lockheed's rival in Europe, would be involved in the next step of any investigation into the Prince's dealings. Several major Dutch newspapers had teams working on the Prince's ties to Northrop. Its former chairman was apparently one of Prince Bernhard's closest friends. However, nothing more emerged on this subject. It would certainly have added an extra frisson if Bernhard had turned out to have been conducting a private 'Dutch auction' between the two US aircraft-makers for his commissions.

Among other repercussions, Nel reported on 7 September that a plan for Queen Juliana and Prince Bernhard to visit the US in bicentennial year was being quietly dropped, citing well-informed sources. It's not hard to guess that the sources includedNel's old friend at the Prime Minister's Office, known in the Netherlands as the General Affairs Ministry.

Another report was written by Nel on 8 September ahead of Bernhard's official resignation from his various posts the next day. The official resignation had taken some time to arrange as it required a royal decree. The report gives more background on the prince, focusing on his pet Bildeberg conferences. Predating the Davos World Economic Forum, these were a kind of private version of Davos founded by Bernhard in 1954. Bernhard was also a patron of Davos.

Bernhard

By Nel Slis

Associated Press Writer

The Hague (AP) -- Prince Bernhard will step down from leadership of the annual Bilderberg conference and is also expected to give up his presidency of the World Wildlife Fund (as a result of the Donner Report), well-informed sources said Wednesday...

Next year's Bilderberg meeting scheduled for April 22-24 in Torquay, England will probably be chaired by an ad-hoc British President, the sources said. The Bilderberg secretariat in The Hague declined comment.

The 65-year old prince cancelled this year's conference scheduled for April at Hot Springs, Va...

Bernhard launched the secret Bilderberg meetings in 1954, explaining that top government and business officials from North America and Western Europe should have a chance to talk with total frankness behind closed doors. The meetings are named after the hotel in the east of the Netherlands where the first conference was held.

Invitations are issued by Bernhard and the list of former participants is formidable -- Gerald R. Ford attended two Bilderberg parlays before becoming U.S. president. Other participants have included Henry A. Kissenger, now US secretary of state, British politician Edward Heath, the ex-prime minister and Helmut Schmidt, now West German chancellor.

The Bilderberg steering committee is due to meet in October in London or Brussels but not at Soestdijk Palace as hitherto, the source said. Several prominent participants have shown interest in continuing the Bilderberg concept, they added.

Bernhard used his wide circle of wartime contacts to get the Bilderberg meetings rolling. He has consistently asserted his only aim is to foster transatlantic relationships and improve mutual understanding.

He has been president of the World Wildlife Fund since 1961. The organisation has its international secretariat in Geneva, Switzerland, and aims at preserving animals threatened with extinction.

Bernhard has travelled to many parts of the world for the wildlife movement to support fundraising dinners and auctions. He also set up its 'Panda Club', an elite of 1,001 top people who each pay 10,000 dollars into the fund for membership.

Meanwhile, a spokesman for the Dutch-based Erasmus Foundation said the prince cancelled his engagement to present the organisation's

1976 awards. Instead, Crown Princess Beatrix will officiate at the September 17 ceremony in Leiden.

The Erasmus Foundation, named after the 16th century Dutch humanist, makes an annual award to persons or institutions contributing to European culture or science. Two awards are being made this year, to Amnesty International and French Professor Rene David.The two posts together (Bilderberg and the World Wildlife Fund) have always been regarded as the major private interests of the prince, who has already announced his resignation from all his official defence and business functions.

However, the Bilderberg movement was one channel through which Bernhard might have hoped to exercise some lingering influence...

The prince has known or been on terms of warm friendship with every American president since Franklin D. Fooseevelt. He had a distinguished World War II record and later bustled around the world in search of big industrial orders to help Holland's postwar reconstruction.

Strictly at Bernhard's invitation, the statesmen and big industrialists came flocking to the annual Bilderberg meetings...(as well as the leading politicians mentioned above, they were attended by) a host of other political and business luminaries including such figures as Giovanni Agnelli of Fiat and David Rockefeller of the Chase Manhattan Bank....

The prince also met the prominent and the wealthy in his work for the World Wildlife Fund.

vi. Vox Pop and Parliament

A poll conducted for Elseviers magazine in mid-September showed that after a little time to ponder the affair, 62 percent of Dutch citizens believed the official inquiry failed to reveal fully the facts on Prince Bernhard's involvement in the Lockheed bribes scandal. Only 27 percent thought everything had been revealed. Two percent said the investigation failed completely to uncover the facts. Fifty-one percent said it was right that Bernhard quit public office. But there was still an astonishing 41 percent who thought he should have stayed on. Despite his disgrace, the poll showed the Dutch firmly backing the monarchy, with 87 percent in favour of keeping it, only 6 percent wanting a republic and 7 percent uncommitted. It also showed 76 percent wanted Queen Juliana to stay on the throne, though 19 percent thought she should abdicate shortly in favour of Crown Princess Beatrix and 5 percent were uncommitted.

The AP report on the poll added some rather more negative 'vox pop' commentary.

> "Since the report was published, I've been looking twice at pictures hanging in public buildings of Bernhard and the queen," declared Jos Lenteren, a 28-year-old bank clerk from Amsterdam. "If he's been in this deep with Lockheed, it makes you wonder what else he's been up to…"

Willem Burg, a 22-year-old student from Alkmaar, asserted: "It's the worst example since Watergate of what so-called top people can get away with. He should have been prosecuted."

> "It brought me to tears," declared Wilhelmina Smits, 82, a widow from Arnhem. "I've been through two world wars with this royal family but I've never experienced anything like this. It's terrible, just terrible."

> "What bugs me," said Johan van de Heuvel, a 47-year-old engineer from The Hague, "is that Lockheed should even think of the idea of bribing a member of our royal family."

The comparison with Watergate is interesting as this US scandal had happened quite recently, in 1972-74 and was evidently still on people's minds.

One other AP piece, on the government's legislative moves following the scandal, had some interesting insights about the royal family. Apparently, legislation aimed at more control over and supervision of the Dutch royal household stranded on differences of opinion between Queen Juliana and the government on the definition of a member of the royal household. This part of the piece reports:

```
The  queen,  they  said,  is  loath  to  have
differences  established  between  any  of  her
offspring, children and grandchildren alike.
```

```
The government  for both  reasons of  cash  and
responsibility wished  to  limit  the  number  of
members of the  royal household to the Queen and
Prince Bernhard  and Princess Beatrix and Prince
Claus.
```

```
"In  the  period  from  1937  to  19..,  there  was
only one person  defined  in  the  constitution  as
```

an 'inviolable' member of the royal household and that was Queen Wilhelmina. The other princess, Juliana, was the 'non-inviolable' member. Moreover it was a period in which one hardly thought of problems involving government responsibility.

Since then the royal household has steadily grown despite the fact that Princess Irene resigned all royal prerogatives after marrying Roman Catholic Prince Hugo Carlos of Bourbon and Princess Christina did likewise after marrying Cuban born Jorge Guillermo.

The Queen also has another daughter, Princess Margriet, who married Pieter van Vollenhoven and they have four children.

Princess Beatrix has three boys. The question is that the government feels reluctant to undertake responsibility for all of these, but the Queen so far has insisted on this...

If they are, the government is responsible for their public speeches and activities if they undertake functions officially.

It is also a matter of cash, as the four members of the royal household live in government-owned and kept palaces and receive tax-free salaries and a number of less significant prerogatives.

One example of supervision is that when Beatrix and Claus visited Israel earlier this year, they went beyond their official programme and at some point crossed into formerly Arab, Israeli-occupied territory not foreseen by Dutch government planners for political reasons...

Stricter control of activities of members of the royal household will mean, among other things, that they must submit texts of public speeches and inform their government of their whereabouts as well as asking permission for the use of government transportation. Meanwhile, some members of parliament, in particular the PPR's Bastiaan de Gaay Fortman, have urged the government to supervise the secretariats and members of personnel of the members of the royal household.

Authoritative sources said that, often, Dutch royalty is too much surrounded by yes-men. People with their own opinion usually do not stay long.

> These same sources feel that the example of the
> British royalty should be followed by
> appointing independent, worldly-wise advisors
> with a solid legal background."

Still, those worldly-wise British advisors didn't seem to be much help when it came to Queen Elizabeth's offspring, especially in the case of Prince Charles' very public breakup with Princess Diana, not to speak of all the other divorces littering the family from the queen's own sister Margaret onward. Then there was Princess Anne, Andrew and Fergie… it was hard to keep track of all those royal divorcees. It's true there were no political scandals like Lockheed, but luckily for the world's gutter press and gossip magazines, there were plenty of personal ones.

The report quoted above was not attributed to Nel, but it seems certain she contributed to it, with her vast experience of the Dutch royals.

vii. Friso's Scoop

Returning to the Lockheed scandal, Nel's fellow-journalist Friso Endt told me the story of how he got a scoop from Prince Bernhard himself, though as a result he unsurprisingly lost Bernhard as a willing contact. When Time Life rolled up all its non-American foreign correspondents in 1973, Endt had started working for Newsweek. In this period, Endt maintained close contacts with the royal household.

> "I had a good relationship with Bernard, dating from my
> publications on the Hofmand affair, when for instance I
> did a story for Fortune. This helped Bernard, as it helped
> to curtail Hofmans' role. He was grateful and said, call
> me any time. When I had important news, I would call
> him, three or four times a year, at Soesdijk Palace for his
> viewpoint."

Friso went on:

> "When the story about his involvement with Lockheed
> was in the Wall Street Journal, his secretary told me, 'I
> know it's not true'. But I wanted to hear it from
> Bernhard. The Government Information Service was not
> talking either. There was a bulletin on Reuters and the
> AP from the Senate committee saying that the President
> of Lockheed paid money to a 'Dutch government
> official'. Bernhard was a patron of Davos so I went there
> to Bernhard's hotel, where he was having dinner with
> Wagner, the head of Shell. He came out and I told him
> that we were called by the palace and told they know it's

not true but I have to hear it from the prince himself. Your Royal Highness, can you say it's not true? 'Friso', he said, 'I cannot say that it is not true'. Bernhard was as poor as hell, he didn't have a penny... I immediately phoned NRC Handelsblad but they did not dare to publish it. Newsweek did dare. I never spoke again with the prince after that."

Friso here provides a clue about why Bernhard may have got involved in the bribery business. After all, he was married to one of the richest women in the world, so it must have been a little galling for him to be strapped for cash on his own account.

The Lockheed affair was also to have serious consequences for Beatrix's depressive husband Prince Claus. Because Bernhard had to resign all his public functions, Claus was never able to take up any significant function. A serious and intelligent career diplomat, many people believe this contributed to his growing depression. Nel got along with him very well, as the photos in the chapter on the Foreign Press Association show. In fact, almost the only thing he was allowed to do was be the honorary patron of the Foreign Press Association and he took a genuinely keen interest in the FPA.

In Beatrix's reign, the protocol of not quoting the queen and other royals was strictly enforced, though there was the odd slip up. One was during a visit to the Netherlands in the early 1980s by the US rising star of the day in black politics, presidential hopeful Rev Jesse Jackson. After Jackson met with the Queen, AP Bureau Chief Abner Katzman managed to get into a car with Jackson and he reported his remarks about the interview with the Queen. This created quite a diplomatic furore but Katzman was naturally happy enough as his story was already well reported around the US. Katzman was the successor to Nel's last bureau chief, John Gale

Sitting on my desk in the AP-Dow Jones corner of the AP office, he made a charming and clever apology over the phone to Jackson, ending: "Just remember, when you visit the Netherlands as President of the United States, I'll probably still be an unknown journalist in Amsterdam."

In 1995, when Crown Prince Willem-Alexander met the foreign press, a German journalist claimed that the prince had spoken in favour of dropping the 5 May National Liberation celebration as a national festival, though this was subsequently denied by other sources.

Helmut Hetzel, chairman of the FPA from 1990 to 1998, recalls getting into a battle with Beatrix over this incident on the question of whether members of the royal household were speaking on or off the record at FPA gatherings. Hetzel's German fellow-journalist had rushed away from the table where the prince was chatting, in order to phone in immediately to the German Press Agentur with this 'big scoop'. Naturally, it quickly got back to the Netherlands. Apart from this contretemps, the meeting was a success and the amiable, easy-going prince enjoyed the excellent gossip provided by his FPA 'minder' for the occasion, my good friend Irish journalist Isabel Conway.

In 1999, a visit by Queen Beatrix to the society of chief editors produced a fracas.

> "Over-hasty talent reported that the sovereign had said of the press that 'lying reigns'. The context in which she had said that was not made clear," the Dutch ANP news service sniffed later. A television programme was actually launched under the title 'Lies reign', in which journalists' behaviour was examined.

As far as I know, Claus never made any faux pas, probably helped by his diplomatic background and considerable personal charm. However, he did have to overcome the initial problem of being German and of learning Dutch.

11.
The Foreign Press Association

Nel and the FPA, Prince Claus, Ruud Lubbers and many others

Nel's fruitful if sometimes stormy involvement with the Foreign Press Association spanned almost her entire life as a journalist. She joined the association in 1945, when she became the first Associated Press correspondent in The Hague. As she became an honorary member in 1982, her name will live on in its annals forever.

i. Getting Known: Press puts flooded Holland on the global map

The Foreign Press Association in the Netherlands (FPA), or Buitenlandse Persvereniging in Nederland (BPV), was founded by 15 foreign correspondents in 1925 to promote the interests of foreign journalists working in the Netherlands. Appropriately for a press association, it owes its origins to a gathering in a bar, 'De Twee Steden' in The Hague, on November 14, 1925. All 15 founding members were male but, a month later, it acquired a lone woman member, French-born Livia Jars de Gubernatis. The initiator, Paul Derjeu, appears next to Nel along with foreign minister Willem Beyen in a photo taken at a reception held by Beyen for the FPA's 30-year anniversary celebrations. The other women are Beyen's wife and Jars de Gubernatis, who was a Le Monde reporter.

The 'well-established and respected correspondents for foreign media' who formed the first board were Chairman W.J. van Ditmar, Secretary Paul Derjeu, Treasurer Dr.H.J. de Lange and board members Henri Asselin and Dr E.K. Huebner. Derjeu said the association was needed because

> "on several occasions, even of important and international interest, the foreign press simply didn't exist in the opinion of the organisers."

The early leaders of the association worked energetically and put in long hours to build it up. They did have more time though. It was a rather more peaceful journalistic environment compared with the hectic 21st century world of computers, mobiles, tablets, video cameras and instant news flashing around the globe. This is what Friso Endt and Isabel Conway wrote about the early years for the FPA's 75th anniversary magazine:

> "Strong and idealistic chairmen like Herman Bleich (also founder of Nieuwspoort International Press Centre in The Hague) and Henk Kersting, the legendary Bureau Chief of the Associated Press in Amsterdam were the workhorses of our association in those early days. The eternal Secretary and 'Mr BPV' was the Hungarian-born Pal Balasz.

> "These gentlemen - they would fire off 4 and 5 letters daily to each other on a myriad of press-related topics - took their calling and their new organisation very seriously. But it was a different world to now. Deadlines were softened by hot metal production, uncertain telegraph wires, the queue at the telex office. One could attend a meeting of one's professional organisation without the constant pealing of a mobile phone and demands for instantaneous emailed copy.

> "Through them, the Foreign Press Association became a powerful and influential institution. So powerful that at the 50th anniversary in 1975 the then Chairman Herman Bleich had the courage to invite all foreign press associations in Europe to the Ridderzaal (Knights Hall) in The Hague in an unsuccessful effort to establish a World Federation of Foreign Press Associations.... in many ways a visionary plan."

Writing in the FPA's 30th anniversary magazine in 1955 when he was Chairman, Nel's boss Kersting complained that the 'jardinièrе' (dinner) that followed its annual meeting had not yet acquired the reputation that it had in other countries, where these dinners "have commonly inspired government members to disclose world news." But even if government officials didn't spill any newsworthy beans on these occasions, the FPA had by then become firmly established as a respected body. The press association proved its worth over the decades and officials gradually learned that both sides needed each other.

The most dramatic way the Dutch establishment came to realise the value of the foreign press was in the catastrophic floods of 1953. Endt recalled:

> "The world rushed to Holland's aid in response to harrowing reports of the tragedy filed by our members. During the clean-up, Premier Drees told us that he had never realised how vital and valuable a Dutch-based foreign press could be. In recognition of our contribution, trees were planted in Ouwerkerk, on Schouwen-Duiveland, where a street was also named 'Weg van de Buitenlandse Pers'."

Endt was among other journalists ceremonially planting the first trees there.

Two years later, Prime Minister Drees put his appreciation in writing in a foreward to Kersting's 30th anniversary magazine:

> "The work of the representatives of the foreign press is important, for our country and the people as well. Reference has already been made many times to how much importance this had in the disaster days of February 1953, when it was precisely the modern communication methods that carried the news of the calamity across the world in the twinkling of an eye, as a result of which sympathy and help was awoken and offered from all quarters.

> "The foreign press, however, also has great value for us in everyday living because, through their correspondents here in the country, they project the picture of our country abroad so that understanding is created for our ups and downs. And seen in a wider context, the journalists who are taxed with such a task can contribute to people having more understanding of one another throughout the world.

> "The foreign correspondents in the Netherlands have in general shown a high devotion to duty and great feeling

of responsibility. I have extremely good memories of my contacts with many of them. I sincerely wish them success with the anniversary of their organisation, which is very much valued by the government."

There was also an extremely polite forward by Queen Juliana's husband Prince Bernhard:

"Now that the Foreign Press Association in the Netherlands is celebrating its 30th anniversary, I would very much like to add my sincere congratulations to the many that will undoubtedly pour in.

The foreign correspondent always fulfils a role which is of great significance to the country where he has his temporary abode.

The readers in his native country see the country on which he reports through *his* eyes. They read *his* praise but also *his* criticism.

It is clear that this fact lays a great responsibility on the shoulders of the correspondent.

With gratitude it can be said that the members of the celebrating association have in fact always shown awareness of this responsibility.

They have become good friends of the Netherlands. Perhaps sometimes the friend that 'points out shortcomings', but still a friend.

I express at the celebration of the milestone which is being passed the hope that this relationship will endure.

People have more need than ever of a better understanding of what goes on outside their own borders.

Those who truly help with the broadening of that understanding earn the thanks of the people whose merits and shortcomings they describe.

Let me then right now express these thanks on behalf of our people.

The same 1955 magazine featured Nel's decorous article quoted in Chapter 4, 'We - Women Correspondents Want to be Taken Seriously'. It is worth noting that compared with a sole woman member at the start and a tiny handful by 1955, 40 percent of the FPA's 120 members were women by the year 2000.

FPA 1955 anniversary reception, Nel with FPA founder Paul Derjeu and Foreign Minister Johan Willem Beyen

As Chairman, Nel's boss Kersting wrote a lengthy and thoughtful but rather turgid piece on the 'Task and Role of the BPV'. David Post, who was later vice-Chairman to Nel, described the Dutchman Kersting as:

> "A very nice guy, very proper, almost German in a way,
> he was so correct, and always beautifully dressed."

Perhaps this super-correctness weighed on his prose as well. He was clearly an effective Chairman of the association as well as being a very supportive boss for Nel. Kersting stressed the FPA's task was to maintain a high standard, which only admitted 'only bona fide and accredited correspondents of daily papers and press bureaux'. Membership requirements were also the basis for the articles of association. These remained unchanged when the organisation was resuscitated after German occupation in World War II. However, a few years later, foreign reporting began to take off and correspondent numbers grew. Soon the requirements had to be tightened up again. He wrote at length about this:

> "The membership committee applies the stipulations
> with the greatest meticulousness. This strict procedure
> ensures for the correspondent that once he is admitted,
> no doubt can exist regarding his position in the

Netherlands for any single body or individual. He can count on it that the BPV will foster and defend his individual interests alongside the professional interests of the group as a whole. He himself has by his membership submitted to the unwritten code of honour. The preventive functioning of membership is so effective that management has only twice felt obliged to voice its censure of unacceptable behaviour."

He does seem to labour the point, but there was a good reason. The tightening up of membership regulations actually became necessary because of a spy who passed himself off as a foreign correspondent during the Cold War period. The fake journalist then tried to get access to strategic information via his FPA membership.

Kersting also revealed a surprising British honorary member of the FPA,

"Sir WINSTON SPENCER CHURCHILL,
spontaneously appointed after the war to honour the
former foreign correspondent as liberator.."

ii. The lure of Brussels

Herman Bleich, who had preceded Kersting as Chairman, was responsible for the creation of the Nieuwspoort International Press Centre. Helping him was parliamentary journalist Nico Cramer, who became a good friend of Nel's. Bleich wrote a somewhat self-congratulatory article about this and the relationship between the FPA and Nieuwspoort in the 1985 anniversary magazine.

An exodus to Brussels had begun in the 1950s, when many foreign correspondents of global papers such as The New York Times, Neue Zürche Zeitung and Time/Life chose Brussels as their location rather than The Hague. Bleich wrote:

"With the result that The Hague as a centre for
international reporting slipped sharply behind Brussels.
A feeling of uneasiness and even disquiet arose… "

He reckoned one reason was that the Netherlands had to catch up with other countries in Western Europe on facilities for the press. In 1959, he decided it was high time the country had a 'pied-a-terre' for its press. So he teamed up with Cramer and after years of struggle, the first Nieuwspoort press centre was officially opened on March 5, 1962. Bleich called Cramer

> "A motor of invaluable significance towards Nieuwspoort, with his inventiveness, flow of ideas and powerful will. Together we lived through ups and downs, triumphs and disappointments."

Warming to his theme, Bleich ended with a flourish of pure self-indulgence and sentimentality:

> "When one sees now how day in day out young colleagues from far and near have taken possession of this press centre, that fulfils such a highly important function, that is indeed something heart-warming. They do not know how much sweat and tears lay behind this achievement and that is not important any more either. What finally counts is the result and that is good both for the BPV and for journalism in the Netherlands as a whole. The 60-year old BPV looks tenderly at the young Nieuwspoort in its full glory - may both experience many more journalistically rich and thus happy years."

Bleich was well-respected and played a powerful role in the FPA as well as setting up Nieuwspoort. However, there could, of course, be tensions within the board from time to time. David Post recalled Bleich - and Nel - when he was Nel's vice-chairman:

> "She could handle anyone. But she was more or less a dictator, things were done her way or they weren't done at all. When I joined, I was the youngest person by far, it really was an old person's club. Because I was an American, I was very welcome there. Particularly by Friso and Nel, because the Germans ere trying to take it over.... Herman Bleich was one of the Germans, he wanted to run it and there were awful fights."

Endt, Bleich and Nel often talked about the gradual decline in the FPA's influence as the EEC became more important and siphoned off international journalists. By 2000, the Brussels press corps of around a thousand was to surpass even that of Washington. As things turned out, other journalists replaced those that left in Holland over the years, partly thanks to the growing international importance of financial news. For a tiny country, Holland has a disproportional number of big global companies as well as a number of international bodies whose activities need to be reported on. Many of these are legal, probably the best-known abroad being a relative newcomer, the International Criminal Court in The Hague.

Mainly as a result of these two factors, the FPA was still flourishing at the beginning of the new millennium, which would have delighted Nel.

iii. The lighter side of life

The later FPA anniversary magazines made sure to include a few jokes. Nel's boss Kersting hunted in his archives for the 1985 FPA magazine and added a contribution from the war years. War or no war, occupation or no occupation, he said, AP New York continued to ask its correspondents for 'smiling briefs' on dull days. On 9 November 1940, this story appeared in American papers:

> War and occupation have not squelched Dutch humour. We Netherlanders are going to erect a statue to the unknown cow at the end of the war, one Dutch farmer solemnly remarked. When asked to explain, he said: "Well, the daily official reports of Britisch (sic) bombings on Dutch soil always state that only cows were hit"
>
> A Dutch woman entered a shop at the same time as two German soldiers. Politely the Germans insisted, "After you, madam." Her retort in untranslatable Amsterdam slang was, "No, thank you, gentlemen, after you. You are in a hurry, no doubt. You have to go to England, don't you?"
>
> A number of Dutchmen and a German soldier, sipping their beer at a pub, were discussing the width of the English Channel. The German warrior insisted it would take only half an hour to get across. The Dutchmen challenged this assertion. They brought a map to prove their point. The soldier ended the argument with a gesture of disdain. "Oh well," he said, "just British propaganda."
>
> Rationing is a fruitful theme to Dutch jokesmiths. The following question and answer combine butter, gasoline and textiles, all of which are scarce and rationed, in one joke. Question: What is the acme of impossibility? Answer: To clean a grease spot on a woollen coat with gasoline.

Nel also contributed to the jokes column in the 1990 magazine. As well as the story quoted earlier about Luns relieving his anger about the 1963 German-French "traite de l'Elysee" by changing Couve de Murville's name to De Murstadt, she had a nice linguistic faux pas by a Dutch minister and a piece of British humour about Margaret Thatcher.

> Dutch environment minister Irene Vorrink left her French colleague and his aides speechless when she introduced herself as *"Ministre du Milieu."* Later, the mistake was explained to her. *"Well,"* she retorted, at a time when speaking French in The Netherlands was considered elitist, *"I don't speak 'buitenlands'"* ('foreign')

> Shortly after Margaret Thatcher first became Prime Minister of Britain, a journalist was seated next to the British Ambassador at a European Covenant luncheon. The journalist allowed as how she admired Thatcher for her courage, intelligence and articulateness, but wondered aloud about her experience abroad. With dry British wit the ambassador replied: *"She once danced with Mugabe."*

Frank de Jong had another one:

> Not long after the world famous "Flying Enterprise" shipping disaster in the 60s the first officer (British) of the tugboat which saved many lives married a Dutch girl in Amsterdam City Hall. The magistrate presiding over the ceremony thought he had done a good job preparing his speech to the bride and groom. But British reporters covering the event burst out laughing when at the end of the speech he said: *"And now I consummate your marriage."*

And Friso Endt's:

> Some years ago Wim Dik, then State Secretary for Foreign Trade and Export gave a speech at the World Trade Center in New York. He made the following closing remark: *"And that, ladies and gentlemen, is another cook"* (a Dutch expression, andere koek, literally meaning 'a different biscuit' but normally translated as 'another story')

Nel's former AP bureau chief John Gale contributed:

> My wife at home at 7 am: "Would you like dressing gown in your breakfast?"

iv.1990 - The fall of communism

In 1990, when the FPA celebrated its 65th anniversary with Friso Endt as Chairman, the world was undergoing huge changes. The fall of the Berlin Wall, German unification, Soviet Glasnost and Perestroika and the emergence of Eastern Europe were among the momentous developments taking centre stage. Nel was in a serious vein in this anniversary publication, now called 'The Foreign Correspondent'. Her article on the EEC and Eastern Europe is cited in the last chapter. Helmut Hetzel, who took over from Endt as chairman later that year, wrote on German reunification and Herman Bleich also had a somewhat paranoid article on the same subject. It is however only fair to recall that many people who still remembered the war were extremely anxious at the time about the possibility of a resurgent Germany.

A Russian, Sergei Melnikof, who had been TASS correspondent in the Netherlands since 1985, wrote a short, optimistic piece about perestroika and the press, saying his work had become more difficult but also more interesting since TASS lost its monopoly. Friso Endt updated his review of the BPV: 'BPV 65 years old: Not pensioned off!' Jan van Groesen wrote about the new, improved Nieuwspoort being built in The Hague and Frank de Jong reminded readers of how technology had changed:

> "Back in the 60s I worked as AFP's bureau chief in Jakarta and the only way to file copy was a morse-cast transmission of up to two pages, twice a day, to Singapore. Even worse, during the four-week telecommunications blackout after the aborted coup attempt in 1965, I had to go to Jakarta's airport twice a day and ask passengers to take my copy to Singapore, where my AFP colleague would pick it up…"

iv. The Prince and Nel

Prince Claus was for years the FPA's guest of honour at the anniversary celebrations that took place every five years, in a tradition established soon after he married Princess Beatrix and he got to know Nel well even before she chaired the association. As Friso recalled in 2000,

> "the prince has always held close ties with the BPV of which we are very proud. This year Her Majesty Queen Beatrix is our guest of honour. It is not the first time she is with us. In the 1960s she attended with Prince Claus

the first Press Ball we organised at the Amsterdam Hilton hotel, where - after the gala dinner - a performance of the Edwin Hawkins singers produced such an enormous voice volume that the electric current in the hotel blew. We sat with all our guests, including the royal couple, in the dark. Princess Beatrix and Prince Claus were clearly amused and enjoyed the rest of the evening with us by candlelight."

David Post told me about what was probably the rowdiest Foreign Press dinner in Hotel des Indes in The Hague in the 1970s, when Joop Den Uyl was Prime Minister:

"It was during the oil crisis and only Holland and America were being boycotted because of their support for Israel and there was this popular song in the country at the time, "Den Uyl is in den olie" (*Den Uyl is in the oil, ie in the shit*) and the Prime Minister actually got up and sang it. It was the rowdiest one I was ever at, it was out of control."

At the 1990 celebrations held in Ootsmarsum in the east of the country, Friso Endt reminded Prince Claus of his speech at the celebrations ten years earlier in the Kurhuis hotel in Scheveningen, the seaside suburb of The Hague. Friso described this as:

"An exceptionally witty, somewhat ironic text, in which the prince interviewed himself and dredged up all the stereotypical questions which he had had to deal with in his life in the Netherlands…. Claus said to me: 'Did I really say that then?' I told him I still had the original text. 'It still sounds completely topical', Claus replied.

Claus was also at the 70th anniversary five years later in 1995, again back in Scheveningen's Kurhaus under Helmut Hetzel's presidency. But he missed the 75th celebrations in 2000 due to ill health. In fact, at the 1995 celebrations, it was Crown Prince Willem Alexander's presence that made the biggest impression, as Endt and Conway recorded.

"The Foreign Press Association even made headlines itself in the Dutch media. We had succeeded where it had failed… in meeting Crown Prince Willem Alexander, who spent a couple of hours chatting with our members… Naturally he was queried about his love life, views on the disastrous goings on at the time in the British monarchy and his ambitions at this extraordinarily frank and fun-filled get-together."

The keynote speaker on that occasion was underwhelming. European Commission President Jacques Santer could chiefly be congratulated for saying absolutely nothing for 20 minutes.

Nel herself chaired the FPA for eight years from 1978 to 1986 with characteristic style, vigour and vigilance, though, as David Post said, she could be quite autocratic. Probably like most FPA chairpersons, she had her trials and tribulations, the main one in her case being the scandal of temporary Treasurer Erich Hoos. He was an excellent BPV secretary who ran off with a chunk of the BPV's cash towards the end of Nel's term. Friso Endt told me the story:

> "Hoos, who had been a very good Secretary, was temporary Treasurer and one day Nel came on the phone yelling and crying, in tears really, in a panic, and said Hoos took 9,000 guilders from the BPV's cash, which is a lot of money... He falsified the signature on the cheque because the bureau chief should have signed it. And he disappeared.

> "He went to a hotel in Maastricht. I went there, and I checked that he stayed the last night, and then he crossed the border and was away…. Frank (de Jong) and I went to the bank, ABN Amro, and I said you accepted a cheque with a false signature, you shouldn't have done that.

> "So they paid it all back. Months later, when I had succeeded Nel as Chairman, I got a phone call and I visited his wife, because she was in great trouble with two childern and somebody came and said that they had seen Erich Hoos on top of the Brenner Pass, I said *what?* 'There is a little pension (bed-and-breakfast), where he is staying'. And Hoos said he was working for Agence France Presse and spoke to Dutch people. I asked him if he was he alone and he said yes. I thought he must be crazy. A couple of months later, his wife called me and told me he was back, so I went there and there was Erich, now undergoing psychiatric treatment. He was fired by AFP, of course, so the (Hoos' family)were in great trouble. I think she later divorced him.

> "He looked at me and asked me what I thought. I said listen, if you would have taken 300,000 or 500,000 guilders from AFP – not that we have that kind of money - and you had escaped with a girl with big boobs, that's understandable. But this is just stupid.

"But Nel was in great trouble. We kept it out of the public prosecutor's office because it would be very bad for the name of the AFP. We got our money back and that was it."

Paul Bremer (tweede van links), Amerikaans ambassadeur, gast van de BPV.   FOTO: CEES ZORN

FPA lunch with US ambassador Paul Bremer as guest

After Friso took over as Chairman, he stressed that Nel remained a vigilant watchdog of press interests.

"When I was Chairman, Nel often called and said we should not take this, we should protest, and I did."

Nel herself presided over two particularly memorable anniversary celebrations, the first being the 55th anniversary, actually held on St Valentine's day, February 14, 1981, when Prince Claus made his famous speech. The programme shows her speech coming after the main course, followed by Prince Claus' speech, followed by a decoration for Balazs, so guests had to wait a while for their dessert.

Nel's speech, minus the odd illegible or garbled sentence, ran as follows.

"Your Royal Highness, excellencies, ladies and gentlemen. We have some sad news tonight as well as much to celebrate. First, the ambassador of the United States, Gery Joseph, returns home soon. She tells us, however, that she also is looking forward to joining our ranks. She will write a column three times a week for a Minneapolis (paper).

We will miss also Willem van den Berghe, who shepherded us through the inauguration of the queen and news of the Dutch royal house, and (*illegible*).

Finally, a few words for a very old friend of mine and of this organisation, Pàl Balasz, the only secretary of the association since 1945, finally is taking his retirement from this arduous task. It will be impossible to fill his shoes and we will miss him sorely.

Pàl and I can attest that there have been many changes in the world of the press since this association was formed in 1925. One thing has remained constant in this country- the right to carry on our tradition of informing readers and listeners as we see fit without restriction.

As our Vice President once put it: this is an open society, open not only to the press but also to new ideas, particularly in the social field. He said: the Dutch do many things in weird and wonderful ways which means that there are interesting stories to distribute around the world.

Our colleagues elsewhere in the world often face physical danger gathering the news. They are often under pressure from governments that seek to manipulate or distort the news. We are grateful for our freedom in this country.

A redeeming feature in our business is that the number of women journalists has grown steadily. I think it is not as difficult for my younger female colleagues as it was for me in 1945 to get a start in this game. They had never heard of a woman reporter...

This organisation seems to be coming of age - it has elected a woman President for the first time in 55 years - who knows - as the least of all evil.

Technological innovation also is changing the working life of journalists. Forty years ago the morse key was still in use to move the news from one country to another. Now the news is sped to the papers at speeds of 1,200 words per minute, using satellite circuits and computer systems.

> John Gale of the Associated Press can tell you there will be an ultra high speed news transmission system operating in Holland by the end of 1981.
>
> Presently a 100 word a minute bulletin filed in Istanbul can be read simultaneously in Paris, London and New York within minutes of clearing a central computer. In future, it will be even faster and huge amounts of information will be transmitted just by pressing a button."

Boy, was she ever right. And this was before mobiles, iPhones and iPads, social media, Facebook and all the other paraphernalia of technological progress with which we have to cope nowadays.

A report of the event in the Haagsche Courant was titled 'Great hilarity in Kurhaus -Prince Claus interviews himself at press ball'. Describing the Kurhaus as 'generously decorated with beautiful flowers and sparkling as of old', it quoted much of the prince's speech and commented on his good English. Photos showed Claus buying a lottery ticket for the tombola from a 'charming kaasmeisje (cheese girl)', and Claus and Nel dancing and laughing. Another shows Foreign Minister Chris van der Klaauw rather dashingly sweeping the American ambassador around the floor.

The original typescript of Claus' speech is shown in the Appendix.

The following year, 1982, Nel was elected honorary member of the FPA, joining a short list of people 'who have made themselves of exceptional service on behalf of the association or the foreign press in general'.

In 1985, Nel presided over one of the FPA's most splendid anniversary celebrations, held in Erestein Castle in Kerkrade, near Heerlen in the southern province of Limburg. Prince Claus was guest of honour and Prime Minister Ruud Lubbers gave the keynote speech.

Nel's speech was in three languages this time, not that she couldn't have still made one in five. The English version went:

> "Your Royal Highness, excellencies, ladies and gentlemen. It is 60 years ago that the foreign press association was founded in November 1925. Its first president was a Dutchman, Van Ditmar, correspondent for the London Times.
>
> During the Occupation, the association was kept alive by Paul Derjeu, correspondent for Scandinavian papers. The association was languishing and mainly concerned with helping members in need.

Twenty years later, in 1945, Pal Balasz, originally from Hungary, unfortunately ailing and not with us tonight, blew new life in the association. Few of the then members are still with us.

Prince Bernhard was guest of honour at the association's annual dinner 16 years ago in 1961. Queen Beatrix then Royal Princess and Prince Claus attended the annual occasion later in the sixties.

Continuity is the life blood of any organisation. For that reason we are particularly pleased to have with us Your Royal Highness, who has always taken an interest in the media.

Prince Claus was with us at our 55th anniversary and we hope he will so honour us at our 65th.

I speak of the importance of continuity because, while the reporting of our members makes the world a little smaller, geopolitical realignments over our six-decade history have also changed and in many ways reduced the Netherlands' significance.

This is reflected by the fewer number of papers that have representatives in the Netherlands. Their dwindling number makes the high quality of those that are left here all the more precious.

Reporters go where the stories are, as they should. But because of that, the spotlight is not on our beat the way it used to be.

Is it because Europe is in decline? Afflicted with Eurosclerosis as some journalists would have us believe? True there is plenty of action and there are plenty of journalists in Brussels, but many of them specialise in and are limited to specific economic areas.

Are fewer foreign correspondents covering the big picture because there no longer is a big picture in Europe?

Perhaps with another visionary like Robert Schumann, De Gaspery, Churchill or Paul Henri Spaak, the EEC would again be a heavyweight?

We hope Premier Ruud Lubbers, who kindly agreed to be our guest speaker -- and also because Mr Lubbers has a soft spot for this southern province -- will answer this question.

Fortunately, the Netherlands still remains a financial and economic centre, and a seat of international law. We are honoured to have with us tonight some eminent specialists in international law from several nations."

At this celebration, Nel received yet another honour. Endt said:

"To her unspeakable amazement and surprise, Nel was promoted by Lubbers from Knight to Officer in the Order of Oranje-Nassau."

According to Endt, the AFP board - vice-Chairman Laura Raun, secretary Frank de Jong, penningmeester Helmut Hetzel, Geert Linnebank (who was to become Reuters Editor-in-Chief by the turn of the century), Ron van der Krol and Endt himself - had cooked the proceedings up with the head of the government information service, Hans van der Voet.

"Van der Voet's deputy Fred Loertzer had the decorations in his inside pocket. Nel was extremely moved. Afterwards, the Limburgers created an exuberant feast with a brass band and flag-waving. Claus enjoyed it all to the full. When he wanted to go home, Beek airport was already closed. The AFP board then called in the governor of Limburg; the airport was opened up again and Claus could fly back to The Hague."

Prince Claus presented the decoration to Nel and one newspaper photo shows her looking quite overwhelmed just afterwards. Numerous other photos show Nel in sparkling form presiding over the celebrations in Kerkrade.

Sandwiched between the two awards from Dutch premiers, in 1982 Nel received "La Croix d'Officier de l'Ordre National du Merit." Nel was honoured by the French government as a 'friend of France' and the title was awarded to her by the French Ambassador, Claude de Kemoularia, in his residence. She told a Dutch paper, which was impressed by her fluent French:

"I received the award for my journalistic efforts... I worked in Brussels from 1961 to 1973. At the EEC. The French gave the lead at that time."

Honouring her work on behalf of his government, De Kemoularia said:

"In her character we recognise courage, loyalty and dedication and above all also love for France, for the country, its culture and its civilisation."

He also outlined her remarkable career, especially her resistance work in London when she was monitoring radio for the BBC.

FPA 60th anniversary, Erestein Castle, Kerkrade November 1985 Nel introduces Prince Claus to FPA members Vera Vaughan Bowden, Caroline Studdert, Laura Raun

FPA 60th anniversary, Nel and Claus tête a tête

DE journaliste **Nel Slis**, voorzitter van de Buitenlandse Persvereniging, is zaterdag in kasteel Erenstein in Kerkrade bij bevordering benoemd tot Officier in de Orde van Oranje-Nassau. Zij kreeg de onderscheiding uit handen van **prins Claus** op een feestelijke bijeenkomst ter gelegenheid van het 60-jarig bestaan van de vereniging. Tot de aanwezigen behoorden o.a. **premier Lubbers** en zijn echtgenote (links op de foto), **minister Van den Broek** (buitenlandse zaken) en Europees commissaris **Andriessen**.

FPA 60th anniversary. A new award for Nel

Foreign Press Association

A witty moment during the Prime Minister's speech. Seated at the table, facing the camera flr: Mrs Lubbers, HRH Prince Claus, Mrs Sfs

FPA 60th anniversary. Premier Ruud Lubbers' speech

FPA 60th anniversary, Nel and Claus dancing

Nel joined the celebrations in Ootmarsum for the FPA's 65th anniversary in 1990 and in Scheveningen's Kurhaus for the 70th anniversary five years later. She was no longer able to attend the 75th anniversary celebrations held in 2000 in the Ridderzaal or Knight's Hall in the old government buildings in The Hague. But she was not forgotten in the anniversary magazine. She would doubtless have been pleased that a woman again headed the FPA, as Vera Vaughan Bowden had become president in 1998. Also, that Queen Beatrix, who had eluded Nel's own efforts to get her to meet the FPA, was guest of honour.

Nel would have applauded Vaughan Bowden's short, dignified address in Dutch, possibly would have had a few criticisms of Foreign Minister Jozias van Aartsen's not uninteresting but somewhat self-promoting speech and definitely would have laughed her head off at Haagse Courant columnist Floor Kist's brilliantly hilarious one. Kist's best joke had Beatrix rolling around in her seat along with everyone else in the room. Talking about how Dutch tulip-growers liked to name tulips after famous people as a good way of getting some publicity, he said Eleanor Roosvelt was one of these. The then first lady said she did feel quite honoured at first to have a tulip named after her, until she read the description of the tulip in the catalogue: 'No good in bed, but good up against a wall'. It was a grand and pleasant millennium occasion for the FPA, which Nel would have enjoyed enormously.

12.
After the AP

The Light that Failed

After retiring from the AP in 1979, Nel maintained a full working life as a freelance journalist right through most of her seventies, and would probably have carried on into her eighties had her memory not failed. As late as 1991, she could list Europe Magazine, Washington, McGraw-Hill Publications, New York, European Chemical News, UK and Oilgram News, New York as her main publications, and she was also still working for Agence Europe at that time.

In the 1980s, one of the topics she regularly followed was the difficult Iranian claims court. Her friend Flora Lewis said she was one of the very few journalists covering it at all. It was a special court handling cases including claims on Iran and Iran's claims on assets that were frozen or seized. Her reports are too specialised to quote nowadays without a mountain of explanation, but it was typical of Nel to take up such a complicated and technical matter which most people avoided.

She also kept a special eye on Europe. Following the collapse of the Soviet Union, her old EEC beat was now joined by the new world of emerging Eastern Europe.

i. Europe after the Fall of the Berlin Wall

In the March 1990 Foreign Press Association (FPA) anniversary magazine The Foreign Correspondent, Nel looked back on the events which had just taken place in Eastern Europe and assessed their implications for the EEC. Her report headlined 'Eastern Europe crowds EC agenda'pinpoints the palpable nervousness about German reunification at that time: 'The West European countries have clearly not forgotten World War II. They fear super-patriotism. All hope that a European Germany will emerge, and not a German Europe'. The report is historically interesting on account of the momentous events taking place at the time, though the sparkle was beginning to fade from Nel's writing.

Nel enjoyed a final burst of journalistic life covering the 1991 EU Maastricht Summit for Agence Europe, rediscovering her old expertise and gusto from the Brussels years. In the run up to the event, she joined the Foreign Press Association on a visit to the Roman ciy gem on the Maas river. The city, on a limb of the country stretching deep into the south and surrounded by Belgium and Germany, has a completely different atmosphere from the Calvinistic northern and western part of the country. The local dialect is soft and sometimes quite incomprehensible to those of us from the north. Women are smartly dressed, and the food is excellent; the historic streets are beautifully preserved. On that visit, a highlight was the old Town Hall and the glory of its dark colonial-era wallpaper covered with fabulous birds and flowers.

The FPA was also taken to inspect the Maastricht Exhibition & Congress Centre (MECC)in which all the journalists were to be corralled, attend press briefings and meet the European Commission and EEC ministers. A very modern complex, it looked quite confusing. Nel hissed: "Always make sure to see where the lavatories are."

Nel wrote a well-composed curtain-raiser for Europe Magazine on her favourite politician Ruud Lubbers and the country under his premiership. This was when he was about to take over the presidency of the EU for the important six months culminating in the Treaty of Maastricht. Though Nel's piece may have needed quite some editing by that time, it encapsulated an impressive amount about what was going on in the Netherlands and in Europe. For once, I am including it here in full, as it struck me as an extremely solid piece of work at age 78.

```
Maastricht Summit curtain-raiser: Ruud Lubbers
and the Netherlands

Lubbers recently outlined his goals for the
important six-month stint during which the
```

Netherlands will preside over the Community. "To hold the Community presidency," he said, "does not in our view mean chalking up as many spectacular achievements as possible. We need to ensure that the Community continues on a course of balanced development and responds adequately to the challenges that arise." He underlined that special attention must be paid to the completion of the single market and to the satisfactory conclusion of the IGCs (intergovernmental conferences).

Other issues Lubbers regards as a priority during his E.C. presidency are the continuing discussions on Community financing-the "Delors Package" covering the period 1988-92-and the reform of social and other funds, especially the Common Agricultural Policy. He also hopes that one of the issues he proposed at the June 1990 Dublin Summit-discussions on an European Energy Community-will take off during his presidency. This policy would coordinate energy activities by both E.C. member states and other European countries. In foreign policy, the Dutch Prime Minister has said that relations with Eastern Europe, including the Soviet Union, will require much attention.

The Dutch team in charge of the E.C. for the next six months appears confident. Most of the key figures have been in government for nearly a decade and have become adept in their dealings with the Community. Lubbers, a Christian Democrat, has been Prime Minister since 1982, and Hans van den Broek has been Foreign Minister for the same period of time.

Lubbers' first and second governments, from 1982-86 and from 1986-90 respectively, were right-of-center coalitions. Yet he is equally at ease in his current left-of-center administration, which he runs with the Socialist Deputy Prime Minister and Finance Minister, Wim Kok.

The Netherlands has definite views on what it would like the outcome of the two IGCs to be. Politically, it would like to see the E.C.'s powers to be commensurate with its economic weight. This would mean that the European Parliament and the E.C. Commission would cooperate more closely with one another and that both institutions could be given more decision-making powers. In international affairs, van den Broek says the Dutch wish to safeguard the U.S.-European link in foreign and defense policies.

On EMU (economic and monetary union), the Netherlands sees the need for a central bank that acts independently of national governments, and for a single European currency. The country, however, is acutely aware of the dangers of proceeding with such goals while wide disparities remain between the economies of the member states.

Other areas of concern Lubbers hopes to address during his six-month presidency are cross-border problems that the Netherlands shares with its European neighbours, especially in the run-up to a borderless European market.

The environment has been an issue of primary concern for Dutch governments since the early 1980s. Since national borders do not stop water and air pollution from spreading into other countries, the E.C. began to formulate an E.C.-wide environmental policy in 1986. The Netherlands has been a consistent advocate of going further and faster on environmental policies. The country is in a good position to do so: The Dutch are already advanced in dealing with pollution problems, having already implemented one of the most revolutionary environmental plans to come to grips with industrial and agricultural pollution in their own country.

The Netherlands' strategic location makes it central to world trade. Rotterdam is the world's largest port and Amsterdam's Schiphol airport is Europe's fourth largest airfreight center. Thus the Netherlands is a key transportation center for all European import and export traffic. Since cross-border traffic by rail, road, sea and air promises to increase as barriers come down, the Dutch hope to reduce border controls and tariffs with the Community to ease such traffic.

On the domestic front, the Netherlands is facing some serious realities. Regarded by some as a "social paradise," The country is now facing the prospect of severe financial cutbacks.

The Dutch built their progressive welfare state on the revenue of gas riches that were found in the country after World War II. The export of natural gas made the country one of Europe's richest, enabling it to establish a generous welfare net. However, as gas resources start to dwindle, the Dutch can no longer rely on that natural resource as guaranteed income. As a result, they are finding that they have to painfully adjust-by tightening the belt on social services.

The Netherlands' budget deficit stands at 4.25 percent of its gross domestic product. Yet the country spends an estimated 80 billion guilders ($41.5 billion) on social benefits each year. For many, such funds have become an acceptable way of life, even replacing work. The Ministry of Social Affairs estimates that social fraud runs at a level of six billion guilders ($3.1 billion) a year. One example: Although the unemployment rate officially stands at 5.1 percent, the number of persons on unemployment benefits is higher than this. Thus the outlays on social security payments are clearly above the European average, even though the relatively high benefits are subject to tax.

Lubbers is confident that his country's domestic woes will not sidetrack his efforts to guide the E.C. closer to "1992""

According to the Central Economic Planning Bureau, absenteeism figures in the Netherlands run extremely high-nearly twice as high as in Belgium and 60 percent higher than in Germany. Research has shown that the health of the Dutch population is better on average than in many other countries. Yet the Dutch socio-cultural climate makes it acceptable for people not to work. The government wants to remedy this situation by reducing the number of young people leaving high school without a degree and by raising the qualifications of those already working by stimulating employers to improve incentive structures.

Despite these efforts, however, the Labor Party fears that the Netherlands' carefully constructed social edifice, which the party regards as sacrosanct, could crumble. This will undoubtedly create problems when the Conservative-Labor coalition sits down to draft next year's budget. For, despite the necessity of budgetary restraint, Labor will insist on maintaining one of its basic political principles-the link between private-sector wage levels on the one hand and all kinds of social benefits, ranging from unemployment and pension

benefits to welfare and disability allowances,
on the other.

Although the outlook does not seem bright on
all fronts as the Netherlands launches its
presidency, Lubbers is confident that his six-
month stint at the helm of the Community will b
a successful one, and that his country's
domestic woes will not sidetrack his efforts to
guide the E.C. into 1992.

At the Maastricht summit, Nel was bustling around happily, working with her Agence Europe friends and tipping fellow-journalists off on anything she thought might be useful to them. I had a chance to experience at first hand there how bewildering the EEC could be to a newcomer, just as Nel had found when she first went to cover it in the early 1960s. In Maastricht, the EEC nights were every bit as long as those described by Nel in her Brussels period. I remember I slept for four hours the first night, two hours the second and not at all on the last night. I could also see how she became fascinated by the process of teasing out what was going on.

Nel's former FPA board colleague Laura Raun, who was my second boss at AP-Dow Jones, was there for CNN News wearing a dashing pink suit. BBC heavyweight John Simpson criss-crossed the floor looking grumpy; John Cole, known for his years of excellent Northern Ireland reporting for the BBC, snoozed cosily through the night on a sofa. This was the summit when British premier John Major extracted the UK's opt-out clauses to the Economic and Monetary Union plan, so the UK's formal press briefings were always packed out. They were run cabaret-style by a young successor to Margaret Thatcher's famous or infamous, depending on one's point of view - press chief, Bernard Ingram.

Any official that appeared through the long nights acted like a magnet, instantly attracting a big clump of reporters, just as Nel had described it. In the absence of any available official, people tended to go on trawling around talking to anyone, including other journalists. On the first night, I was surprised to be interviewed by a TV station from somewhere remote, I think in Australia. In the depths of the second night, I found a small group of Eastern European journalists from Latvia and Estonia encamped in an otherwise empty room somewhere in the depths of the MECC rabbit warren. They explained to me how it had been necessary before the collapse of the USSR to report to the KGB both before and after doing an interview. There was no alternative. Either one complied or one could not work. This was a glimpse of a very different world.

The summit produced the important Treaty of Maastricht, setting the conditions for Economic and Monetary Union (EMU) and the single currency. To the surprise of many, the exchange rates of 12 EU countries went on to be irrevocably fixed as early as in 1999, when the notional euro was introduced. The historic launch of the euro as legal tender followed in 2002, forming the biggest European currency union since the Roman Empire. Today, it looks decidedly shaky but so has the whole European enterprise at many stages and I remain a euro-optimist.

In Maastricht, the Economic and Monetary Union part of the proceedings was settled fairly quickly. At an early morning Dutch press briefing, Wim Kok, then Dutch finance minister, had one bright red eye after his long smoke-filled night but looked reasonably content. For the rest of the summit, all kinds of other bizarre issues were on the agenda. As usually happens in this evolving European institution, many issues ended up being glossed over or swept under the carpet in some kind of blurry compromise.

Concluding the summit, an extremely weary Prime Minister Ruud Lubbers confessed his disappointment that more had not been achieved. He was also unhappy about the UK opt outs, but he did express satisfaction about the EMU agreement. He must have been pleased when this was crowned by the successful introduction of the euro currency a decade later.

Nel would have been pleased about the eurozone too. She would certainly have appreciated not having to change money between countries so often on her tours around Europe to see her friends. But she would also have been delighted with the symbol of a solid and growing European union - despite remaining ever prone to the odd seismic upset.

ii. Friends' Tales: Adventures and Tribulations

The last decade of the century began as a glorious celebration of Nel's life, with a series of anniversary parties and interviews marking her achievements. But all too soon dark clouds would start to gather.

During the last period of her life, Nel had four key people who looked after her and her interests in The Hague: Tyna's brother Piet Wackie Eysten, the lawyer she had known her whole life; producer Yolanda Frenkel Frank and fellow-journalist Friso Endt. Another journalist, Frank de Jong, also helped out in the earlier stages before he himself became ill. Friso Endt bore much of the day-to-day brunt as Nel became more difficult as her memory loss took hold.

Still, whenever people recalled the difficulties and sadness, they were also inclined to remember Nel as she was earlier. Her long-standing friendships persisted well into these troubled years, as long as her more elderly friends were able to drive or were at any rate still alive. She also continued to travel to, and with, her friends.

David Post, Nel's former FPA vice-Chairman recalled signs of eccentricity long before the memory-loss became evident.

> "She had one horrible habit of asking questions at press conferences and then never listening to the answer because she was in a private conversation with her neighbour. I remember being at Fokker (the aircraft-maker which later went bankrupt) with her and she asked (Chairman) Frans Swarttouw a very complicated question and then she started talking to me. Swarttouw was saying Mevrouw, Mevrouw..... . Towards the end, she wasn't doing that much any more, I don't think, but she did a lot for McGraw Hill like weather reports and news services for agriculture."

Post also remembered a hair-raising drive with Nel:

> "I was at the Hilton in Rotterdam, I think it might have been an AmCham (American Chamber of Commerce) lunch, and Neelie Smit-Kroes (former transport minister) was there, I guess she was the speaker. There was a Foreign Press meeting going on in the evening in The Hague, and I took the train knowing it would be quite a boozy day and she said oh, I've got my car here and I'll drive you back to The Hague. It was parked right on the pavement in front of the Hilton Hotel and she came out and the doorman started yelling at her. She said there wasn't time to get a parking place.

> "So I leapt into the back seat, knowing it would be awful. It's 4 o'clock in the afternoon in Rotterdam and we're driving back to The Hague on that busy highway. She had some sort of DAF car that journalists could get 10% off in those days and she decided she wanted to talk to me. I was in the back seat, so she just turned around, looked me in the eye and kept talking while big trucks were zooming all around us. We finally got to the Binnenhof (parliament courtyard) and she parked the car right there and a man came up. 'Oh, it's you, yes, all right,' he said.

> "I think she was a very generous person, particularly with young journalists. Yes, she introduced you to everyone, and if you ever needed to know something, you could call her up and she'd tell you who you could get hold of and she usually would call them up first so they'd know

who you were. She was extraordinarily kind to younger journalists, particularly Americans like me and Jim Smith."

Jim Smith was a young AP reporter in The Hague in the late 1970s who was later Nel's vice-Chairman at the Foreign Press Association before David Post.

David also knew Nel's old friend Rudolf 'Peek' Pekelharing, who was once slapped by Nel but forgave her. He used to visit her regularly, 'up to the last time he could drive a car'.

> "They were really good friends. Rudolf would always talk about her in a very nice way. And this Dan Schorr was one person she would have married but this Jim Smith at the AP - despite being young enough to be her grandson, she would have married him too."

I myself met quiet-spoken Jim Smith briefly in the AP office on Amsterdam's Keizersgracht just before he moved to South Africa in 1981. Thanks to Nel's introduction, I was working there for the AP-Dow Jones financial news service, now called Dow Jones.

Flora Lewis remarked that Nel was a very loyal friend. When her old friend Jacqueline who lived near Biarritz became ill, she would go and stay with her and help her for long periods.

> "So Jacqueline left her house to Nel but by that time, Nel wasn't able to keep it up, so she finally sold it. She had a lot of friends whom I didn't really know, going way, way back to her childhood. There was a woman in Geneva I didn't know that she would go and see all the time, she kept up her friendships, and some of these went back 50 or 60 years."

Tyna Wynaendts said Laura de Jonghe, who had lived just outside Brussels, was one of Nel's greatest friends. After Laura was widowed, they would travel together frequently. Nel had met her in London when she was working for the BBC. After Laura died,

> "it was more Jacqueline; she spent summers with her in her little house near Biarritz and she would travel with her."

Jacqueline was also a journalist, who had got to know Nel when she was working for Agence France Presse in Holland.

Tyna also explained that Nel did not actually nurse her friend Jacqueline, as some had said she did nor did she nurse Tyna's mother.

"She didn't want anything to do with nursing. She went to Jacqueline in the last months, but more to hold her hand. Also when my mother was dying and she came often, my mother sometimes suggested it. We had nurses in and out all the time and when one was going on holiday, she asked Nel would you maybe stay? No, no way. She was probably afraid that she no longer knew how to do it. Yes, she wouldn't do it unless she could do it well."

"Often, after visiting Tyna's family, she would visit friends somewhere in the Dordogne, then go to Jacqueline and then she would go to Switzerland, to see her bank account. Then she went to see her counsellor and that was always a big joke because she was called Madame Corrupt, a wonderful name for a financial advisor. She didn't stay with her, but she always took her out for lunch. She stayed in a Salvation Army place because in Geneva apparently the Army has a hostel for women only, nice and clean, and Madame Corrupt had given her the address. Going to the bank was just habit, that's what she had done in previous years, and I don't think it was really needed."

"When Laura was alive, she had a brother in Portugal and Nel stayed there - Portugal used to be on the circuit too. And when my husband and my children would go for holidays to Gult in the south of France and stay in the house of a friend of ours, Nel would take a little apartment in a village quite near. She would spend the day with us or go out for lunch."

It was Tyna who told me Nel had actually wanted to move to Portugal. Because of Laura's brother, Nel at one point thought that she would move there when she retired.

"That's what she originally planned to do. She didn't like the climate in Holland. She got rheumatism, and she said she would move to a warmer climate where she would not suffer from that. She had gone to Portugal for a holiday and met Laura's brother and there was an elder brother and a whole circle of friends. But they were all elderly, she was probably one of the youngest of the group. So when the time came, it was too late because they had all died.

"But I think she would have liked it. Sometimes, I asked, wouldn't you be afraid to be on your own, not knowing anybody? And she said, well, I've settled in so many places, I would go to the yoga class and see if there's a nice woman and I could take her out for a coffee and then one thing would lead to another - it doesn't scare me at all."

Tyna also told me that Nel gave Dutch lessons to Portuguese workers after she retired.

Probably the lessons were not very good, she was already (losing it), but she could explain things to them in Portuguese as she spoke that language a little bit too."

On one occasion when Tyna was at Bel Ile, off the coast of Brittany, Nel came to visit with her friend Clara Meyer from the European Commission.

"We went for a walk with the two old ladies and I said now, Clara, you have the choice, you can go left back to the house or right - this way is a bit more difficult but that is a bit longer. So Nel said right and Clara said no, no, that's too steep, left, and there was no way of making them give in - they were exactly the same kind of person. So we ended up taking a middle road that wasn't really a road, it was terrible - I didn't know which one to go with because they were determined to go their own way and I felt as I was the hostess that I couldn't leave one or other by themselves."

"My children got on very well with Nel, too. When she came to stay, she always took them out shopping. Sometimes when I said no, you can't have that dress or that pullover because you don't need and I don't like it, they'd say, we'll ask Nel and Nel would buy it for them."

iii. Gonne Hollander's story

Though most of Nel's old friends were scattered around Europe, she had acquired a few other good friends along the way in The Hague. Two of them also went travelling with her.I met Gonne Hollander in her elegant house in The Hague in 2002, soon after Nel died. She was the same age as Nel; a stout, smartly dressed woman, only slightly lame. She told me she had first met Nel in 1958 through her husband. "I liked her from the first meeting, she was so keen, fierce - open." She went on:

"I travelled with her too, in the South of France, Spain. In Biarritz, where her friend Jacqueline was in hospital, we went to live at her house. It had all sorts of weird noises in the night - Nel got a bit afraid. Perhaps it was the heating, or the fridge, but it would burp in the middle of the night. In the daytime, we visited her friend in the hospital.

"In the north of Spain, I had a friend who had been an au pair living there. Nel made a great impression on those people, they always wrote and asked how she was getting on. Nel always drove - I didn't dare. She always smoked at the crucial moment and at one moment, she drove straight through a barrier. What an adventure!

"Later, we went to Berlin and knowing how Nel was afraid of airplanes, we had to go by train. It took an enormous time, and we had difficulty finding a hotel that wasn't a skyscraper, with no lifts. So we found somewhere, and we were walking along and Nel had a brainwave - we'll go to the cabaret. It was just after the Berlin Wall had fallen - they had lots of East and West Berlin jokes. I didn't like her smoking the whole time but she was fun to be with."

In 1975, Gonne had started giving "eettafels" - informal dinners for the various single people in town. Nel still managed to make it to these social events until well after her memory loss became serious – sometimes being quite obstreperous, Gonne recalled.

"She also made rows, she could be so unreasonable. One time at an eettafel, a gentleman said something about the Red Cross. "Red Cross", said Nel and launched into a whole tirade - nothing good about the Red Cross. And he was president of the Red Cross! I didn't like it, her fighting with words, I had to smooth it over. She could hurt people.

"She would arrive at my eettafel when we were sitting having our dessert. I didn't like it very much, having to open up a place on the table. She had such strange stories about coming late - I forgot the way, the taxi didn't come, I walked. Nel was very energetic. I was energetic too when we went on holidays together.

"Once, she wanted to go to the doctor for a driving examination; she was very, very past her best. The doctor phoned and said, are you sure? But she didn't turn up to her appointment so I said I'll take her. The doctor asked her if she knew what day it was. No, she didn't. Which month? She got that wrong. The doctor was very nice. If you were my mother, he said, I would say, let go, don't do the exam any more. But she took it badly and went home in a huff. Even now, she thinks she's still driving. Piet eventually sold the car, so she came to me by taxi or with Yolanda but she was always looking for the keys... Oh, the last years were tragic.

"She had a lot of dear friends; she was very friendly with the neighbours, a gay couple, she loved them. There was also a woman who made clothes for artists.

"Rudolf Pekelharing, they smoked and drank together the whole time. He was a bit short of breath as he smoked too much but he was a very nice man. Clara Meyers always asked after Nel. She was a bit of a tease, and would arrive at my house hours too late.

"Nel loved telling the story about when she got the second Officer of the Order of Oranje Nassau decoration, that someone wrote to her and said, I always associate you more with officers and their language than knights.

"Piet was an angel to her but it was Tyna who inherited. I used to say to Nel, remember Piet too in your testament. I don't know whether she took any notice. He didn't need the money; Tyna needed it a lot. Nel didn't like Piet's wife very much, I don't know if she showed it, one could understand Piet would take his wife's side. Nel was so dependent on Piet. He paid all her bills at the end, organised the furniture, everything. She also had a dear Indonesian charwoman, Sandra, who did everything for her.

"Nel had a heart of gold, everyone who knew her well, knew that. Tyna said at the funeral - remember they lived in Goeree, they were provincial girls and boys - that Nel opened the world to her; 'Thanks to Nel, we had a wider view of the world'."

iv. Elizabeth de Jong van Beek en Donk's story

Nel's last trip was with her own and Gonne's mutual beautician, who had the remarkable name of Elizabeth de Jong van Beek en Donk. A tiny woman in a lilac tweed skirt and jersey with neatly curled hair coloured dark-blonde, she talked to me in her light and airy working room with beautician chair, steamer and other tools of her trade around. She gave me delicious coffee and cakes.

Elizabeth met Nel at Gonne's eettafels and became her friend as well as beautician. Nel, she told me, would come regularly once a month for a facial and massage. Elizabeth also once travelled with Nel to Brussels to the funeral of one Sylvia Fentener van Vlissingen, a member of a famously wealthy Dutch family, who had died in a car accident.

In the second half of the 1990s, when Nel was suffering from serious loss of memory, she suddenly wanted to go to St Petersburg. Tiny, fragile-looking Elizabeth arranged for a three-day bus trip there and back, with three days in St Petersburg. Though it must have been very difficult to cope with Nel by that time, Elizabeth insisted it was great fun. She also said the other passengers on the bus looked after Nel to allow her a break from time to time.

Elizabeth said that Nel was not so keen on the drive right through Germany, threatening to start making unpleasant noises about the war. But by the evening, they were in Copenhagen and could stroll around its great park. Then they drove across Sweden, took the ferry from Stockholm to Helsinki and the bus again to St Petersburg. They had three days there, and then the whole long trip back again. This was a remarkable achievement for Nel at that time, and possibly even more so for Elizabeth.

> "What I miss about Nel? The atmosphere, openness - everyone was welcome, the warmth. She was really trustworthy. And also her candour, honesty - she would say, I don't want that. Yes, she could be difficult, but that was also her power. Perhaps because of her lonely childhood, she became so strong - I was very protected as a child, but then you are not so combative as if you are alone like Nel - it had its good side, in her independence. She was really a big figure in the world as a woman - you could see that at her 80th birthday celebrations."

v. The New Generation: Grande Dame vs Queen Bee and other colleagues

Yolanda once remarked that Flora Lewis was 'very much the same kind of... tough old lady journalist (as Nel), no way to fight them'" Friso Endt claimed Nel imitated Flora; perhaps there is something in it but, whereas Flora seemed to positively enjoy intimidating or upstaging more lowly journalists, Nel was unfailingly kind to those starting off in the business.

British journalist June Dole was among those:

> "I was a newcomer to The Hague when Nel Slis, the colourful grande dame of the FPA introduced me to the then Dutch Prime Minister Ruud Lubbers with the maximum of impact and the minimum of protocol. 'Her boss can be pretty tough and if you don't answer her questions, she will be fired'... This first sip of vintage Slis was heady, leaving me somewhat stunned. But politicians of all labels knew her as one who shot remarks from the hip in a multitude of languages so the Premier wasn't at all flustered. He reacted with humour, courtesy and candour in answering the questions we raised."

All the same, Nel certainly understood herself to be the Grande Dame of Dutch journalism and clashed fiercely with AP-Dow Jones' Victoria English, another strong character. Short, somewhat stocky and intense, with abundant short dark hair, Victoria was not inclined to give any quarter to the older journalist. Nel, always so immaculately turned out, was genuinely outraged by Victoria's American bobby-sox and lack of stockings. Victoria claimed years of modern dancing enabled her to focus her energy, for which I can vouch. Victoria was my first boss and taught me the trade of journalism. She certainly rated herself a Queen Bee in financial journalism and so did others. By way of confirmation of her status, Dutch Central Bank President Wim Duisenberg, the future first President of the European Central Bank, came to her leaving party in the AP office when she, like Nel years ago, was moving to Brussels. This reminds me that Victoria was somewhat piqued to be given a lady's shaving kit by Philips as a leaving present:

> "All those interviews when I thought they were pondering my astute questions, they were just looking at my legs and thinking, why doesn't she shave."

vi. Such sweet sorrow: Parting with the FPA board

Louis Metzemakers had gone on to me at some length about how Nel would pester him in Brussels years ago when she was unsure about something; Friso Endt explained how hard it became to cope with this habit in Nel's later post-AP years.

> "I called Henk Kersting, her former boss, and I said what am I to do, Nel sometimes calls on Sunday morning 8 o'clock and starts yelling. Towards the end, 20 times a day. Henk said, Jesus, Nel is so difficult, if she starts yelling, you yell back, it's the only thing she understands."

As noted earlier, by October 1999, Friso estimated that her memory lasted 5-7 seconds.One of Friso's hardest jobs was getting Nel off the board of the FPA which she had chaired so successfully. Other board members also remembered that having her on the board became a real problem. These included Vera Vaughan Bowden, who became FPA President in 1998. (She changed the job description from chairman). Vera told me:

> "She would sit at the annual meeting, and she would say, where's that bloody Italian who walks his dog every day and lets it shit in my garden. And then another day she would say, the bloody Brits, they think they're journalists, no way they're journalists, and she would go on about that and then another day it would be the French. It depended on the mood."

Nel had remained on the board after first Friso and then Helmut Hetzel took over as Chairman. Friso continued:

> "Already she had this sort of Alzheimer but she was a big, big nuisance. Hetzel was President and I was Vice President because I had stepped down as I'd been ill but Hetzel said stay on as Vice President so I said ok, I'll do that. So one day Hetzel said Friso, we can't stand it any more, she is a pain in the neck because she always talks about other things suddenly or explodes in a rage for nothing and already for 5 or 6 years, when the new board comes in, she says well, I'm signing on again, when she promised the year before that she would go. So he said you have to fix it because you know her.

"And I called Henk Kersting, who was still alive, he said congratulations, quite an assignment, how will you do that? I said, I don't know. We had a meeting at Reuters in Amsterdam, and I said to Nel, why don't you drive with me in my car. She said ok, fine, and halfway to Amsterdam, I said, and what are we doing with your farewell party? She said, what farewell party? I said well, last year you said you would resign and she said, oh no, I signed on for another year.

"So then I had to come clean and I said then you will be in trouble, because the young lions on the board won't take it any more. 'Oh, that goddam German, that goddam mof'. I said no, it's also your friend Christian Chartier. 'Oh, him too?' 'Yes, and Ron van der Krol (*Financial Times correspondent*), who was the treasurer, thinks so too.' Chartier (*a charming Frenchman at Agence France Presse who himself later got into a monumental fight with Hetzel*) was Secretary. She went very pale, and a bit shocked, so I said, 'you had better resign, and I give you that advice as an old friend'.

"Oh no, Nel said, if you want me to resign, I will only do it if you will too. So I said ok, that's good. So we had the board meeting, and when it came to me, I said, it is for you to decide, but I've been on the board for a long time, I'm now over 70, so I think I probably should go. But Ron van der Krol said hey, look, you sit on the board of Nieuwspoort as FPA Vice President and you are dealing with the move from that little old building into the new one, you'd better finish that, so I protest if you resign, I'm against that. So the board said Friso, you stay on.

"So I saw that Nel got paler and more angry. Then I had to drive home, so I said to Hetzel, you took the train, drive back with me, you have to protect me from that angry old woman. He said yes, ok. Ron told her that she was unfair to me, he had the guts to say what we wanted.

"So we were driving through Amsterdam, down Laressestraat and there was a red light - it was 11 in the evening - and it just turned green so I drove on. Nel said, you drove through the red light, and she banged her fist on my knee. She refused to talk to me for a year and she said to everybody in Nieuwspoort: I hate Friso, he has kicked me out of the board, in a very nasty way and I couldn't do anything against it.

"When we had the annual meeting, Hetzel suggested I give her the farewell speech, I said Nel isn't talking to me but he insisted. So I said Nel, you are already an honorary member, you are a member for life but we have a medal - I think Ballasch invented it - for people who did a lot for the FPA, it's a nice silver thing and it says in gratitude for everything you did. You know what Nel said? I have that already - but it was a lie! So she got it anyway."

Hetzel thought that in retrospect Nel might have understood a tougher approach better, along the lines of Kersting's advice to Friso to shout back at Nel.

"It was very difficult... We tried the diplomatic approach, maybe for her it was a bit too elegant, we should have told her now, Nel, you are being kicked out! I'm sure she would have understood that better. All the time, we had a strategy, to get her in a good mood, offer her a whiskey."

Hetzel had first met Nel back in the early 1980s.

"My first impression? I was very much shocked because of her impoliteness, straight words and strong voice - not fitting for a lady! But after getting to know her, I found she was an interesting person. But very impatient, of course, and very choleric. She could shout in all languages - French, English, German, Dutch."

But Nel, who had certainly attacked Hetzel on occasion, along with many of her other fellow-journalists, would have been pleased with his final assessment:

"Most important, was her attitude, she was completely independent, criticising the government. She was a critical journalist, as a journalist should be. She did not believe what politicians said, she was investigative and critical... Like a bee, buzzing around to get the honey out of the story... And she had tremendous power, she was like a volcano who could explode again and again.

"There's a good Dutch saying - she was a 'vreemde eend in de bijt' (*the odd one out, an intruder or outsider - literally, a strange duck in the hole*). She was provocative - the opposite of the average silent, reluctant Dutch journalist.

> "In 1985, the first time I attended a FPA official celebration, she was still President. It was a very good anniversary with Lubbers and everyone… She was well respected by people. It was sad how quickly she lost her memory, very sad."

The last regular press events Nel still went on attending were Prime Minister Wim Kok's press conferences. In an obituary on Nel, Friso wrote:

> "When Kok appeared at the annual pre-budget day press conference with the new Secretary General of the prime minister's office, Ad Geelhoed, it was Nel who asked: 'Mr Kok, who is the gentleman who is sitting next to you?' A young reporter said later: 'We were all thinking that but Nel asked it'. That's how she was: the right question at the right point."

vii. Into the nursing home: Yolanda's story

Eventually, the day came on 8 June 1999 to move Nel into the nursing home, the Gulden Huis on Steenhouwersgaarde in The Hague. The move was well managed, but was quite nerve-wracking, as Yolanda recalled:

> "Piet took Nel to the hairdresser while Sandra and I packed stuff and put it in the moving van. She did care about clothes, she never threw them away, ones she'd had 20 or 30 year ago were still there, hundreds of pairs of panties, cardigans, silk blouses - really a lot…. Nel was quite a striking lady, very pretty when she was younger…"

Tyna Wynaendts was also impressed by Nel's huge quantities of clothing, as well as how very well organised they were, possibly as a result of her early nursing training. Tyna also remembered Nel insisting on 'hospital corners' when making beds with her, when she would remark: You know, I'm a Swiss nurse and this is how it must be'. Over the years, Nel squirreled away and hoarded everything.

> "Thousands of doubles of everything. But it was very well organised, in neat piles, and every spring, everything came out of all the cupboards and was put back again. She was a bit of a hamster. Yolanda wasn't exaggerating,

I've never seen anything like it. She had all her old lipsticks that were not quite finished, about twenty of them. We were trying to give things away and clear things out, and then we would open another cupboard, and there was more and more of it - it was incredible. Even in the cellar, there were suitcases full of clothes that were still taken out, cleaned and put back again. That was a bit of nursing mentality."

While they were still struggling to deal with all the clothes,

"The hairdresser called, Nel was finished and wanted out and we were not ready at all. Piet rushed over and plonked her by the television at his house, after some yelling and screaming. She really loves him. Piet's brother and I put up her things, hung up curtains... We had come up with the idea of saying the house is being painted, you have to go out for a while."

"I had to go with her to her room. When she saw all her stuff, she sat down and stopped grumbling. She loved chocolates and especially cheese, she stuffed them in. A lady in the home came in. It was really very funny, with an enormous list of questions, what do you like for breakfast, porridge? Nel hooted, you must be absolutely crazy. A question about hobbies - her eyes were nearly closed, she was tired. '*Hobbies*?' She said, 'Hobby, I never had a hobby, don't be silly'. Working was her hobby.

"Piet and I were really sad - such an amazing woman, kicking and screaming. Why am I here with all these mad people. After the first day, she took over one of the chairs by the elevator, made it her chair for a couple of months. The nursing staff liked her very much, the only one that was more or less alive and kicking. Nel was quite nice to the other people too. There was one old lady, she would come by and offer her chocolates. They were playing bingo - can you imagine? She hadn't got a clue what everyone was doing."

This gusto for favourite foods was an enduring characteristic. For Friso's 70th birthday, he hired a boat and invited all his friends on a boat trip. Yolanda said he wanted Nel to be there, even though she was already pretty far gone.

"No problem, I said, I'll take her. She made for the herrings, she loved herrings and Friso had only reckoned on one per person; she ate about three. Typically Nel. She sat down on the boat and it was lovely to see her with all her old mates, probably old enemies, the way they told stories - everybody in Nieuwspoort still watching her - how much admiration they had for her, it was really quite stunning."

The best part about the move, said Friso, was that once she was in her room, with some of her furniture around her and the pictures put up on the wall by Yolanda, she looked around and said it was quite nice though half the time she thought she was in Brussels. Nel had started to go walk-about from her flat, wandering all over The Hague completely lost, and sometimes being picked up by the police. There were other distressing stories about incontinence and tantrums at the Nieuwspoort press centre but the staff there always remained completely understanding and kind to her. But getting lost was frightening; she would feel safe and be well cared for physically in the home, Friso felt.

A number of people continued to visit her in the home. Yolanda found she could make her laugh over a pile of old photos but as her memory got shorter and shorter, it could be painful. Tyna said Flora didn't like visiting Nel:

> "It drove her crazy, Nel asking the same question. But I gave her the same answer, why vary it when she asks exactly the same question. And that kept her happy. And it doesn't really matter so long as you are communicating. People found it annoying when she couldn't remember them but I would always get her to talk about the past and my mother when they were small. Then she remembered a lot better."

The end of Nel's life was particularly distressing, Yolanda said, as she simply stopped eating but still took some days to depart. Even at the end, her will remained strong.

Nel Slis died on 17 December 2001.

Celebrations and Reflections

A series of interviewers, myself included, made their way to Nel's apartment in The Hague in the years after her retirement from the AP to record and transmit her story to the public on some particular anniversary, or simply because they had got wind of it. As well as the many gaps these filled in putting together Nel's earlier history, they give a series of thumbnail sketches of Nel in later life. As Dutch newspaperman Robert Schouten remarked,

> "Journalists are not supposed to interview each other, is the normal opinion in journalism. But Nel Slis simply has to be an exception to this rule. After all, she also belongs to the category of women-who-have-made-a-career".

i. The magnetism of Nel

Nel finally retired on 1 May 1979. As she told Schouten, she had wrung an extra eight months from the AP.

> "Completely exceptional for AP. It is an iron rule that you have to go when you're 65. But among other reasons because they thought that the queen would abdicate on her seventieth birthday, and I am well-informed about royalty, they wanted me to stay on a bit longer. But that abdication is now no longer expected for the moment."

Keith Fuller, who had succeeded Wes Gallagher as President and General Manager of the AP, said in a letter to Nel:

"I know you will look back with pride on the big stories you helped cover, including the Moluccan siege, the Prince Bernhard story and the Common Market. It will seem strange to think of anyone else covering the tough political scene".

One of the press interviews with Nel on her retirement inspired a 77 year old woman from Gouda to write a letter to Nel which must have touched and amused her.

"What you have achieved borders on the unbelievable. Nurse, Sorbonne, Oxford, almost psychiatry, English, French, German, Italian, translating from New York for the Netherlands Purchasing Commission, AP correspondent in a man's world, and then still to look so nice!"

Schouten described his encounter with Nel in an article headlined: "Give me the nub of the business":

"Madam, you are blessed with a strong voice". Nel Slis glances, not a bit surprised, at photographer Kurt Boekenkamp, who is setting up his camera. Behind her back, men are apt to compare her voice to a foghorn. But the awe-inspiring noise that this astute woman can produce - if necessary also in English, French, German and Italian - is undoubtedly one of the qualities that has made her, as correspondent of the powerful American press bureau Associated Press since the war in The Hague and Brussels, into a professional difficult to circumvent.

At the foreign affairs ministry, people talk derisively, but nonetheless with respect, about the way Ms Slis puts her questions on the phone. "No long stories, please. Give me the core of the business. What are you doing there the whole goddam day, if you can't do that."

Nel Slis is retiring from the AP. In her flat in The Hague, where the dunes can just be seen, the telex still rattles away in her study. "I shall miss that thing, not the noise, but the information," she says.

Then, looking rather helplessly at enormous piles of newspapers and reports on the floor, looking for photos that refuse to appear, she says: "I can't find anything any more. One of these days, I must just chuck everything out; I don't believe there's any point in keeping anything".

Fortunately, the typical journalist's reluctance to throw stuff away prevailed, otherwise it would have been impossible to write this book. Schouten also quotesNel complaining about paying taxes for "emancipation," and denigrating marriage.

> "If it was for crèches, ok. This whole legislation here, that's why I have been a member of the bachelors' union from the start. Not because I don't like men, on the contrary, but because of the neglect of singles compared with married people. This whole marriage business, anyhow I find it idiotic".

As we know, there was one man she would have married, though that was a long time ago by then. The dig was mainly to do with Nel's perpetual irritation about relatively heavier taxes paid by single people in the Netherlands.Nel once said she would not like to have had children herself as it would be "tedious to have to give a good example all the time". But she remained very interested in other people's children, who in turn found her fascinating. Yolanda said:

> "She was always interested in children of friends knew all their names, who they married, their jobs, everything. It also showed when we were clearing up through her desk, there were lots of pictures of small children".

Igor Cornelissen's interview in Vrij Nederland in 1982 was headlined: 'And on top of that I had the good fortune that I had a nose for news' It was Cornelissen who made the comment quoted in Chapter 5, that it would have been nicer and more to the point, if she went down in Dutch press history as "That woman who stopped Molotov", rather than "that difficult broad". Nel Slis, he went on,

> "undoubtedly belongs to that group of people that the English delicately and without condescension call a character. In the AP house magazine she was once described as vivacious and charming. Charming we would not want to dispute, but vivacious is definitely too weak a word. Slis is the writing tornado of the Foreign Press Association".

In November 1988, when Nel was 75, the Foreign Press Association celebrated her 45 years as a journalist with a reception in Nieuwspoort. As I was attending the reception with Nel's former FPA vice-chairman David Post, a friend from England was astonished when Prime Minister

Ruud Lubbers strolled casually in and amiably heckled Nel from the back of the room, without a bodyguard in sight.

Endt, who had initiated the celebration, had assembled a book of multilingual appreciations from dozens of friends. Among their contributions, Herman Bleich called her "the terror of press officers" and Manuel Santarelli, director of information at the European Commission, "la personnalite la plus craquante, la plus attachante" at Brussels press conferences.

An article in the Haagse Post to mark the occasion was headlined by her favourite tag on how she became a journalist: 'I fell into it like a hair in the soup'. It portrayed her as still very much a working journalist, at the age of 75. About her career, she told the paper it was "a long and often also a hard time. But I would do it all over again with pleasure",

In 1991, Monique Smits' portrait of Nel Slis appeared in the Mediakrant headlined by that modest remark of Nel's: "If it's about news, I trample them all into the corner": Smit, too, was impressed by the dynamism of the 78 year old journalist, still in harness. though becoming a little chaotic.

> "Who sent you?" In the hall of her flat in The Hague, where bulging bookcases line the walls, she looks me up and down curiously. While she impatiently awaits my answer, I remember the character sketches by journalists who worked with her: "During the Indonesian crisis, she put the wind up at the foreign affairs ministry. The terror of many an authority and spokesman, but with a soft heart. *Never a dull moment* with Nel
>
> Nel Slis (78) quickly displayed her charms, with a sonorous voice from the back of her throat, deepened a fair number of octaves by cigarettes. First she wanted to know the reason for my visit, before she rushed irrepressibly hither and thither and in a bird's eye view unveiled her wanderings around the world and landing up in journalism.
>
> Since retiring from the AP ("they palmed me off with a rotten little pension"), Nel has been writing for American publications like Europe Magazine, Oil and Chemical News and for the Agence Europe press agency ("Because I still find it fun and because I need the cents to be able to travel")…"

Later in the interview, Nel produced a framed photo of Han Boon, Foreign Affairs State Secretary under Joseph Luns, inscribed by Boon:

"To Nel Slis. Dynamic, intrepid, a true friend over the years." At the end of the interview, Smits has Nel already getting back to work again:

Talking about the Bosio affair ("I can't make head or tail of that") reminds her of a lunch date with the French ambassador. "Perhaps I should ask him about it, but he will certainly think twice about giving an opinion on it"….

ii. 80-year War

Ageeth Scherphuis' extensive and sympathetic portrait, in Vrij Nederland, was one of several marking Nel Slis' 80th birthday in 1993. It also had some vivid vignettes of Nel in action. The introduction recalls Nel's early battles:

```
Nel Slis' 80-year War

The only women among a hundred wily
correspondents. 'That difficult woman' on facts
and checking and bolting barefoot to that
godforsaken telephone. The news must get onto
the wire. On her male colleagues: nit-pickers.
And on women: milksops, they were, and still
they don't do anything.

A nice girl from the South Holland islands at
Associated Press, one of the biggest press
agencies in the world. She had to hammer away
harder than such a nice little man from NRC. It
made her more aggressive than she was, she
says, and it gave her a bigger gob. Definitely.
But there will hardly be another like her in
The Hague.

A big gob and a smart face, these are her
biggest qualities, she says herself. 'And then
if you are also a bit intelligent.." Eighty
years old, she is, and certainly for sixty of
those, she has made it herself. She is better
known in the world than here: in Brussels, she
is La Slis and in New York every journalist
knows her. In The Hague, she's that difficult
woman, who always wants to hear everything
twice before she reports it. Or better still,
she was that difficult woman. "She is a lamb
now, compared with earlier," says Gijs van der
Wiel, former director of the government
information service.

He gives a perfect imitation of a dialogue
which he had had a hundred times with The
Hague's correspondent for the Associated Press.
```

"By night and at breakfast she called me with this heavy, smoky voice, put her questions and drew her conclusions. If I then said: 'Nel, that's not how it is,' she shouted back: 'How is it then, goddamit?' And I came back again: 'That I can't goddam tell you yet'. A manner of conversation that I did like, but the younger spokesmen were not all charmed by it.

"She has an extraordinary journalist's intuition," says Van der Wiel, "she is very persistent and she has unheard-of energy. Intuitively, she knows what's going on and then she sticks to it, stopping at nothing. But nobody will run aground with this woman - she is trustworthy. Never have I heard a minister or civil servant interviewed by her complain: *that I did not say.* They can be shocked by their own remarks, especially because it goes to the world abroad.

'I will read (what they said) over to you,' she phones then.

And me: 'Yes, but can't there be a word in between, it is really so very strong'.

'They goddam said it like that'

'But if you tone it down a bit'.

'No, then it would be such goddam flabby trash'".

Commenting that her knighthood from Den Uyl did not make her any softer or easier, Van der Wiel said to Scherphuis:

"Difficult she is, and impatient. Always with the hot breath of the competition on her neck. 'Don't you goddamn have anything for me yet, UPI will soon be running away with it.'"

Scherphuis finishes up:

The interview ends: "So", she concludes her tale, "now you know my whole history.

Why should people be afraid of me? As you see, I am a lamb".

Algemeen Dagblad reporter Sjef van Woensel was impressed by her 80th birthday "reception for a trustworthy big mouth", at which she was presented with an entire edition of Europe Tomorrow devoted to her, asking his readers:

"To whom does it happen that the prime minister comes to address you because you are having your eightieth birthday? And who gives you a free reception with hundreds of people attending? This happened yesterday to Nel Slis, a very well known journalist in The Hague who worked as correspondent for the Associated Press in the Netherlands from 1945.

Slis began working in the Netherlands for this American press agency, which supplies news reports to virtually all newspapers in the world, as a jong broekie (greenhorn) immediately after the war and remained there, with an interruption of a number of years in Brussels. The European Commission yesterday offered her a reception where many prominent people came to shake her hand. Such as foreign affairs minister Kooijmans and prime minister Lubbers. Lubbers praised the journalist for her tenacity in questioning and the trustworthiness of her reports. The premier also put up happily with the big mouth that made Slis a colourful and resonant figure in The Hague ('in het Haagse')......

What do you think of the Dutch press after 48 years experience?

She hardly pauses for thought and with her harsh, penetrating voice she says that it could sometimes be a bit more critical. "They could hit home a bit more often. That does not have to be hard or improper." In general, she finds the news media "not bad". Every day she mines part of her information, but this never goes out around the world without being checked with the original sources.

What irritates Slis is that the Dutch news media has so few correspondents abroad. "You are a little country (Nel often distanced herself from her own country), but the papers should really invest more money in correspondents. Young dogs that build up experience abroad and can accomplish very good work in their own country after that. They would also be more critical then".

She is not unhappy about Dutch politicians. She just finds it a pity that some able people do not want to give time to politics or choose to hold better paid jobs at international companies like Philips and Unilever.

Have you seen clear developments in the Netherlands?

"Oh yes, certainly. The Dutch have evolved very much in their opinions. Earlier, when I began here, they were very reserved. Now they are much more free, for instance in the political area and as far as sex is concerned"

How long will you go on with your work?

"As long as I can talk and walk. So I hope a long time yet".

iii. "If Lubbers goes, I go too"

Finally, Ineke Geraerdts had a piece in October's Nieuwspoort Nieuws. When Geraerdts complained to her editor that Vrij Nederland had covered everything conceivable in its three full pages on Nel Slis, she was advised to ask Nel what she had missed in that interview. The piece she wrote has considerable atmosphere and a revealing sad note:

"News has become second nature to me"

Eighty-year old Nel Slis: "If Lubbers goes, I'll go too"

She lights up another cigarette. A slim, well-dressed woman, with lively brown eyes that assess me curiously. "What I missed? Something about my work. There is a lot in it about my career, but my work never came up. It is still very important for me. I could not do without it, that would bore me to death". Her home on The Hague's Ranonkelstraat breathes the atmosphere of a student flat. Furious clean-up attempts stranded on the impossibility of throwing away books, magazines and other valuable piles of paper. The walls are good for reminders of former times, well-loved people, foreign countries: a print of a San Francisco swimming bath, a photo of a good friend who is no longer around, a water-colour of a country lane on Goeree Overflakkee…

"I owned land in Zeeland and I now live in the proceeds of this" She looks around. "Good, isn't it? But now and then I have to get away for a month or two, when I've had enough of this fiddling around here. Moving again? I couldn't think of having to drag all this mess with me. No, just now and again going away for a couple of months is a fine solution for now. It is like the Rock of Gibraltar here in the winter. Then I go to the south of France. If I

was not Dutch, I would only like to be French.
I still have a few good friends, but they are
becoming fewer. Sometimes I think: what have I
done to deserve it that I'm still here. All
these boys that I have known, apart from a
couple, are already in their coffins..."

*In 1986, you poured your heart out in
Nieuwspoort Nieuws on "the lack of
understanding of the*

*Government Information Service RVD for the
interests of the Foreign Press Association".
You were then chairing the FPA. Has the
situation improved since?*

"Yes, considerably. My criticisms applied at
the time mainly to the RVD spokesmen for the
departments and for the major cities, who with
a few exceptions were not very accommodating.
Since then, people here in the Netherlands have
made great progress in the way in which they
handle the press. 'Cooperating with us' is
better realised. Earlier, many bodies were
scared stiff of us. That is over now, all the
doors are open. I think that the EEC has played
and still does play a big role in that. A
United Europe is a good idea. It is the only
way to ensure that something comes out of all
these different countries. I called for that
already in May 1948 at the meeting between
Churchill and Adenauer".

"My big trump card was of course my knowledge
of languages. I still remember that Gijs van
der Wiel called me up one time with a cry for
help: 'Can you come to the Portuguese prime
minister's press conference? I'm stuck here
with twelve young press guys who don't even
understand a word of French'. Underestimating
the importance of languages is a mistaken way
of thinking".

Like others, Geraerts quizzes Nel on what she
thinks of Dutch journalism:

"A bit sloppy perhaps, but in general I enjoy
reading what's being written. From time to
time, I buy Vrij Nederland and I have a
subscription to De Volkskrant and NRC. One for
themorning, the other for the evening. That
keeps a person informed. And then there is the
TV. I find it awful if I miss the news one
time. News has become second nature to me.

"What has struck me recently: it is so quiet. That is not just Dutch journalism. The whole of Europe is 'quiet'. Europe is preparing itself. This lull will not last for ever".

'It is quiet. I try: You had the nickname in The Hague of "the terror of Luns" (Dutch foreign minister, later NATO chief). Were you so difficult for him?

"Of course not. I was maybe not the easiest, but Luns was such a conceited man that he was actually scared of everyone. Do you know who I really have admiration for? For Lubbers. After Drees, Lubbers comes top for me. If he goes, I go too. Lubbers is an extraordinary man. Exceptional. The fact that he is Catholic, I don't blame him for that. You might as well know, I'm not mad about these fine Holland Catholics, but I find Calvinists just as creepy.

Back to Lubbers. I have known him so long, first as MP, then as economic affairs minister. He has only had 10 years as premier after all. He has flair, talent for ironing out messes. I do not believe that he has many enemies. An international career should suit him. Delors (EEC President) is stepping down next year….

After Lubbers we may get Brinkman. He has the best credentials. I'm not afraid of his piercing eyes. Six month ago, I suggested in the FPA, 'let's quiz him', and we invited him to a lunch. A great success. He was like a lamb. Ach, it will all turn out all right".

Nel Slis is now 80 and not yet "at peace". She still takes care of reports from the Dutch country for "Europe, agence internationale d'information pour la presse", writes features for Europa Magazine (an EEC publication in New York), writes articles for the "chemical magazines" of DSM, Akzo and Gist Brocades. And so on, and so forth. She has a telex and a fax. No computer. "I don't have to have that any more at my age?"

In the winter months her car is parked in the Lange Lombardstraat every Thursday evening. Nel Slis polishes up her Italian now. Soon she is going to start learning Russian as well. "I met such nice White Russians in those days in France at the Sorbonne."

Oh yes, some people are unstoppable….

Robert Schoten interview on retirement from AP, 1979

Ivor Cornelissen interview, 1983

THE LADY OF THE PRESS

Ageeth Scherphuis interview: Nel Slis' 80-year war, 1983

Nel and NATO Secretary-General Joseph Luns feature in Netherlands
Press Museum exhibition

iv. Reflections

On Nel's enthusiasm for Lubbers, Yolanda Frenkel Frank said she thought Nel was secretly in love with him, "absolutely smitten by him." Nel also liked Prince Claus very much. The many photos of her with Lubbers and Claus show how well she got on with both of them.

In 1995, Nel featured as '*the grand old lady of the press*' in a centenary exhibition mounted by the Netherlands Press Museum, entitled Voor alles journaliste - Journalist before everything. The exhibition guide remarks: "She distinguished herself from her male colleagues by her direct approach, tenacious persistence in asking questions, and lack of respect for authority"; its centrefold is the photo of Nel with Mansholt.

Asked what she missed most about Nel, her friend Flora Lewis said:

> "Oh, just an old friend. Comfort. We had little junkets, excursions, which I couldn't bear to do later, because she insisted on driving and she was a terrible, awful driver. Oh, in France, places we wanted to go, or I had some reason to look at, or because we thought there might be a story. We would look for something in a place that I was eager to visit, or that was attractive. No, I'm not a mountain climber - Nel is, but I get tired, it's not my thing. She was adventurous. There were places that I wanted to see, that had some artistic or historical or picturesque interest. For the reasons that people go away on junkets. For years after, she was always nagging me to go somewhere for a holiday, which I didn't want to because she had become difficult".

Musing on Nel as a journalist, Flora said:

> "I think she was a kind of role model, rule-breaker, that made it easier for women… I think her contribution was just steady, honest reporting. Sturdy, sober, getting the information, reliability, credibility. She was honest. She would ask tough questions because she wasn't about to play softball - to give someone an easy ride because she liked them. But on the other hand, even if she didn't like someone, she wouldn't ask mean questions, she wouldn't ask trick questions, it was all very straightforward. The sources who knew her, because it's a small country and they all know each other quite well, learned quickly that they could rely on her. She wouldn't distort, pretend, twist. She didn't try to trip people, but she didn't give them a puffball either.

"She was a very straightforward, hardworking, uncomplicated reporter. My sense of her was always very open, very straight, she was about exactly what she said she was about. (*From childhood, she was very curious*) That's what makes a reporter. She had some problem with her father... She said that was one of the reasons she was eager to get off and be a newspaper woman, because she wanted very much to reach this stage of independence.

"She would try very hard, she was very persistent, but she wouldn't do anything improper. She wouldn't pretend to be somebody she wasn't, call up and say I'm so-and-so.

Lots of people do that. Woodward and Bernstein tell in one of their books about Watergate that they broke into an apartment and stole documents: Nel would never do that. Oh yes, they did that, and you get - particularly with television people - this pretending to be somebody that they're not, pretending to want to ask about one thing, when they're really trying to go for something else. Making appointments giving the wrong information about yourself. Nel was always honest.

"Practically everybody who knew Nel was fond of her. You saw that Lubbers was also.

Well, because one admired her, it was exactly this independent-mindedness, this honesty, this certainty that you knew who and what she was, and that's extremely attractive. Particularly in a society where that kind of woman was unusual".

As I was writing, Laura Raun, another fellow-FPA board member and friend of Nel's, e-mailed from Texas with this charming image of Nel in the kitchen:

> "Oddly enough, my most vivid memories are of Nel in her personal life, not her professional one. For example, Nel was meticulous about cooking.

When she made an oil and lemon dressing, she was very careful about measuring out the ingredients and mixing them thoroughly in a small, clear bowl. I can still see her in the kitchen, the sun silhouetting her, stirring that dressing.

I loved Nel's flat in The Hague because it had windows in every room. It was a virtual glass house, close to the water. We would go for walks on the beach, sometimes stopping for a coffee on the boardwalk.

I would stay overnight and she was a perfect hostess. Nel adored having a captive audience to hear her colourful tales of friends and colleagues across Europe. Her throaty voice painted the picture, her cigarette-wielding hands accentuated it".

Yolanda, too, remembered Nel's salad dressing.

> "It always tasted better than anyone else's, even if we made it exactly the same way. She was a very good cook, liked to make salads, that type of thing".

Smoking a Cigar at Home

v. Lubbers on Nel

Nel's favourite politician Ruud Lubbers, who promoted Nel to Officer of Oranje-Nassau at the second FPA anniversity celebrations over which she presided, has the last word on her, both as a journalist and a person. Lubbers, who went on after his premiership to chair the World Wildlife Fund and in 2001 became UN High Commissioner for Refugees, phoned me very quickly after I wrote to ask for his help for the book during my early struggles with it, in autumn 1999.

Lubbers said he was coming to the Nieuwe Kerk in Amsterdam to see the Dalai Lama and told me to come along there and "say you have an appointment with me". A very young lad on the door looked totally disbelieving when I muddily dismounted from my bike in the pouring rain and told him this as instructed, but at that moment, Lubbers rushed out, grabbed my arm and whisked me inside, saying "I need this woman", leaving the door-boy gaping.

Sitting on the steps of the crowded Nieuwe Kerk, Lubbers said:

> "I liked her – the strangest thing is that she was a Francophile and I also am – I was intrigued by the fact she was a Francophile. Though in the European context, she was more British – communitaire – a no-nonsense approach to Europe". (Lubbers himself was famous for his "no-nonsense" politics).

> "A very straight lady, and open. And I found her typically Dutch – Les Gueix. In the beginning of the 16th century, the aristocrats joined with the ordinary people, and when

> Charles V left to go to Spain, they protested – if you go, we go too. It's the French for beggars. So Nel was one of Les Gueix, and I had something in common with her.

> "She was plain-speaking, and the fact that she was a Francophile gave me an intimate feeling with her. As a journalist, she was good – direct, not scared, not impressed by authority. But I had the impression she was a colleague as well. She could team up with people in the British press, managing essential, vital contacts with colleagues.

> I had the impression she was old-fashioned in a way as a journalist, not looking for headlines. I always felt secure – it's not normal with modern journalists. She was a very

> civilised lady. Open, not respectful of authority, but at the same time, you could trust her.

> You are a bit scared of journalists, sometimes they abuse you, but she did not.

> I found she had a good grasp and analysis of Europe, remarkably good. Not only contributing as a journalist, but in her own right, you could learn something from her. I learnt a lot from her. I had a good relationship with her, very positive".

Postscript: Ave Atque Vale

On a squally, showery April day, I set off by train from Amsterdam to Rotterdam, excited and a little nervous, to visit Nel's island for the first time. I want to sniff the air she breathed and feel out the place where she grew up. Hopefully this will be an inspiration as I go on trying to assemble the jigsaw of her exciting and sometimes tumultuous life. So many pieces are missing. I have known Nel for a fairly long time, but I have never really been with her for more than for odd hours or the odd evening. I have learned Nel in very small slices, forced to reflect her world in broken fragments. But now at least I will have a glimpse of the island of which she was so proud. Something about an islander...

It's only a short metro ride from Rotterdam to Zuidplein to catch the bus to Goree-Overflakkee, a very straightforward trip compared with Nel's epic outings to Rotterdam as a child. On the bus, I crane eagerly through the window like a child myself, looking out for the crossing to the island. Every detail of the trip becomes riveting, crying out for some significance, some meaning, some Nel association. As the bus reaches the long bridge, tall white wind turbines line the mainland shore, one inexplicably immobile but the others briskly circling their skinny arms. Nel's island is just visible in the distance. On the other side, another line of turbines waves us onto the island. There, ponies and black cattle graze between swathes of water, as if the land is reluctant to part from the sea. Then the heavens open and blinding sheets of rain blot everything out.

In Middelharnis, the rain abates. As I search for the town hall, I'm excited to recognise Nel's old school from photos I've seen. The town hall turns out to be at the previous bus stop and is closed for lunch. A group of some thirty teenagers cluster around a dark, barn-like café nearby. Do they perhaps have a distinctive Goeree-Overflakkee physiognomy? The girls are blonde, but seem distinctively thin and wiry like Nel, not blonde and bovine as elsewhere in Holland. And they look a lively lot. The boys look like boys anywhere. The burley middle-aged café landlord says the place has changed since the bridge was built, with people from Rotterdam settling here "for the nature" and nobody speaking the old dialect any more. Perhaps Nel spoke that dialect as a child.

When the town hall opens, the enthusiastic Mr Both has me enthralled for hours with his descriptions of early 20th century island life referred to in the first chapter of this book. Then there is just time to visit Middelharnis graveyard before catching the bus back. A large and imposing-looking group of Jewish gravestones faces the only slightly larger group marking the graves of the Protestant island dignitaries. And this group is dominated by the Slis family. That large Jewish community on the island reminds me of the only man Nel really loved, Dan Schorr. I wonder again whether the child Nel was perhaps a little fascinated by that community.

Here we have come full circle and at last encountered the island of Nel's beginnings. Something about an islander… Back on the bus, I scramble to do my daily translations via laptop; it runs out of battery in Rotterdam and I rush into an Etos drugstore and borrow some electricity to finish my work. So has it always been, always trying to do the Nel book along with too many other things. That's the story of my life. From Rotterdam, I travel on to Scheveningen, The Hague's seaside suburb, to stay the night with Vera. (Vera Vaughan-Bowden, Nel's third successor as president of the Foreign Press Association) The next day, I talk on the phone to Nel's nephew Hans Nieuwenhuyzen, who is feeling terrible as he is having chemotherapy, but still wants to find an old photo of four generations of the Slis family including Nel, and to photocopy the Slis genealogy for me.

Later, Vera and I take the tram together to visit Nel. I'm so happy Vera is coming too. On the last two visits on my own, Nel was sleepy and far away in some other world. I found it heartbreaking and could only bear to stay a few minutes. Her carers tell us things are not too good and Nel refuses to put her teeth in. I knew that she had become aggressive in the autumn; I feel it must be the frustration of not remembering the end of any sentence you begin. The last I heard, from Friso, some old man in the home was convinced Nel was his wife and kept trying to hug her, but got a few kicks from Nel in return. "Tragic but humorous," said Friso. There was life in the old dog yet, I thought.

We start the usual hunt for Nel, who is inclined to wander into someone else's room and fall asleep. Then, at the end of the corridor near her room, we see an unmistakable tiny figure silhouetted against the window and we rush to corral her into her room. She looks fragile and birdlike but still smart in a brown Chanel-type wool suit. Vera's soft Belgian chocolates are a big success; she can hardly wait for Vera to open the box and eats one after another. Often she stands by the window and gazes out at the sky, far away somewhere else.

She is quite wide awake and several times attempts some sentences but they die away unfinished, sometimes causing a flash of anger. The nearest to a coherent one was about some girl that disappeared: we wonder where that came from. She also walks companionably with us to the lift when we leave, uttering more half-sentences; we can feel flashes of her old charm. Vera and I talk later about how these kinds of sociable manners can persist. My mother, for instance, who was pretty much in a daze in her last few years, still invariably rallied to say: "Have you eaten yet?" Vera also reminds me of Nel's reluctance to part with us until Vera said we were going to see Frank de Jong, a name that produced a slight flash of recognition.

While we were visiting, I talked determinedly at Nel about the book, told her it would be inished soon, and showed her photos from her archives and the ones of her father and mother that her nephew gave me. She gazed over my head for a while, but eventually started looking at the photos. She seemed interested in the ones of her father and Dan Schorr and then the ones with Prince Claus, Lubbers, Stravinsky and other famous people. For a while, perhaps she was transported back in time to her days of power and glory, as the AP's Slis, La Slis of Brussels, Hellcat of The Hague. We tiptoe away but she comes friendly with us to the door.

***

Rage, rage, how does that poem go? I feel it now.
So sad to see Nel like this, her battle almost done.
She has fought a most glorious fight
Hacked her way through that Great Grey Male Jungle
Adding colour - clearing the way for us other women to follow.
Always her sharp, clear eye for detail and what lies beneath
Her Nose for News, her probing quest, never flagging, never giving up.
Her Iron Goeree Constitution, tireless to the end.
And then - her endless kindness to all new journalists, especially empowering women
Her raucous laugh, her smoky voice, cutting through the cackle - or cackling!

We celebrate the Life of Nel.

***

It's hard to believe that this trip was more than 12 years ago, as I finally launch Nel's book into the world. Such is the strength of the fascination Nel and her life and times have had for me and others.

Appendix A:.
Speech by Prince Claus to the FPA, 14 February 1981

The original typescript of Prince Claus' famous speech to the Foreign Press Association in Scheveningen's Kurhaus on St Valentine's Day, 14 February 1981.

Madam Chairman, ladies and gentlemen

It is a pleasure to be here with you tonight attending this annual dinner of the Foreign Press Association in the Netherlands. Your association is celebrating its 55th anniversary. Well - actually it should have been celebrated last year because the Buitenlandse Persvereniging was founded back in 1925. I am afraid it is due to problems with my agenda that you had no dinner last year. But then you will have two in 1981. Anyway, I congratulate you, Madam Chairman and all the members on your 55th anniversary and wish you many happy returns.

Your association has many friends in our country which is shown by the number of

supporters, or as we say: donateurs. In fact you have even more donateurs than ordinary members - A situation not unknown in the world of sports. I hope they, the DONATEURS, as their name suggests, have indeed paid for the excellent dinner we have enjoyed here tonight.

Ladies and gentlemen, when I was asked to take the floor tonight, the question arose: What, other than proposing a toast to your association, should I talk about and how. An after-dinner-speech? Now, this is a very tricky thing to try for anyone who has not been brought up in the tradition of this very specific genre of speeches. That is to say - for anyone who is not British. An after-dinner-speech, l.+g., has to be short and witty. To make a speech short - like a short letter - as Pascall observed so rightly - you need a lot of time to prepare it. Which I did not have. You always seem to start thinking about a speech when time is running short. And witty. Well, you either are witty or you are not. Wit can be acquired to a certain extent but on the whole I have found that the opposite to being witty is to try to be witty. It mostly fails and results are painful, especially for those who have to listen.

So, as a result of a more or less frank and honest self-assessment I discarded the idea of a typical after-dinner-speech. What then? Somebody suggested that I speak about: My position of Prince-Consort.

My answer was: Why not? Since I knew my audience tonight would consist for no small part of journalists, foreign correspondents, I said to myself: Why not an interview? After all, many of your colleagues, maybe some of you present here, are said to be of the opinion that we, members of the Dutch Royal Family are much too tight-lipped; anyway, give far too few interviews.

Well, then, here is one. A fictitious one. Off the record, please, and almost off the cuff. An interview where I ask the questions and will try to answer them as honestly as possible.

Here we go - First question

Sir - I presume an English speaking journalist would commence his question like this. (Possibly, tell me prince, or what's your name). This little word, Sir, I wish we had some equivalent in our language. It would save quite some people a lot of tongue-twisting exercise in trying to find the right form of address. But back to the first question.

Sir, what is it like, how does it feel to be a Prince-Consort"?

Well, there is this problem of being called Prince-Consort or Prinsgemaal in Dutch.

As you certainly know, Prince-Consort or for that matter Queen-Consort, is the title conferred upon a Queen's titled husband or a King's wife. Again: a very British institution. The last Prince-Consort was Queen Victoria's husband, Prince Albert. The Duke of Edinburgh - to my knowledge - does not have this title. Neither had my father-in-law nor I. It just does not exist in Holland officially. It only means to say in colloquial language that you are the Queen's husband. So when my wife became Queen I - in this colloquial sense - automatically became Prince-Consort. - Prinsgemaal. The wife of a King on the other hand becomes Queen. Some sort of discrimination - one could argue.

But please don't jump to conclusions now. Otherwise we'll have headings like: CLAUS: DISCRIMINATION - WHY NOT KING FOR ME?

To answer your question: What is it like to be a Prince-Consort. Well, to be quite frank, I don't feel so much of a difference with my previous position of prince tout court - husband of the Crown Princess. You know my background; A commoner who at the age of 39 came here from a foreign country to say the least, and got married to the Crown Princess. This was back in 1966. Now we write 1981. All I can say is this: 16 years of learning and adaptation. The Role and the real person - if you know what I mean. Some sort of an identity syndrome - to use a modern term. Not easy. And I am a bad actor...It still is not easy. I go on trying in my new position.

But mind you: The change in my life in 1966 was a much more drastic one than the change which took place on the 30th of April last year (when Beatrix was crowned queen).But that very human problem or, if you want, the tension between official role and private person remains. But then many people who have come to public prominence later in their lives have to cope with this phenomenon.

Q. Sir, talking about adaptation and learning, what was and maybe is the single most difficult problem you had to cope with?

A. Without any doubt the Dutch language. Does that surprise you? I know, people in Holland are very nice, very complementary about my command of the Dutch language. But I myself know better. I agree, I do speak Dutch fairly fluently. No small wonder after 16 years of trying. But it just remains - as far as I am concerned - quite a handicap to always have to speak in a language which is not your mother tongue. And I think the dilemma increases with the number of languages you speak. The result being that in the end you don't speak any single language quite correctly any more.

So I do not believe in what Emperor Charles V allegedly has stated, namely that man acquires a new additional personality with every new language he masters. But then he used the different languages in a very specific way: To his God he spoke Spanish; to women Italian; to men French and to his horse -- German. Today we would call him a multinational emperor.

As to myself, I speak Dutch to my wife and to my children and all the animals - pets - around. If you want to know exactly how good my Dutch is, just ask my children. They are the most unbiased and merciless critics and I still learn a lot from them. What does irritate me at times is the fact that they who took up Dutch years later than I did speak it so much better.

Q. Sir, I read recently in a serious French newspaper an article heading: "Un Prince-Consort de Gauche". A leftist Price-Consort. The article, Sir, was about you. What is your reaction?

A. Oh, yes, I have read that article myself. Quite some fancy conclusions based on a lot of hearsay. You know, a ruling Queen's husband like, for that matter, the Queen herself or any constitutional monarch should not publicly give evidence of any political preference. But since this is a confidential interview, off the record, I shall try to answer this tricky question as frankly as possible.

To begin with: The notions right or left as pointing to the outer ends of the political spectrum of our pluriform system of Parliamentary Democracy have never meant a great deal to me personally. I really don't know what I am. It depends so much on the issue in question. I am not an homogeneous person in this respect, I'm afraid. Some sort of a sujet mixte, a political hybrid.

Why then the reputation of "Prince-Consort de Gauche"? Maybe I owe it partly to the fact that when I came to this country and had to find myself some meaningful work I got engaged in things like ecology, city planning, conservation of nature, development cooperation with Third World countries etc. etc. Some people then thought these to be the domain of the so-called political left. Maybe there was some truth in this reasoning in the very beginning. But now we have in this country - with gradations - quite a consensus on most of the problems connected with the aforementioned sectors of modern society. They are not really controversial. And that is also the reason why I can still be active in them.

You know, once you have got this sort of reputation - be it left or right - it is very difficult to change it. There seems to be an urge to stick a label on people. The problem is that those who label you can get very disappointed whenever you do not act or react according to what the label suggests. I think you have to live with these sort of things. Again it is a problem all people in public functions have who for constitutional reasons are not supposed to have an opinion of their own on politically controversial matters. Which of course is nothing but a legal fiction….

You know, I once chaired a committee set up by the Government to advise it on

matters of subsidizing activities within our country meant to alert the Dutch public opinion about problems of the so-called Third World. Soon it was called the "Committee Claus". And soon somebody found out that we were indeed dealing with some rather tricky questions. Politically sensitive problems. And then we were hailed by the one side of the political spectrum as doing the right things whereas the other side was screaming blue murder: "Prince Claus - or as some preferred to put it: Princess Beatrix's husband - is engaging in politics, he is a leftist fellow-traveller and what have you. The label was printed and stuck onto the man… Prince Philip, one of the most experienced and certainly most eloquent and witty of the living Prince-Consorts, has - in this context - said this: I quote:

"One of the greatest weaknesses of Monarchy is that it has to be all things to all people... It cannot do this when it comes to being all things to all people who are traditionalists and all things to all people who are iconoclasts. We therefore find ourselves in a position of compromise, and we might be kicked by both sides. The only thing is that if you are very cunning, you get as far away from the extremists as possible, because they kick harder." Unquote.

Q. What can you do, Sir, to let the real person be known to the public?

A. Well, I'm not so sure I really want the real person to be known. This was a joke – you understand. But seriously, I think the only way is to meet as many people as possible and speak up frankly as I do here tonight. But mind you: stereotypes are difficult to kill. Q. Sir, you are said to know a lot about the Third World, the North-South problem. As a Journalist, I would like to know your opinion about the so-called New International Information order.

A. Well, let me confess in general that I do not believe in all sorts of plans for New Orders. The advent of a New Order of any sort is a question of evolution. It takes time. Changes take place almost continuously, and by little steps. New Orders... are not made on drawing Boards nor indeed in conference halls. That does not mean that we should be drifting along into the future without any well formulated goals. Such a goal could be a New Order of sorts. So if you talk about this New International Information Order I do not mind people to think and talk about shortcomings in the flow of information around the Globe and how to improve the general situation, especially the quality of information. Provided - and this to me is a condition sine qua non - the principle of the freedom of the press is not jeopardized. And by this I do not only mean the free flow of information from North to South but also the freedom of expression within countries.

I believe - or stronger: I am absolutely convinced - that the existence of a free press .In any given developing country enhances the terms for an economically efficient and socially more just development. The watchdog function - to name only one - of a free press should not be underestimated - neither here nor there.

I know by experience and I hope you will forgive me when I state this quite frankly: the press - like the dentist - can be a nuisance. Of course only when they write nasty things - true or not - about you. But we should never forget: "Sans la liberté de blame, il ný a pas eloge flatteur". (I hope you speak French).

As you may know, I have served in my previous career in a Latin American country. In those days the press there was indeed not free. With respect to people in high places there were only eloges flatteurs. It was sickening. When I went back last year and was asked by a local journalist what in my view was the single most striking change I had observed I said without hesitation: "Reading your newspapers and realising they were obviously free to write and publish what they saw fit to write and publish. Certainly not only to please but also to blame - and very much so.

Q. Sir, may I ask you a last and rather personal question?

A. You did nothing else but ask personal questions so far - so go ahead.

Q. Are you a happy man?

A. I more or less expected this question. It seems significant for the time we live in that people are so much concerned about personal happiness. Materialistically the terms for "la condition humaine" in our affluent or welfare societies of the Western world have never been more favourable. But what about happiness? Are people now happier than, let's say a hundred years ago? Are they happier here than in the poor countries down South? A very difficult and also intriguing question. Especially for those among us who, either here or there, with the best of intentions and quite disinterested, are trying hard to help the poor countries in their development. It is too much to be treated in a short interview. The fact, though, is that we in the materialistically rich countries have come to question the rightness of the equation: Material welfare and affluence equal personal happiness. And some have for that matter introduced the dubious distinction between welfare and wellbeing. Personally I realise of course very well that in many respects I am in a very privileged position. But all I can say as a first reaction to your question is: Sometimes I am happy, sometimes I'm not. But then there is nothing in a normal person's life like a permanent state of happiness. At least when one is aware of what is going on around you, in the world at large. Hunger, deprivation and the ultimate threat of global annihilation through nuclear holocaust. You have children and you worry about their future. And there are many other worries, small and big which concern our country and people and the world as a whole.

But within these limitations which bear heavily also on one's personal feelings, I think, although not without some hesitations, I can call myself a happy man..."

Appendix B
Obituaries

Durable Associated Press correspondent dies in The Hague at 88

By ANTHONY DEUTSCH=
Associated Press Writer=
AMSTERDAM, Netherlands (AP) _ Nel Slis, a tenacious correspondent who pioneered European political affairs coverage during more than three decades with The Associated Press, died in a nursing home Monday. She was 88.

Slis won renown, and reference in journalism textbooks, for her aggressive reporting style, which was said to have intimidated even the toughest of politicians. She was one of the first women to cover the forerunner of the European Union, the European Economic Community.

"Nel was a feisty and determined reporter who covered Common Market and Dutch government affairs with a breadth of knowledge and vision that encompassed virtually all of postwar European politics," said AP's president and chief executive officer, Louis D. Boccardi.

"And being one of the first women to cover day-to-day politics in the Netherlands, she was a role model for Dutch women journalists," Boccardi said.

Slis started her journalism career in 1938 and worked in England during World War II. She worked as a nurse during the Finnish-Russian war in 1939.

After returning to Europe on a coal ship from America in 1944, she joined the AP and spent 35 years in Amsterdam, Brussels and The Hague.

After 10 years as a Brussels correspondent she returned home in 1973.

In the Netherlands, she reported on armed hostage-takings by Moluccan independence fighters, the role of Prince Berhard, husband of then-Queen Juliana, in the Lockheed pay-off scandal and the assassination of a British Ambassador.

Veteran journalist and commentator Daniel Schorr worked very closely with Slis in The Hague from 1948 to 1953, when he was stringing for publications, including the Christian Science Monitor and the New York Times.

Schorr spoke of her knowledge of the issues and fierce dedication to getting the story.

"Her great quality was her general warmth and passion for what she was doing, with the result that when she had to interview sources, she sort of overwhelmed them, " Schorr said. "She had very pronounced views of her own."

On one assignment, in the fall of 1975, Slis witnessed the takeover by Japanese Red Army terrorists of the French embassy in The Hague. After scrambling to the rooftop of a nearby bookstore, she lay crouched in the shadows as they emerged with heavy weapons. She later told the story in an eyewitness report.

She was awarded a Dutch knighthood for her service to journalism. The honor followed a recommendation from then-Prime Minister Joop den Uyl, who said: "she is certainly difficult, but I still love her a little."

After a long and fiery career, she retired in 1979, keeping herself busy with free-lance assignments. She devoutly attended the Dutch prime minister's weekly press briefings in The Hague until well in her 80s.

Slis is survived by her nephew. Memorial services were planned in The Hague for Thursday.

Associated Press - Anthony Deutsch
Npnieuws - John Buckley

Notes from the BPV
Nel Slis †

Since the last publication of this column, the Foreign Press Association said its last goodbye to its former president Nel Slis, who died in The Hague at the age of 88 on December 17. Those who knew her, and many who didn't, will surely concur with Friso Endt, who in his appreciation of Nel in the last edition of Nieuwspoort Nieuws dubs her a "legend in her own time". Rarely is this often-used phrase so appropriate. Some 60 to 80 people traveled to the funeral in Ockenburg to bid farewell to Nel, according to Friso. "Not only the journalistic community was there, but also

people like former State Secretary Ernst van Beughel and the European Economic Community's former Director-General Wellenstein," according to Friso, who succeeded Nel as the BPV's president when she stepped down in 1985 after eight years at the helm. "Newsweek's former European correspondent Scott Sullivan came from Paris, and then there were the people from Nieuwspoort, her second home in the last years, especially when life became difficult and her memory began to fail her."

Friso and others remember Nel as a reporter whose tireless tenacity raised standards of

journalistic quality in the Netherlands – this while working for years as The Hague's only female Dutch career, as her biographer and close friend Caroline Studdert points out. While various government leaders and spokesmen may remember Nel as a source of terror, I personally knew her as someone who, despite the legends surrounding her and her formidable circle of contacts, was warm, welcoming and encouraging when I began covering the Netherlands in 1991, and who was always ready, willing and available to show a new reporter in The Hague the right doors to knock on. Thank you, Nel.

Caroline Studdert spent the last years of Nel's life collecting her reminiscences and those of her contemporaries. She looks back here on the life of a journalist, in heart and soul:

A feisty, ground-breaking journalist who gave no quarter and expected none, Nel Slis was far from unhappy with her domestic sobriquet "Hellcat of the Hague." When she retired in 1979, her Associated Press bureau chief John Gale wrote: "Junior ministers have been known to quail under her questioning, but she could also charm the birds out of the trees." Fierce and combative, Slis was nevertheless extremely kind to people starting a career in journalism and would do everything to help them, as many can testify. As a journalist, she said, "you must have done your homework, you must have a tremendous interest in the subject and finally, you must possess tenacious stamina. On top of this, I had the good luck that I also have a nose for news".

Slis and veteran U.S. journalist and commentator Daniel Schorr, a close friend and colleague in the early days, pioneered together, higher standards of American journalism in postwar Holland, providing a model which the best have followed. Schorr says: "She was a great, great journalist, she knew a news story, she knew how to

interview people. She also had a great temper, but attached to her sense of justice". The sole female Dutch career journalist in The Hague for years, Slis fought a hard battle for acceptance in her indefatigable pursuit of news, and has provided a rare role model for career women.

Her vivid, intelligent reporting covered postwar topics from the loss of Indonesia, Marshall Aid and Dutch reconstruction to the great floods in 1953. Always a strong believer in Europe, Slis plunged with gusto into the complex world of the European Union's forerunner in 1963, when she became the AP's first Common Market reporter. After her last stint covering the AP in The Hague from 1973 to 1979, Slis continued to write for U.S. publications and the Brussels-based agency Europe. Sadly, in her last decade, the loss of her brilliant memory caused her frustration, rage and perhaps fear. But she was well cared for by fellow journalist Friso Endt, friend Yolanda Frankel Franck and lifelong friend and lawyer Piet Wackie Eysten as well as by the entire staff at Nieuwspoort.

Slis was among those who built the Foreign Press Association into a powerful, influential body. As its president, she presided in 1985 over one of the most memorable anniversary celebration since its 1925 founding, at Erenstein Castle in Kerkrade. There she was elevated to Officer of the Order of Nassau-Oranje by Premier Ruud Lubbers, who has praised her persistent questioning, trustworthy reporting and remarkably good grasp of Europe:"I learned a lot from her," the current UNHCR chief has said. International Herald Tribune columnist and former Brussels reporter for the Financial Times Reginald Dale, recalls 'La Slis' in her prime:"Everyone knew her, she was a charismatic figure... As you go through life, you meet a handful of people who are clearly larger than life. It's a privilege to have known them, and Nel is one of those".

John Buckley

Irene van Geest weg bij VWS

Irene van Geest is met ingang van 1 april directeur Communicatie bij de Nederlandse Voedselautoriteit (NVa), een onafhankelijke organisatie die onder meer de kwaliteit van voedsel en niet-voedselgerelateerde producten controleert. De NVa valt onder twee ministeries en wel Volksgezondheid, Welzijn en Sport en dat van Landbouw, Natuurbeheer en Visserij. De benoeming van Van Geest betekent haar vertrek bij het

ministerie van VWS, waar zij directeur Communicatie was. Zij verlaat ook het algemeen bestuur van Nieuwspoort, waar in zij de VoRa, de voorlichtingsraad, vertegenwoordigde. Verwacht mag worden dat haar opvolger pas zal worden benoemd na het aantreden van een nieuw kabinet. Niemand zal verbaasd zijn als Richard Matthijsse bij VWS als gekende 'vliegende kiep' zal optreden tussen 1 april en dit najaar. ~

Hans Goessens overleden

Begin maart is in zijn woonplaats Nuth (Zuid-Limburg) de journalist Hans Goessens overleden, laatstelijk hoofdredacteur van het Limburgs Dagblad. Goessens maakte lang deel uit van de redactie van De Volkskrant, bij welke krant hij in de turbulente jaren zestig en zeventig nauw betrokken was bij de modernisering van dit dagblad. Hans was parlementair redacteur, chef nieuwsdienst en later chef van de parlementaire redactie. In 1967 werd hij

adjunct-hoofdredacteur van het Utrechts Nieuwsblad, in 1994 hoofdredacteur van de Amersfoortse Courant en in 1995 hoofdredacteur van het Limburgs Dagblad.

Hans was een beminnelijk mens. Hij kon evenwel, als hij dacht dat hij gelijk had, voor collega's ook hard zijn. Zijn werkdrift en zijn strijd tegen een opkomende slopende ziekte dwongen bewondering af. Hans heeft de strijd niet kunnen winnen. Hij werd 53 jaar. ~

Obituary, John Buckley

Dutch press: NRC , De Journalist, Npnieuws, Volkskrant - Friso Endt.

Volkskrant:

Journaliste Nel Slis: grof en gedreven

18/12/01, 00:00

Bot benaderde ze menig hoogwaardigheidsbekleder. Zelfs kousen en schoenen gingen uit bij de run voor nieuws. Nel Slis, een van de eerste vrouwelijke journalisten, is overleden....

IN JOURNALISTIEKE kring gold Nel Slis als 'een vrouw met kloten', die voor geen autoriteit opzij ging. In de jaren vijftig en zestig bestookte ze excellenties met scherpe vragen in plaats van hen te vleien met de hypocriete nederigheid die velen van haar collega's eigen was. Niet: 'Heeft u een goede reis gehad?' Maar: 'Wat heeft u in dat land bereikt?' Slis overleed gisterochtend in het Haagse verpleeghuis Gulden Vlies, 88 jaar oud.

Slis was jarenlang correspondente voor het Amerikaanse persbureau Associated Press (AP) in Amsterdam, Den Haag en Brussel. Toen ze al in de tachtig was, bezocht ze nog elke vrijdag de persconferentie van de minister-president in Nieuwspoort, en stond de telex nog steeds naast haar te ratelen.

Na enkele avontuurlijke omzwervingen kwam de op Goeree-Overflakkee geboren Slis in de journalistiek terecht. Als verpleegster maakte zij in 1939 de Fins-Russische oorlog mee. Bij het uitbreken van de Tweede Wereldoorlog kon ze niet meer terug naar Nederland en monsterde ze aan op een kolenschip naar Amerika. Een militair schip bracht haar naar Engeland, waar ze op het vertaalbureau van de BBC een baan kreeg. Ze luisterde Duitse gesprekken af en vertaalde ze in het Engels.

Via de BBC kwam ze bij het persbureau AP, en na de oorlog keerde ze terug naar Nederland, waar ze correspondente werd in Amsterdam en de politieke berichtgeving verzorgde vanuit

Den Haag en Brussel. Ze bleef grof in de mond, en gedreven. Tegen Vrij Nederland zei ze vier jaar geleden: 'In het Vredespaleis, met die verdomde gladde vloeren en trappen, deed ik onder tafel vast mijn kousen en schoenen uit om zonder uit te glijden het eerst bij die godvergeten telefoon te zijn, die verdomme altijd beneden was.'

Na een veelbewogen leven en tot het laatst toe liefdevol verzorgd in Verpleeghuis "Gulden Huis" is overleden

Nel Slis

oud-journaliste
oud-correspondente van Associated Press
Officier in de Orde van Oranje-Nassau
Draagster van de Medaille van Verdienste, in zilver,
van het Nederlandse Rode Kruis
Officier de l'Ordre National du Mérite
Erelid van de Buitenlandse Pers Vereniging in Nederland

Ooltgensplaat, 2 september 1913   Den Haag, 17 december 2001

Delft, Lars Wackie Eysten
Den Haag, Piet en Mick Wackie Eysten · Noervoort
Parijs, Tyna Wackie Eysten

De plechtigheid voorafgaande aan de crematie zal plaatsvinden op donderdag 20 december 2001 vanaf 11.00 uur in de Kleine Aula van het Crematorium "Ockenburgh" aan de Ockenburghstraat 21, Den Haag/Loosduinen.

Na de plechtigheid is er gelegenheid tot samenzijn in de ontvangkamer van het crematorium.

Funeral Notice

I also discovered **Leiden University's Parliamentary Documentation Centre** has filed a synopsis of Nel's life. The short introduction in the synopsis below says:

Vigorous assertive journalist who as Associated Press correspondent after the Second World War in The Hague and

Brussels was the terror of many pr people and ministers. An intelligent, tenacious, but somewhat unbridled personality, who could pose tough questions in her heavy smoky voice to each and all foreign politicians in their own language. And still to try and often succeed in being the first to send the news out into the world. For those who understood her, a warm-hearted woman, who once given trust never disappointed, and who also had access to the world of classical music.

University of Leiden, Parliamentary Documentation Centre

N.A. (Nel) Slis - Hoofdinhoud

Vitale assertieve journaliste die na de Tweede Wereldoorlog als correspondente van Associated Press in Den Haag en in Brussel tientallen jaren de schrik was van veel voorlichters en bewindslieden. Intelligente vasthoudende, maar nogal ongeremde persoonlijkheid die met haar zware doorgerookte stem iedere buitenlandse politicus in zijn eigen taal hard kon ondervragen. En steeds probeerde de eerste te zijn die het nieuws de wereld inzond en daar vaak in slaagde. Voor wie haar begreep een hartelijke vrouw, die eenmaal geschonken vertrouwen nooit beschaamde en die ook reçu was in de wereld van de klassieke muziek. in de periode 1945-1979: opinievormer/journalist

voornamen (roepnaam)
Neeltje Adriaantje (Nel)
personalia
geboorteplaats en -datum
Ooltgensplaat, 2 september 1913
overlijdensplaats en -datum
's-Gravenhage, 17 december 2001
Loopbaan
verpleegster in Lausanne, Metz en Genève, vanaf 1938
verpleegster bij de ambulance van het Nederlandse Rode kruis in Finland, van maart 1940 tot juni 1940
secretaresse bij de Nederlandse Aankoopcommissie te New York, van november 1940 tot mei 1941
verpleegster in New Cross Hospital, Wolverhampton (Engeland), van augustus 1941 tot november 1942
monitor bij de Luisterdienst van de BBC te Londen, van januari 1943 tot 1945
journaliste bij Associated Press, van 1945 tot 1 mei 1979
nevenfuncties
medewerkster voorlichtingsdienst EEG te 's-Gravenhage
medewerkster Europe, nieuwsbulletin EG, van 1960 tot 1985

voorzitter Buitenlandse Persvereniging, van 1982 tot 1988
opleiding
voortgezet onderwijs
Hogere Burgerschool te Middelharnis
Kennemer Lyceum te Overveen
academische studie
farmacie Rijksuniversiteit Utrecht, van 1933 tot 1934
overige opleidingen
cursus Sorbonne te Parijs, van 1931 tot 1932
cursussen te Oxford en München, 1934
opleiding voor verpleegster te Lausanne, van 1935 tot 1938
psychiatrie te Rome, van 1938 tot 1939
wetenswaardigheden uit de privésfeer   Haar vader was herenboer
pseudoniemen   Adriana Dykes, Len Koert
woonplaats(en)/adres(sen)
Parijs, Rue Tournefort, vanaf 1933
's-Gravenhage, Javastraat 11 3hoog, van juli 1950 tot juli 1963
Brussel, Avenue Molière 168, van juli 1963 tot juni 1973
's-Gravenhage, Ranonkelstraat 53, van juni 1973 tot juni 1999
's-Gravenhage, Steenhouwersgaarde, verpleeghuis Gulden Huis, vanaf juni 1999
ridderorden
Ridder in de Orde van Oranje-Nassau, 29 april 1976
Officier in de Orde van Oranje-Nassau, 2 februari 1985
buitenlandse onderscheidingen
Dapperheidsmedaille in brons van Finland, 1940
Officier de l'Ordre National du Mérite, 3 december 1982
overige onderscheidingen en prijzen
medaille van verdienste in zilver Nederlandse Rode Kruis, 1940
gouden speld, A.P., oktober 1969
relevante buitenlandse reizen
vluchtreis van Patsamo (noord-Finland) met klein Fins vrachtschip Brita Thorden via Tromsö (Noorwegen) langs IJsland en Groenland door zware stormen in de Noordelijke IJszee en op de Atlantische Oceaan naar Baltimore in de USA, van oktober 1940 tot november 1940
publicaties/bronnen
artikelen in "Religious News Service, New York", "Ladies' Home Journal", "The New York Times", "Newsweek", "MacGraw Hill World News" -
artikelen in "Vrouwenbelangen"
"Dikes and Bikes" (1953 met illustraties van Hugh Jansz)
Interview met Ageeth Scherphuis, Vrij Nederland, 1993

Londense dagboeken O.C.A. van Lidth de Jeude, ING 2001, p. 796

familie/gezin   vader - J.A. Slis, Johannes Aren, moeder - L. Koert, Lena

Bovenstaande gegevens zijn ontleend aan het biografisch archief van het Parlementair Documentatiecentrum (PDC) van de Universiteit Leiden en betreffen vooral de periode waarin iemand politiek en bestuurlijk actief is of was.

Aanvullingen en gemotiveerde correcties ontvangt PDC graag. U kunt hiervoor de "reageer-keuze" aan de rechterzijde van deze pagina gebruiken of uw aanvullingen per post sturen naar PDC, antwoordnummer 10801, 2501 BW Den Haag of per email aan info@biografieen.com.

Appendix C.
Notes & References

Chapter 1

Selma Lagerlöf, the author favoured by Nel's best friend Jenneke's mother, was winner of the Nobel Prize for Literature in 1909. A Swedish writer and secondary school teacher (1858-1940) wrote poetry from her childhood but did not publish until 1890 when she won a literary competition and published excerpts from her most popular book, Gösta Berlings Saga, published in full in 1891..

Johannus (Hans) Nieuwenhuyzen died of cancer about a year before Nel. He had very much wanted to provide a photo of four generations of the Slis family for the book but sadly was unable do so. But he did photocopy the Slis genealogy. Below is the family tree, showing Nel's father Johannes Ahrend (circled) plus the excerpts giving the names of his first two wives and children, and the Slis coat-of-arms, from GENEALOGIE DER FAMILIE SLIS, A.K.VINK, Leiden 1917.

Chapter 6

Government Information Service (Rijksvoorlichtingsdienst RVD)

Nel spoke about some of the Government Information Service spokesmen of the day, who would arrange contacts with the royals.

Willem van den Berge was "a nattily-dressed man, also usually with a bow tie, and his boss was first Joop Landre, and later, Dr. Lammers. Where Joop Landre could be an understanding soul if circumstances permitted, Lammers and Rebel were tremendously scary gentlemen, who did not take female correspondents in particular wholly seriously, and/or were afraid of them". Van den Berge proved elusive in an internet search, but it finally came up with a photo of him, unexpectedly plump and hearty-looking, but indeed sporting a bow tie.

Chapter 7

Refugee Relief Act

The Refugee Relief Act provided for admission of those who qualified as relatives of persons already in the United States, those who were victims of war, and those victimised by natural disaster. The German invasion of the Netherlands in World War II and the floods in Holland in 1953 fitted the last two categories for the Dutch. The act expired 31 December 1956, but four more months were allowed to use visas granted before that date.

Chapter 8

In light of former UK Prime Minister Margaret Thatcher's recent demise and the film about her starring Meryl Streep, it is interesting to see how Nel felt about the Iron Lady and the then apparently intractable Ulster Question. This is from her August 1981 interview with me:

> "A great breakthrough was Britain joining the EEC, because of the Channel and their physical (and psychological) difficulties. Even now, it sounds horrible, but they can see the (IRA) terror hasn't stopped at the Channel. I'm a great admirer of Thatcher. I'm very happy to see a woman premier anywhere; I think she is remarkable in the sense that she's courageous and articulate, and she's intelligent, But at the same time, she's a smug Conservative who doesn't understand the FIRST thing of what's going in 1981 among the youth and the world at large - that's why I think it is a damn good thing that this shows her that terror has not stopped at the Channel. Perhaps it will slowly dawn on Margaret that she has to give up Ulster".

Chapter 11.

Honorary FPA members

D.J. Lambooy (1946), H.G. Kersting (1972), Pal Balaz (1976), Herman Bleich (1977), H. George Franks MBE (ex-honorary president, 1980), Willem Vuur (1982), Nel Slis (1982, then chairman). The other five were: Gijs van der Wiel (1983), Frank de Jong (1991), Gerry Peterson (ex-Reuters, 1991), Friso Endt (ex-chairman, 1995), Helmut Hetzel (ex-chairman, 1998).

Appendix D
References

Articles and typescripts

Articles and typescripts consulted include:

1. 1957 Slis typescripts on emigrant ship Waterman's collision with Italian freighter, trip to New York, articles written during her stint at the AP's New York and Washington offices and on her trip around the U.S.

2. Slis typescript: Interview with Queen Fatima of Libya 1954

3. Foreign Press Association - Buitenlandse Persvereniging in Nederland 30th anniversary magazine. 1955. Forwards by Prime Minister Willem Drees and Prince Bernhard, articles by Henk Kersting and by Nel Slis (We - Women Correspondents - Want to be Taken Seriously)

4. AP World Service item NEWSMEN AT WORK, on Common Market summit conference November 23-29, 1969

5. Slis typescripts on changes in the Netherlands in the 1960s and 1970s and on the Den Uyl and Van Agt cabinets

6. Article on departure of Slis to Brussels, 'Hartelijk Afscheid van Nel Slis' in Het Parool, 23 August 1963.

7. Article by G. Toussaint on departure of Slis to Brussels in De vrouw en haar huis (Woman and home), October 1963

8. Slis typescripts on Waterman collision, trip to and around the United States and work done there, 1957-1958

9. Slis typescripts on Staphorst story, November 1973

10. Miscellaneous Slis typescripts covering members of the Royal Family

11. Article on Slis in Brussels Bulletin magazine, The Dutch in Belgium, undated

12. Slis typescripts on Joseph Luns and Sicco Mansholt

13. Slis typescript for Kennemer Lyceum reunion on her life so far, written on Les Freres Charbonnel paper, plus typescript of Schmal's contribution, 1974.

14. 'Het Europese journalistenwereldje' (European journalists' world) in Vrouwen en hun belangen (Women and their interests) Vol 39, no. 3, june 1974

15. Slis typescripts on hijacking, independence for Surinam, politics and politicians and other topics from 1974 onwards

16 .Slis typescripts on Lockheed affair, 1976

17. AWCA (American Women's Club of Amsterdam) Guest speaker 2 March 1978, interview with Slis by Madeline Landau in November issue of AWCA Bulletin.

18. AP World item 'Nel Slis retires' by John Gale, Amsterdam Bureau Chief, 1979

19. Vrij Nederland interview with Robert Schouten, 'Nel Slis: "Geef me de kern van de zaak"' (Give me the nub of the business), 1979

20. Haagsche Courant, 'De Franse ambassadeur Kemoularia reikt Nel Slis de onderscheiding uit'

(French ambassador Kemoularia presents Nel Slis with the decoration - La Croix d'Officier de lÓrdre National du Merit, 14 September 1982

21. Vrij Nederland interview by Igor Cornelissen, (And on top of that I had the good fortune to have a nose for news'), 1982

22. Het Parool item in Apropos roundup on women in a man's world, Een handvol luizen in een mannenpels (A handful of lice in a male hide), 11 October 1984

23. Unattributed article partly about Nel Slis by Jeanne Roos, 1983. Roos was a Het Parool journalist after the war, the first person seen on Dutch television on 2 October 1951 and also appeared in Theo van Gogh films. She died 30 June, 2001.

24. ' Foreign Press Association celebrates 60th anniversary', Worldwide News May 1985

25.. Haagsche Courant interview, 'Ik viel erin al seen haar in de soep (I fell into it like a hair in the soup), 19 November 1988

26. De Mediakrant interview by Monique Smits, 'Als het om nieuws gaat, trap ik ze allemaal in de hoek' (If it's about news, I trample them all into the corner), 1990

27. Algemeen Dagblad interview by Sjef van Woensel, 'Afscheid van een betrouwbare grote mond' (Reception for a trustworthy big mouth), 3 September 1993

28.Vrij Nederland interview by Ageeth Scherphuis, 'Nel Slis' 80-year War: The Lady of the Press", 28 August 1993

29. NIEUWSPOORTNIEUWS interview by Ineke Geraerdts, "Eighty-year old Nel Slis: 'If Lubbers goes, I'll go too', October 1993

 30. Radio interview in 'Wie bent U eigentlijk' series 1990

31. NPnieuws, 'Invloed van de BPVsinds 'Brussel' danig geslonken' (Influence of the FPA much reduced since 'Brussels"), September 2000

BOOK: Nel Slis, journaliste Een levensschets door Piet Wackie Eysten, August 2001

Author's interviews

Interviews include:

1. Jan Both, Middelharnis archivist (4 April 2001)

2 . Randoll Coate, maze-maker, former diplomat and friend of Nel in The Hague and Brussels (21 March 2002)

3. Isabel Conway, journalist, former FPA vice-president (sometime in 2000)

4. Reginald Dale, Financial Times journalist (17 June 2001)

5. Friso Endt, journalist, friend and carer (3 August 2000)

6. Yolanda Frenkel-Frank, producer, friend and carer (29 March 2000)

7. Helmut Hetzel, journalist, former FPA president. (23 April 2002)

8. Gonne Hollander, The Hague friend and travelling companion (sometime in 2002)

9. Elizabeth de Jong van Beek, Nel and Gonne Hollander's beautician and friend in The Hague (February 2003)

10. Flora Lewis, renowned American journalist & columnist, friend of Nel and Daniel Schorr (20 January 2001)

11. Ruud Lubbers, former Dutch Prime Minister, World Wildlife chairman, UN High Commissioner for Refugees

12. Jan Nkeuwenhuyzen, Nel's nephew (3 October 2000)

13. David Post, journalist, FPA vice-chairman and friend of Nel and author

14. Daniel Schorr, renowned American print, TV & radio journalist (NBC, CNN,) and the man Nel loved (19 December 1999)

15. Allan Tillier, journalist, friend of Reginald Dale

16. Vera Vaughan Bowden, journalist, former FPA President (2000)

17. Tyna Wynaendts, librarian, daughter of Nel's childhood friend Janneke (November 2002)

18. Piet Wackie Eysden, lawyer, brother of Tyna

Also several interviews with Nel by the author in 2000, plus her first interview with her in 1981 which was published as 'Hellcat of The Hague' in Holland Life magazine, August 1981

Appendix E.
Files & Archives

Chapter 1

I found this local newspaper article from the island of Goeree-Overflakkee in Nel's archives and have made a free translation of it below. This is partly because I felt it gave something of the harshness of the island life. Nel could see when she was growing up how hard life was for the women of the island, slaving away for their menfolk throughout their lives. She must have certainly have known the oppressive patriarch Keesje de Graaff and as she kept it, it obviously meant something to her. The other reason the article resonated for me is that it also talks about his unmarried sisters living together for years awaiting death, grim but clearly with a certain status Nel's heir Tyna Wynaendts said Nel had two elderly aunts who lived together:

> "That was done then, if girls didn't marry, they would live together and be a sort of entity, the ladies De Graaff - these spinsters living together. They had a status in the village; they had money and they were important people."

> I wondered whether the tragi-comic story reminded Nel of her aunts.

'The Last Will of a Hard Gentleman Farmer'

A HALF MILLION FOR THE DOCTOR - NOT A CENT FOR NEPHEW AND NIECE

The power of the patriarch extended to way beyond his death

Keesje de Graaf died in December 1968, "in good health, one could almost say, at the well-nigh patriarchal age of 82. So no buckets of tears over his departure. But certainly something more than the normal commotion. Because his inheritance – money and property worth more than half a million good Dutch guilders – did not go to his nephew and niece MAART and NARDA DE GRAAF. But to village doctor P.R. BAKKER, 42, and his three sons EELCO, 12, REMCO, 9, and PAUL, 7. Some home nursing services and a union that occupies itself with fishing up drowning people from the South Holland and Zeeland waters received some legacies."

The black sheep among Keesje's four siblings, Maart and Narda's father "mad Dries," apparently offended the family, became intractable, broke his word in some way and "saw salvation in a merry servant girl hopping around in his neighbourhood." The family judgement was that "1) Driesje should in future be called Dries, 2) that he must leave the house to marry the servant girl, 3) that he had no right to any family capital, nor of farmlands with or without barns creaking in the wind and plodding labourers". Dries was apparently happy enough to leave, and "earned a living for later, son MAART (not Maartje) and NARDA (not Nardtje) as milk inspector and as inseminator attached to the institute for Artificial Insemination". Obviously it was a serious matter to lose the diminutive.

The paper quotes regional novelist J. Knape as saying such situations were completely normal on the island for centuries:

'The power of the patriarch extended to way beyond his death. Children sighed under the yoke of their father and no mother could do anything about it'. At any rate, Keesje, 'with an iron will and stony inflexibility, carried out the last will of his father – Jantje – and has now completely consistently disinherited Maart and Narda. All in all, a lingering family history that stretches out over more than a century and can compete with the sob-story in the evergreen *Winden Waaien Om De Rotsen* (Winds Blowing Over the Cliffs).

Meanwhile, the siblings complete with diminutives, Keesje, Kommertje, Jansje and Keetje led a sober and very frugal life in the old family house in Middelharnis' Voorstraat. The women were reportedly 'stern figures, robust and proud of visage. There the four of them sat for decades behind the little windowpanes, stoically awaiting their end. Kommertje and Keetje went first, and a couple of streets away, Dries and his wife also died (Dries was allowed in the family grave, but not his wife)'.

Then Jansje got sick and was treated by Dr. Bakker, who believed he won Keesje's heart because Jansje refused to take her pills and he told her, go ahead then and burst. "That, I believe, aroused the boundless admiration of the old fellow. Someone that at last told his stern sister the truth for once", says Bakker. The doctor adds ironically that De Graaff showed repeated signs of a certain degree of profligacy in his last years, for example in swapping his daily drink of cheap Dutch brandy (vieux) for a French cognac, because: 'You can't take your money with you, after all'

Keesje's unreasoning hatred of his brother Dries went so far that he wouldn't have anything to do with his children either, and even told his lawyer that they should be kicked out of the churchyard if they turned up at the funeral. But they did eventually ask the doctor's permission to visit him a couple of days before he died, remarkably inquiring: 'He won't get a heart attack if he sees us?' In the event, his wits had gone and he knew nobody.

The nephew and niece, both well into their forties, must have felt decidedly sour about this stubborn old man's estate going to the doctor and were at the time of the article trying to prove that he was not in his right mind when he signed his will.

The village backed the doctor, though he himself remarked: "Actually it would be better to win the football pools. That is 'nicer' money and no inheritance rights are involved". As to Keesje's mental state, the doctor said he wrote the will 11 months before he died, and plenty of people could bear witness to the fact that Keesie was very much all there until shortly before his death. "A few days before he died, he was pointing out to me that his oil shares (Royal Dutch Petroleum) were at 200 (guilders)"

Harde herenboer

Chapter 5

ADULTERY IN STAPHORST

In her first 'take', Nel typified the right-wing village as "Holland's most unique off-beat spot", placing it for her American readers as "not far from the German border, on one of the main highroads to Scandinavia". Here is a compilation of the rest of the story, from various versions.

Two lovers were punished and condemned here over the weekend by a popular tribunal of some 600 young men in this off-beat village of 10,000 inhabitants spread over a fifty-square mile area near the highroad to Germany and Scandinavia.

A mother of two, 48-year old Marte Schoenmaker and her forty-five year old lover, butcher/carpenter Derk Timmerman, were forced to publicly repent their adultery after the Staphorst community had got irate when it became known that Maarte's husband, Jan, for the second time tried to take his life by hanging himself.

There is a great deal of literature written by sociologists and students of folklore on the quaint customs of this odd group of small farmers who have been wearing their elaborate national costumes for over two centuries.

In Staphorst, 'blue laws' reign on Sunday, and courtship - even today - often culminates in trial marriages with the nuptials following after pregnancy. But the young bachelors meet out justice publicly to the suitor deserting his girlfriend, who he has courted most often through the 'courting' window of the 'opkamer' (side-room) through which the Staphorst bachelor climbs to pursue his wooing inside.

A woman artist living here, 60-year old Stien Eelsingh, admits she once was surprised by a male trying to get through.

Last Friday, towards midnight, Dr. G. De Jong, the village's only medico, said, "the Staphorst 'pathboys' (local name for the teenagers, meaning they are 'on the path') took justice in their own hands", supported by their parents.

They went to Maarte's home and lifted her out of bed, and hoisted her into a pigsty on a farm wagon, under the illuminating lanterns carried by the pathboys. Maarte was not just in negligee, Dr. De Jong explained.

Staphorst women wear four layers of skirts and only doff one before retiring. Atop, Maarte wore the white sack-like cloth all Staphorst women wear beneath the daily wear of tight-fitting black silken bodices. Marte's head was covered only by a black silken under-bonnet, worn in daytime under the pure silver helmet-like hood which is even worn by girls of six.

Amid howling they pushed the wagon to the nearest cafe.

"But", said cafe-owner Gee Waanders, "Derk was not here. He was in a cafe in Meppel - six miles away - and slightly under the weather" (presumably drunk). Swiftly a couple of pathboys motored to Meppel and took Derk along to Staphorst where he, together with Maarte, was taken on the wagon.

The two had three humiliating hours, Dr. De Jong said. They were pushed along the long winding path of Staphorst, amid loud shrieking and howling and wild singing of 'in the gloria'. "It was all very cynical", Dr. De Jong said.

Not until the wee hours of the Saturday morning and under the threat of being drowned in the nearest ditch, did the two solemnly promise to better their lives.

Standing in the cart, each in turn told the crowd: "I promise that it will never happen again", according to Dr. De Jong. Hereafter they were sent to their respective homes afoot.

According to the one and only hotelkeeper, Ge Waaners, in Staphorst the handful of local police purposely ignored the mass demonstration that took place at night under the light of home-made Chinese lanterns.

According to Waanders, the two culprits will take heed to report to the police for fear of a repetition of the public punishment, an old tradition in this quaint village.

The Staphorst people took the law into their own hands after Maarte's legal husband, Jan, publicly complained over Maarte's unfaithfulness and threatened to kill himself after she refused to cook for him any longer.

Although according to a 1961 law, traditional excesses are no longer permitted, and although the police are watchful, they fear to intervene in these mass demonstrations when thousands of Staphorst people manifest their fury, an artist living here, Stien Eelsingh, said.

Commander of the district police, Major W. Vrieze, said after investigation: "My men did not know about it. Otherwise we might have taken preventive action. Presently we can only act if someone brings up a charge, but noone here ever would..."

"The last time a popular tribunal was held", Dr. De Jong said, "was twenty years ago, when a suitor deserted his pregnant fiancee"

But Eelsingh remembers well a 'pathboys' procession of farm wagons to a home of a girl known to be non-fertile. They dismantled the wagons in front of the home, indicating that she was 'dead wood'. "The symbolic demonstration", Stien said, "ended by the pathboys hanging a doll in a tree in front of the farm home".

"Their credo here", Eelsingh said, "is based on very orthodox Calvinism mixed with superstition. They paint the base of their homes a fiery blue to keep the devil away".

To a visitor, the blue-based, whitewashed little farmhouses with their thatched roofs and white impertinent chimneys, all built along a miles-long winding road, boarded by apple trees, look like a picture right out of brothers Grimm fairy tales.

Staphorst is Holland's quaintest village where both men and women are still wearing an elaborate national costume and live their lives based on a strict Calvinistic dogma and a good deal of superstition.

"It is sad", the 63-year old Henderikus van der Wal, the village mayor sighed, "we were so well on the way to clear the Staphorst reputation for backwardness, and now this happened, but the people were mad after Jan tried to take his life".

Alderman Bert Klomp agreed with the mayor, but said the "people's justice had also a preventive quality".

"The popular tribunal is accepted by all Staphorst people," Dr. De Jong said. "Maarte and Derk will not be boycotted, but it will be difficult for them to have close contact with the others because in the eyes of the community they have behaved shamefully".

Rev. Pieter Dorsman last Sunday admonished his flock, saying sternly that "it is the Lord's privilege to punish and not that of us earthly people".

Chapter 9

EDUCATION

A partly illegible typescript of a draft story I found in Nel's archives starts off intriguingly but becomes disappointingly turgid and fails to explain the big educational battle in the lead, but I liked the beginning part for its picture of rampant denominationalism in the Netherlands at that time:

Typescript: Education in the Netherlands (early 1970s)

THE HAGUE, APRIL(illegible date).--For over a century--from 1806-1920--the educational system has been the battlefield of the most bitter and prolonged controversy there was to divide the Dutch Calvinists, Roman Catholics and Liberals. The 1920 Elementary Education Act put an end to this fight. Although there is still friction on a local level occasionally between supporters of the private schools and the public schools it no longer is a national issue.

It has been solved here along denominational lines, like most similar issues. Holland is generally ruled by three official "pillars" (which the Dutch call "Zuilen") --the Protestant, the Roman Catholics and the neutrals--the latter covering anyone from humanist, agnostic, free-thinker and rare communists. The whole social life of the country is similarly fragmented. Radio and television have Protestant, Catholic and Humanist hours and days of transmissions, and there are Protestant, Catholic and neutral trade unions. There are Catholic and Protestant Sheepbreeders' associations and Catholic, Protestant and neutral bakery-hands and building workers associations etc.

FEMINISM

This report is included as it seems so much from a bygone age in its phraseology and ideas. The Dolle Mina movement it refers to was a feminist movement named after early feminist Wilhelmina Drukker (1847-1925) and translates as Mad Mina.

Typescript on feminist magazine Opzij

The Netherlands' only independent feminist magazine Opzij has a 'small catechism', designed to help feminists answer hostile questions convincingly: The suggested answer to: "Aren't women after all much more emotional than men?" is as follows: "Pressured by our culture pattern, men are not allowed to express their feelings as freely as women.

For example, a man may not weep, but he pays for this with ulcers and heart disease".

Dolle Mina's major ongoing projects concern single parents and abortion. Dolle Mina also participates in the 'Ombudswoman' project. Ombudswoman Meta van Beek, employed as a business-social worker by the municipal social service in The Hague, is giving her free time to receiving questions and complaints from working women and women looking for work.

Opzij has experienced nothing but financial difficulties since its inception 14 months ago. Despite its 1,500 subscriptions and 3,500-copy news-stand sales, Opzij remains in the red.

A spokeswoman says the magazine receives no subsidies of any kind, and that the staff work practically for nothing and are mainly dependent on the non-financial interest of the publisher.

The lead article in Opzij's October issue, published in conjunction with the widely-circulated Dutch liberal weekly Vrij Nederland, deals with plastic surgery.

"Women weep for their appearance", writes the article's author, Freke Vuyst. "They suffer because of it... Suffering is central to all the stories of women who undergo such operations. They take the step because they suffered from inferiority complexes, street anxiety, contact disturbances and problems in relationships....

I suspect that Nel probably liked the woman socialist party leader in the interview below better than Vuyst:

Typescript: Woman socialist (excerpts)

Holland has got its own type of Peggy Thatcher, now the Dutch Labor party, late last night, elected Caroline van den Heuvel-De Blank (47) as chairman of the Dutch socialist party (PvdA) for the next two years.

She now is for Holland staying in NATO. In an interview, she said: "I started out being against NATO membership, because I am a convinced pacifist. I do not believe in the army - it is a poor instrument. But later I have realised that if we did leave there will be uncontrollable bilateral defence arrangements. This will lead to national nuclear armament and above all will cause a split in our own Labour party. This means that the conservatives will rule Holland and that will be worse".

A small brunette, she is outspoken and intense and tough. So far she has been engaged mainly in matters like social welfare, the media, development aid but also foreign policy.

Among her European socialist friends she cited West Germany's Anne Marie Renger, Britain's Betty Lockwood, Belgium's Irene

Petri, France's Therese Equiem, Italy's Enrica Lorelli and Luxembourg's Lidy Schmidt.

Ineke is for emancipation of women and wants to see in Holland, like France, a special post created in the cabinet for women's affairs, like Francoise Giroud in France.

"In this country we must start from scratch", she said, "and change the cultural pattern of girls' education".

She has no time for hobbies, she said. Apart from reading modern literature and enjoying theatre and cabaret - if it has a political flavour - she concentrates on party work.

"We must make the party one of action", she told her audience in her Thursday night opening speech.

.Privately she said: "The party must prepare political decisions and make the people participate, telling them why decisions are taken.

"So far all this remains too much with the top level and with too little participation of the people".

Mrs Van den Heuvel feels that Holland's trade unions are "too tame". On nationalisation she said: "This is not a panacea. It has to be considered case by case".

In her opening speech, she pleaded for cooperation among the leftwing parties, "but not with the Communists--that is no credible partner", she said.

SLIS GENEALOGY

The Slis family tree so kindly provided by her nephew Jan Nieuwenhuijzen was a little difficult to follow, but here at least is the Slis coat of arms:

Slis coat of arms

PRESS CUTTINGS

A few samples of articles as they actually appeared are given below. The first shows one of several US newspapers picking up Nel's Japanese terrorists hostage-taking story, the scoop Nel achieved by getting onto the roof of a nearby bookstore. Second is an unusual caravan story which was popular with AP clients, who asked for more like it. Third comes Nel's historically interesting but slightly dull piece at the time of the collapse of the Soviet Union, Eastern Europe crowds EC agenda, from the 1990 FPA magazine The Foreign Correspondent. Finally, from The Foreign Correspondent 1995, there is a piece I wrote on Nel, 'La Slis,' a no-nonsense journalist, and one by Daniel Shorr, Warmest Memory, which mentions Nel.

Japanese terrorists

Finnish Lapland Has Mix of Old, New

By TOM HOGE
Associated Press Writer

ROVANIEMI, Finnish Lapland (AP) — A summer sojourn in Lapland can be an intriguing experience, even if reindeer meat heads the menu at lunch and dinner, and the arctic sun floods your hotel room day and night.

Impressions of Finland's northernmost province can differ sharply, depending on where you get your first glimpse of the vast region billed as Europe's last wilderness.

One tourist, whose plane touched down near the provincial capital of Rovaniemi, was taken aback at the sight of this modern town with its glassy facades and smart shops. They seemed a far cry from any wilderness. And a tethered reindeer munching grass in a backyard looked more like a cow with antlers than one of Santa's helpers.

A couple of hours later, this same tourist, driving in a taxi-bus through towering spruces which make up much of this 40,000-square-mile preserve called Finnish Lapland saw herds of grazing reindeer loping across rolling hills.

Beyond lay greening lakes and winding rivers that stretched for miles, with no house or any sign of man's handiwork visible. Tiny blue wildflowers dotted the ground in this northern Eden where August temperatures hover close to 16 degrees F., even though it lies above the Arctic Circle.

"This is the last real wilderness, except perhaps for parts of Russian Siberia," said Pertti Korhonen, young manager of the Lapland branch of Finland's Tourist Board.

"Even Rovaniemi was once a rural village of less than 7,000 persons," Korhonen said later as he nursed his car through the city traffic. "But that was before World War II when everything was changed."

He referred to the German armies who put Rovaniemi to the torch when they retreated in 1944, leaving it a smoldering heap. When the conflict was over, an army of architects, builders and engineers descended on the ruins of Rovaniemi and built a modernistic city of steel, glass and stone. Today the population has grown to more than 28,000. Rovaniemi is now a main street is part of the great Arctic Highway that leads to the Barents Sea.

Even the back country has changed considerably since the old days, Korhonen pointed out.

DEER FRIEND—A Lapp child leads one of the small number of tame reindeer kept in Rovaniemi, Finnish Lapland.

A tourist who expects to find the original Lapps living in wigwams with witches and magic drums is in for a disappointment. Today the quaint reindeer-drawn sledges that sped across the frozen countryside in winter have been largely replaced by noisy but more practical motor sledges.

There was once a saying that Lapland was a remote corner on the outskirts of the world, surrounded by Polar bears and darkness. It gets pretty dark in the winter, says Korhonen, but the only polar bears you will find are 200 miles southward in the Helsinki zoo.

But the vast forests still remain, inhabited by bear, wolves and wolverines. The ptarmigan, a plump, white, grouse-like bird that is regarded as a great table delicacy, circles overhead in the cloudless sky.

Reindeer roam the area grazing on the lichen, which covers the ground. In winter they dig it out from under the snow. The reindeer total half a million in the entire Lapp country, which covers some 186,000 square miles stretching across the northern parts of Norway, Sweden and Russia, as well as Finland.

The reindeer is one of the last animals to be domesticated by man, and about 200,000 of them are raised in Finnish Lapland alone, roughly one to each of the province's inhabitants.

This reindeer-breeding has become a highly organized business, and the 17,000 reindeer owners belong to a central association.

They butcher about 60,000 reindeer a year, since reindeer steaks, casseroles tongues and smoked reindeer meat are considered great delicacies in Scandinavia. The meat is usually accompanied by a sauce of lingonberries, that resemble the American cranberry.

The Lapps have roamed the Lapp tundra for nearly 2,000 years, but they are now a distinct minority in all parts of the region. There are said to be only 2,500 of them among Finnish Lapland's 200,000 residents. But it is difficult to get an exact count, since many have intermarried with Finns.

In olden days, Lapps were nomads who spent their days hunting and fishing and huddled at night in their tents of reindeer hide. Today some of them maintain small farms, but most Lapps breed herds of reindeer for the butcher shops. The majority of them are literate, but a local law calling for the teaching of the Lapp language in school is hard to enforce since few teachers know the tongue.

Lapland has often been called the Land of the Midnight Sun. Modern French scientists gave it in the 18th century when they discovered that starting in late June, the sun does not set here for three weeks. By the same token, at the northern tip of Lapland it is dark around the clock for 51 days in winter.

Dutch Truck Caravans Head for Middle East

By NEL SLIS

AMSTERDAM (AP) — Trucking companies of The Netherlands have opened a new trade route to the rich Middle East, a sort of desert caravan carrying everything from eggs to modern sports cars.

Some 35 Dutch companies are involved in the commerce, sending about 250 trucks every month on two to three-week round trips of some 7,000 miles.

The route passes through West Germany, Austria, Yugoslavia, Bulgaria and Turkey, and then to the client countries of Iran, Syria, Saudi Arabia, Kuwait and Iraq. Along the way, the drivers encounter extremes of country, rugged mountains and barren deserts.

Much of the freight begins its journey at Rotterdam's giant Europoort where it is unloaded to start the journey south. The lucrative trade is worth millions of dollars annually and one of Holland's largest haulage firms employs British, Belgian, West German and Dutch drivers on the 20 trucks it keeps rolling in the Mid-East shuttle.

"The drivers need a sense of adventure," Director Marinus Rijnart said. "One of our trucks broke down at Erzincan, in eastern Turkey, and it took 19 days for the nearest garage to get spare parts.

Drivers face temperatures which can range from 25 degrees c. below zero to 42 above. The mountain roads of eastern Turkey are said by many of the men to be the most difficult to traverse.

"You're sure if anything happens to you," said Johannes Heeren, 35, a regular on the run to Teheran for the past three years.

"It can take days before you get going again. There are very few telephones in that part of the world and often the only way to get help is to wait for another driver."

Now, Dutch companies are forming caravans of three or four trucks so that if one breaks down another can go ahead for help.

Heeren said there have also been problems with children herding sheep along the roads of eastern Turkey. "They always want cigarettes, and if you don't hand them over they pelt your windshield with rocks."

Hans Van Meenen, secretary of the Dutch Trucking Association, said there was also a lack of hotels and restaurants along the route and drivers often slept in their cabs on dusty roads miles from anywhere.

Some drivers run into trouble with authorities and are arrested. One Dutchman has been held for weeks in a Turkish jail accused of reckless driving. His truck was involved in an accident with a bus.

But business is booming, Van Meenen said, and there is no shortage of drivers prepared to take the risks of the haul.

"One woman even drove the route earlier this year, but when she came back she said it was for the first and last time."

The Dutch are currently looking for ways of streamlining their service. One plan calls for the Dutch to unload their goods at the Turkish border and to let Turkish companies take over for the last leg of the mideast

Fire Engine's Driver Takes It Easy on Road

SAN BERNARDINO, Calif. (AP) — The vehicle Ivan "Pep" Richardson often drives across country is an unusual sight on the highways.

He keeps the speed down, because someone's life is at stake him where's the fire. And when he stops for the night at a motel he climbs clamber aboard.

When Richardson takes a trip it's usually behind the wheel of a bright, shiny, red fire truck.

On his most recent trip he ferried a brand-new $50,000 fire engine from the American-LaFrance factory in Elmira, N.Y., to San Bernardino, a city about 70 miles east of Los Angeles.

Richardson is the chief mechanic for the San Bernardino Fire Department. Whenever they buy a new fire engine it is usually his job to go pick it up.

Richardson, on this recent trip, traveled twice to the Elmira plant, twice to Clintonville, Wis., and three times to a plant in Columbus, Ohio.

Once, he was wheeling a hook and ladder truck across a narrow river bridge when he encountered an oncoming car. The bridge's weight limit barely accommodated the truck, Richardson recalled. "And it was about nine miles to the bottom and the bridge was just wide enough for two cars. And here I was with that big ladder truck."

The motorist barely squeaked past the big rig, and Richardson stopped at the other side at the toll booth. But the gatekeeper just waved him through, saying, "Buddy, you got this far with it, just keep going. I'm not gonna charge you."

turned and found himself in the middle of rush-hour traffic in St. Louis, Mo. He was driving a 25-ton folding boom truck.

"I was scared to death!" he said. "I could just see myself running over someone and I wouldn't be able to stop 50,000 pounds."

But he got through without a scratch on the paint job.

What kind of attention does he get on the road?

"You get no reaction at all," says Richardson. The city's insignia and name aren't painted on the trucks until they reach San Bernardino. Motorists tend to ignore the truck. It isn't until he stops at a motel for the night that he draws attention.

Richardson said by the time he checked into his room and cleaned up, "there might be a half-dozen kids out there."

He said he'd never encountered a fire on any of the trips — and it's just as well. The trucks don't get hoses, nozzles and other accessories until they reach San Bernardino. He does, however, half fill the water tanks for ballast.

Besides being cheaper than sending trucks by rail, the cross-country trips save a sort of shakedown cruise that allows Richardson to check out any defects.

Dutch caravanserai

The Foreign Correspondent

Oostenrijk, Friday March 9, 1990

Page 3

Britain still keen:

Foreign secretary George Brown (l.) kept his Italian counterpart Amintore Fanfani in the margin of negotiations for U.K. membership of the EC in Brussels in the 1960s.

Herman Blaauw, pictured (left.) fled Nazi Germany before World War II, and settled in the Netherlands in 1936. He escaped to Switzerland in 1942, returning to Holland after World War II, a naturalised Dutchman, he reports on Dutch and inter...

Eastern Europe crowds EC agenda

by Nel Slis

Veteran correspondent 'Nel Slis looks back on the events which have taken place in Eastern Europe over the last months and assesses their implications for the EEC.

Bestuur B.P.V.

Peno Enck, *voorzitter*
Laura Raun, *vice voorzitter*
Frank de Jong, *secretaris*
Helmut Hetzel, *penningmeester*
Jef Sins, *lid*
Ronald van de Krol, *lid*
Geert Lauwaarsse, *lid*

Nel on Eastern Europe

‡FOR∃IGN CORRESPONDENT

'La Slis', a no-nonsense journalist

by CAROLINE STUDDERT

Nel Slis

Yearbook

Exhibition

Small World

THANK YOU

Studdert on Nel

THE FOREIGN CORRESPONDENT

Warmest memory

Daniel Schorr began a distinguished international career in journalism in the Netherlands and went on to become one of America's most successful and respected TV, radio and print journalists. Here he shares some memories of the country he grew to love, headline stories he covered and his long association with the Foreign Press Association...

The Prince of Oranje meets Jacques Santer, 'key-note' speaker at BPV's 70th Jubilee held at the Kurhaus Hotel.

DANIEL SCHORR is a Senior News Analyst with National Public Radio in Washington, DC.

Left picture: 2 April 1965. H.M. the Queen receives members of the Foreign Press Association at Soestdijk Palace.

Right picture: Minister Jorritsma, welcoming a temporary BPV member. Stephen Fleay's kiosk, attended a BPV reception.

Board

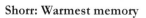

GUY THORNTON

Shorr: Warmest memory

About the Author

An Irish journalist, editor, translator and writer, Caroline Studdert has always made her living from one kind of writing or another but this is her first biography.

She grew up in Waterford, Ireland, with interludes in Germany and England. A keen traveller, she has since lived in Dublin, London, Miami, Paris, Tobruk, Amsterdam and, for the last 12 years, Prague.

After graduating from Trinity College Dublin in economics and political science, she worked in motivational research, later moving into qualitative research with her own consultancy in Dublin in the 1970's.

In Amsterdam in the 1980's, she switched to financial journalism. Today, she continues to work as a freelance journalist, translator and writer.

Like Nel, she says she doesn't have hobbies but enjoys walking, reading, cinema, theatre, opera, parties, people, animals, especially feline and equine, and last but by no means least, family. She has a son and a daughter and two grandsons.

Printed in Great Britain
by Amazon